Feeling up to Par:
Medicine from Tee to Green

Edited by

Cornelius N. Stover, MD

Hunterdon Orthopaedic Associates, P.A.
Director
Department of Orthopaedic Surgery
Hunterdon Medical Center
Flemington, New Jersey

John R. McCarroll, MD

Methodist Sports Medicine Center
Indianapolis, Indiana

William J. Mallon, MD

Triangle Orthopaedic Associates, Inc.
Assistant Consulting Professor
Division of Orthopaedics
Duke University Medical Center
Durham, North Carolina
Class A Member, PGA of America
Former Member (1975–1979), PGA Tour of America

 F. A. DAVIS COMPANY • Philadelphia

F. A. Davis Company
1915 Arch Street
Philadelphia, PA 19103

Printed in the United States of America

Last digit indicates print number: 10 9 8 7 6 5 4 3 2 1

Medical Editor: Robert W. Reinhardt
Medical Developmental Editor: Bernice M. Wissler
Production Editor: Crystal S. McNichol
Cover Design By: Steven R. Morrone

Cover photo by Faustino Sirven/THE IMAGE BANK

Library of Congress Cataloging in Publication Data

Feeling up to par : medicine from tee to green / edited by Cornelius N. Stover, John R. McCarroll, William J. Mallon.
    p.   cm.
  Includes bibliographical references and index.
  ISBN 0-8036-8203-4 (hardback : alk. paper)
    1. Golf injuries. 2. Golfers—Health and hygiene. 3. Golf—physiological aspects. 4. Human mechanics. I. Stover, Cornelius N. II. McCarroll, John R., 1944— . III. Mallon, Bill.
    [DNLM: 1. Golf—injuries. 2. Golf—psychology. 3. Joint Diseases—physiopathology. 4. Athletic Injuries—prevention & control 5. Physical Fitness—physiology. QT 260 1994]
  RC1220.G64F44 1994
  617.1'027—dc20
  DNLM/DLC
  for Library of Congress   94-6576
                                                       CIP

Foreword

....

I have been involved with professional golf since the mid-1950s. During that time, I have played professionally, and I currently follow golf and the PGA Tour quite closely in my job as a golf commentator for CBS Television. During my 40 years in golf I have seen many promising careers ended or lessened by injuries or other medical problems. Although golf is not thought to be a demanding sport physically, the hours of continuous practice and the time spent in the outdoors in all manner of weather conditions force many top professionals and amateurs to play with and through various medical problems.

My own professional golf career is a good example. After starting out as one of the top players in the world in the 1950s, various back and other injuries caused my game to fall off. I was able to come back from this to win the 1964 US Open, but that win also highlighted the dangers that beset professional golfers. On the last day, playing 36 holes with temperatures hovering around 100°F, I suffered from heat exhaustion and was barely able to finish. Although the win resurrected my career, I later developed severe problems with carpal tunnel syndrome in both hands. My hand injuries eventually ended my career.

I was very happy to be asked to write a foreword to *Feeling up to Par: Medicine from Tee to Green*. Prior to this time, no medical book has ever discussed the medical problems that are unique to golfers. Although aimed at medical professionals, I think the book will help golf professionals and other players to understand their own specific set of injuries and illnesses.

The book's three editors—Connie Stover, John McCarroll, and Bill Mallon—have assembled a world-class group of chapter authors, each an expert in his or her own field. Drs. Stover and McCarroll, as orthopedic surgeons, are both well-known for their work with golfers and golf injuries. I have known Bill Mallon since his own days on the PGA Tour. As a practicing orthopedic surgeon, he is able to contribute to this book both as a doctor and with the golf knowledge of a professional player. Together with their contributing authors, they cover all aspects of medical problems among golfers.

I trust you will find this book as enlightening and interesting as I have. My only complaint is that it was not available to doctors during my own playing career.

Ken Venturi

Marco Island, Florida
January 1994

By permission of Johnny Hart and Creators Syndicate, Inc.

Preface

· ·

The game of golf is a participant activity that has grown steadily since World War II. In recent years this growth has accelerated, and now 20 million golfers are active in this country, with nearly half of them more than the age of 40. During this time, sports medicine has also shown rapid growth. Numerous societies and organizations are now involved full or part time with the medical aspects of sports. The American Orthopaedic Society for Sports Medicine has been the fastest growing subspecialty society within the American Academy of Orthopaedics. In spite of these growth patterns, the medical literature does not reveal a comparable increase in publications related to sports medicine and golf. Compared with tennis and other sports, there is a paucity of medical reports dealing with golf. This book recognizes that fact and provides literature reviews, pertinent studies and investigations, and specific therapies.

The time that aging individuals can participate in their sport has been lengthened by technical advances such as joint replacement surgery. Improved equipment and special instruction clinics for older players will result in growing requests for medical assistance to permit prolonged participation. As practicing orthopedic surgeons, we often see patients with a variety of medical problems who ask us questions about participation in golf. This book will give physicians (as well as other health-care professionals and teaching golf professionals) guidelines to help in answering such questions, whether they come from patients with common conditions such as cardiovascular disease or low-back pain, or from those with missing limbs or joint replacements. We include not only advice on diagnosing and treating the most common injuries and illnesses afflicting golfers but also suggestions for preventive techniques (including the avoidance of some highly touted but stressful swing styles) to ward off future pain and disability and permit the golfer to enjoy a satisfying day on the course. Chapter 17, "Medical Control of Injuries and Illness," offers guidance on handling medical needs arising on the course, particularly in a tournament setting. Other chapters discuss training and nutritional and psychological techniques that can help golfers of any skill level to achieve better results safely.

The editors are indebted to the individual contributors to this book. Special thanks are owed to Dr. Gary Wiren for his thoughtful comments and constructive criticism. We would also like to recognize the willing help of the library personnel of the US Golf Association. Greatly appreciated are the many hours given by our office staff to the completion of this project.

Cornelius N. Stover, MD
John R. McCarroll, MD
William J. Mallon, MD

Contributors

· ·

James R. Andrews, MD
Clinical Professor of Orthopaedics and
  Sports Medicine
University of Virginia Medical School
Charlottesville, Virginia
Medical Director
American Sports Medicine Institute
Orthopedic Surgeon
Alabama Sports Medicine and Orthopaedic
  Center
Birmingham, Alabama

Ned Brooks Armstrong, MD
Board Certified Orthopedic Surgeon
Duke University Residency Graduate
Durham, North Carolina
Clinical Instructor
Emory University
Atlanta, Georgia
Member
Northeast Atlanta Orthopaedic Associates
Dunwoody, Georgia

Paul Callaway, PT
Former Director of Physical Therapy for
  the PGA Tour
Director of Physical Therapy
Midwest Physical Medicine
Director of Research and Education

Institute of Physical Medicine and
  Bio-Cybernetics
Oak Brook Terrace, Illinois

Kathy Corbin
President and Founder
Never Say Never Golf School for the
  Physically Challenged
Member, LPGA
Phoenix, Arizona

Glenn S. Fleisig, MS
Director of Research
American Sports Medicine Institute
Birmingham, Alabama

Charles J. Gatt, MD
Division of Orthopaedic Surgery
UMDNJ — Robert Wood Johnson Medical
  School
New Brunswick, New Jersey

Eric Gertner, MD
Department of Internal Medicine
Medical College of Pennsylvania
Philadelphia, Pennsylvania

Timothy M. Hosea, MD
Division of Orthopaedic Surgery
UMDNJ — Robert Wood Johnson Medical
    School
New Brunswick, New Jersey

Walter L. Jenkins, MS, PT, ATC
Coordinator of Sports Physical Therapy
Instructor, Department of Physical
    Therapy Education
Instructor, Department of Surgery,
    Orthopaedic Section
Kansas University Medical Center
Kansas City, Kansas
Instructor, Master of Health Science
    Program
University of Indianapolis
Indianapolis, Indiana

Susan W. King, MS, RD
Sports Nutrition Consultant
Kelly, Wyoming
Nutrition Consultant, PGA Tour and
    Senior PGA Tour, 1986–1988

John W. Kozey, MSc
Assistant Professor
Division of Kinesiology
Dalhousie University
Halifax, Nova Scotia, Canada

Mark I. Loebenberg, MD
Orthopedic Resident
University of Rochester Medical School
Rochester, New York

William J. Mallon, MD
Triangle Orthopaedic Associates, Inc.
Assistant Consulting Professor
Division of Orthopaedics
Duke University Medical Center
Durham, North Carolina
Class A Member, PGA of America
Former Member (1975–1979), PGA Tour
    of America

Terry R. Malone, EdD, PT, ATC
Executive Director of Sports Medicine
Associate Professor of Physical Therapy
Assistant Professor of Surgery
Duke University
Durham, North Carolina

John R. McCarroll, MD
Methodist Sports Medicine Center
Indianapolis, Indiana

Claude T. Moorman III, MD
Sports Medicine Fellow
Hospital for Special Surgery
New York, New York

DeDe Owens, EdD
Director of Instruction
Cog Hill Golf Course
Lemont, Illinois

Edward A. Palank, MD, FACC
Director
New Hampshire Heart Institute
Manchester, New Hampshire

Arthur C. Rettig, MD
Methodist Sports Medicine Center
Indianapolis, Indiana

David Robinson, MD, FACS
Robinson Eye Associates
Lewes, Delaware

Robert J. Rotella, PhD
Director
Sports Psychology
University of Virginia
Charlottesville, Virginia

William D. Stanish, MD, FRCS(C), FACS
Professor of Surgery
Dalhousie University
Director
Orthopaedic and Sport Medicine Clinic of
    Nova Scotia
Halifax, Nova Scotia, Canada

Cornelius N. Stover, MD
Hunterdon Orthopaedic Associates, P.A.
Director
Department of Orthopaedic Surgery
Hunterdon Medical Center
Flemington, New Jersey

M. William Voss, MD*

---

*Deceased.

James A. Whiteside, MD
Director of Medical Aspects
Alabama Sports Medicine and Orthopaedic
  Center
Birmingham, Alabama
Clinical Associate Professor of
  Orthopaedics and Sports Medicine
University of Virginia Medical School
Charlottesville, Virginia

Robert C. Wilson
Executive Director
National Amputee Golf Association
Amherst, New Hampshire

Contents

*Deceased.

PART

1

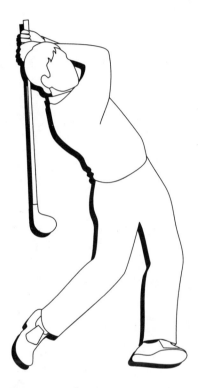

Introduction

1

Injuries and Illness Among Professional Golfers

William J. Mallon, MD

As a group, professional golfers probably have fewer injuries than participants in more violent sports such as football, basketball, baseball, and hockey. Yet throughout the history of professional golf, many of the great names of the sport have been afflicted by a variety of injuries or illnesses. This chapter reviews some of these problems and relates them to later chapters of this book.

THE PSYCHOLOGY OF GOLF

Psychological problems (see Chapter 5) have affected many great players. Bobby Jones, the great amateur of the 1920s believed by some to be the greatest player ever, was considered to have had two distinct periods in his career, the "7 Lean Years" and the "7 Years of Plenty." The lean years were said to have resulted from his inability to harness his mental abilities and control his psychological problems, rather than from any lack of physical talent. Even in the years of plenty, he was tormented by the pressure of competition, often vomiting before rounds and losing copious amounts of perspiration regardless of the weather, from the stress he felt.[7]

Probably the best-known psychological affliction among golfers has been termed the "yips"—putting woes in which the golfer's putting effort not only is unsuccessful but may even be described as pathetic, as the putting stroke loses all rhythm and smoothness. The yips have been said to affect many players as they grew older. The best-known sufferer, Ben Hogan, once described it as due to the toll of many years of pressure:

3

"Well, even the drop of water on the rock is going to wear a hole in it, you see."[6] Jim Flick, a respected teaching professional, described the yips as caused by a combination of psychological and physical factors: a breakdown in mental composure, and the failure of the left hand to lead all the way through the stroke.[3]

The effect of years of pressure on the putting stroke may be seen by looking at the current PGA Senior Tour. Whereas players on the regular PGA Tour tend to putt conventionally, the seniors employ a bewildering variety of putting strokes and putters as attempted remedies for the yips: cross-handed putting, split-handed putting, side-straddle putting (popularized by Sam Snead, a well-known sufferer), and putters with handles up to 2 ft longer than standard.

TRAINING AND CONDITIONING

Prior to the 1950s, training and conditioning (see Chapter 4) were words foreign to most golfers. The first great golfer to espouse physical fitness as a way to help his golf was Frank Stranahan, a great amateur of the late 1940s, who briefly played the PGA Tour in the mid-1950s. To the consternation of many bellhops, Stranahan carried his barbells with him while traveling.[13]

In the early 1960s, Gary Player realized that he could become a great player only if he learned to hit the ball farther. A small man, he enlisted the help of a former Mr. Universe, Roy Hilligenn, to train him and help develop his body.[11] By running and lifting weights, Player increased his distance and became one of only four men to win all four major championships of professional golf.

PGA Tour players now realize the importance of staying physically fit. A fitness trailer travels to all the tour stops, and players frequently use it for postround exercise.

NUTRITION

As happened with conditioning, nutrition (see Chapter 6) has become a more popular topic on the PGA Tour in recent years. The easy availability of fast-food restaurants and

the difficulty of finding healthful meals led many past players to have a poor diet, but golfers now realize that they must eat nutritiously to optimize their chances of playing well. One player, Payne Stewart, even enlists a personal nutritionist to help plan his diet.

Some past golfers who were quite overweight have gone on diets. By far the best-known in professional golf was that undertaken by Billy Casper in the late 1960s. One of the finest players in the world, Casper was obese and also suffered from numerous allergies. When he decided to lose weight, he planned his diet with the help of both a nutritionist and his allergist. Because of his food allergies, the diet contained several rather exotic foods, notably buffalo meat, making it a delight to the media.[8]

Occasionally, dieting has been found detrimental to a player's game. In the late 1970s, Leonard Thompson, who had been quite overweight, lost more than 50 lb one winter. When the tour resumed the following spring, Thompson found that he had lost a great deal of distance with the weight. His scores suffered as a result. Thompson quickly gained back a portion of the weight, his drives lengthened, and his scores dropped again.

GOLF PARTICIPATION BY THE PHYSICALLY CHALLENGED

Many golfers have overcome physical handicaps (see Chapter 9). No amputee has ever competed on the PGA Tour, but Charles Owens has played well on the PGA Senior Tour with a completely fused right knee, the result of an injury he suffered while a paratrooper. He rides a cart.

Skip Alexander enjoyed success on the PGA Tour as a young man in the 1940s. He won several tournaments and made the 1949 Ryder Cup team. At the peak of his career, his hands were badly burned in a plane crash. Pioneer hand surgeon Dr. J. Leonard Goldner of Duke University fused Alexander's left hand into the position of a golf grip, bringing a sterilized club to the operating table so he could get the position correct. The fusion enabled Alexander to compete on the PGA Tour for several years after the accident.

The best-known example of overcoming severe injury to play outstanding golf, of course, is that of Ben Hogan. On February 2, 1949, Hogan and his wife were traveling through west Texas when his automobile was struck by a Greyhound bus. With the collision imminent, Hogan threw his body over his wife to protect her. She was unharmed, but he was nearly killed, fracturing more than 20 bones and damaging several internal organs. After he began to improve slightly, he suffered a massive pulmonary embolism. He was flown to the Ochsner Clinic in New Orleans, where his vena cava was ligated to prevent further emboli from reaching his lungs.[5,13] Just after the accident he was not expected to live; walking was thought to be a lofty goal. Not only did he walk again, but in early 1950 he returned to play in the Los Angeles Open, losing to Sam Snead in a play-off. Later that year he won the US Open. The best player in the world before the accident, Ben Hogan dominated professional golf for the next 5 years and in 1953 performed the still-unmatched feat of winning the Masters, US Open, and British Open in the same year. Some consider the golf he played after his accident to be the greatest of all time.[13]

The accident definitely affected Hogan's career and schedule, however. He needed long recovery periods after tournaments and entered very few events. In 1953, his greatest year, he played in only six tournaments —and won five. He rarely played competitively after 1955, and in later years developed difficulty in walking, which he attributed to poor circulation from the vena caval ligation.[5,13]

THE GOLFER WITH A TOTAL JOINT REPLACEMENT

No one has yet competed on either the PGA Tour or the PGA Senior Tour with a total joint replacement. Several club professionals who have undergone total joint replacements play in local tournaments, however (see Chapter 10).

Two successful professional golfers of the 1950s and 1960s, Julius Boros and Patty Berg, have since undergone total hip replacements.[9] Boros underwent his operation while playing on the PGA Senior Tour but

has not returned; he has also undergone cardiac bypass surgery, however, which may have contributed to his decision. Berg was no longer playing competitively at the time of her operation.

INJURIES AND ILLNESSES: THE BACK

Problems with the back (see Chapters 11 and 12) seem endemic among professional golfers. Frank Beard once commented that virtually all professional golfers have had back problems at one time or another.[2] Lee Trevino, Fuzzy Zoeller, and Dan Pohl have all had surgery to excise herniated discs, and George Archer continues to play on the PGA Tour after several back surgeries, including fusion of several lumbar vertebrae. It will be interesting to see how well he performs.

Jack Nicklaus almost saw his career come to an end because of back problems. In early 1989 he considered surgery, but weight loss and physical therapy have helped him cope with his problems, and he is again playing competitively.

INJURIES AND ILLNESSES: THE SHOULDER

Many professionals also have had problems with their shoulders (see Chapter 13). The best-known is Jerry Pate, who won the US Open in 1975 and was expected to become one of the world's great players. In the next few years, though, Pate began to experience shoulder problems. He has undergone multiple surgeries, both for instability of his shoulder and for impingement problems related to the instability, and now rarely plays on tour. Shoulder pain also contributed to the end of the careers of Jim Simons and Lyn Lott.

In recent years, both Dr. Gil Morgan and Lou Graham have returned to their respective tours after the surgical repair of rotator cuff tears.

INJURIES AND ILLNESSES: THE ELBOW

Although the elbow seems to be a common source of pain among amateur golfers (see Chapter 14), chronic elbow problems have been relatively rare among tour professionals, perhaps because their good swing mechanics decrease stress on the elbow at the time of impact. Chi Chi Rodriguez did require surgery for tennis elbow in the late 1980s. Both Calvin Peete[10] and Ed Furgol[12] have played on the PGA Tour with stiff elbows that would not straighten fully. Furgol's left arm was also slightly withered as the result of a childhood accident.

INJURIES AND ILLNESSES: THE WRIST

Wrist injuries (see Chapter 15) are very common among tour professionals, possibly because of the long rough on so many tour courses. Many players have ganglia about the wrist, although few have required surgery. Tour player D. A. Weibring had a ganglion excised from his left wrist in late 1989 when it did not respond to conservative treatment.

Carpal tunnel problems are not common on the PGA Tour. The best-known case occurred in Ken Venturi. In 1965, he began to experience pain in both wrists, and his play suffered badly. After bilateral carpal tunnel releases, he returned to the tour and won the 1965 Lucky International tournament. His problems recurred, however, and he never regained his previous form.[1]

INJURIES AND ILLNESSES: MEDICAL PROBLEMS

The climatic stress of being exposed to the hot sun for long periods 5 or 6 days a week for most of the year, as experienced by professional golfers, can exacerbate almost any medical condition (see Chapter 17). Many have dealt with the problems well, however.

Mark Lye, Scott Verplank, and Michelle McGann have learned to play with type I (childhood-onset) diabetes mellitus.[10] All take daily insulin and are followed carefully by endocrinologists. They carry fruit with them in their golf bags and are careful to keep well hydrated. Still, Verplank was hospitalized for fatigue in early 1990 and attributed it to difficulty regulating his disease carefully while playing.

Two players, Al Geiberger and Tony Sills,

continue to play despite long bouts with inflammatory bowel disease that have required colostomies. One of the finest female players ever, Mildred "Babe" Didrikson Zaharias, also played with a colostomy at the end of her career. She developed rectal cancer in 1953, necessitating the surgery. Incredibly, she won the 1954 US Women's Open by 12 strokes (still a record) despite this handicap.

In March 1972, cancer was diagnosed in Gene Littler, and it was thought that his career was over. Despite weakness in his left arm and chest from an axillary node dissection, Littler continued to win tournaments on the PGA Tour and later on the PGA Senior Tour.

Lightning

Although professional golfers should recognize the dangers of electrical storms, a few have been struck by lightning. The most famous such incident occurred in 1975 at the Western Open in suburban Chicago, when Lee Trevino, Jerry Heard, and Bobby Nichols were all struck. None sustained life-threatening injuries. It is not known whether the incident is related to the back problems that all three developed over the next few years.

Heat Illness

Heat illness is rarely a problem on the PGA Tour, as the players are well schooled in keeping hydrated; water and usually Gatorade are available on every tee. The most famous case of heat exhaustion occurred at the 1964 US Open and involved Ken Venturi. The psychological aspects of his victory that day make the case all the more dramatic and poignant.

In the mid-1950s, Ken Venturi had been predicted to be the next Ben Hogan. He won 10 tournaments through 1960, but late that year his game fell off and Arnold Palmer assumed the mantle that was to have been Venturi's. From 1961 to 1963, Venturi sustained various minor injuries, began to play worse, and his confidence flagged badly. His endorsements were not renewed, his marriage became rocky, and by late 1963 he was almost bankrupt. In 1963, he won only $3848 in official money, and his career seemed over.[12]

Early in 1964, with the help of a local Catholic priest, he began to bring his life and his game together. He had not won another tournament but was improving weekly and winning money consistently. He qualified for the US Open, and the week before it he finished third.[12]

The 1964 Open was held at Congressional Country Club near Washington, D.C. In those days, 36 holes were played on the last day, Saturday, a day that was brutally hot, with the temperature hovering near 100°F (38°C) and the humidity about 90%. Venturi was not leading after Friday's play, but Saturday morning he shot 66 to take the lead. The heat began to affect him, though, and he bogeyed two of the last three holes. By then he was dehydrated and had become lightheaded and tremulous. Between rounds, he collapsed in the clubhouse and was attended to by a doctor. Intravenous fluids were administered, and he was advised not to play any more.

Venturi, however, felt that he had come too far to quit, with victory in the US Open so close. Accompanied by his doctor and his priest, he walked the last 18 holes almost in a daze. On the last hole, he turned to USGA Executive Director Joe Dey, apologized for walking so slowly, and told him to go ahead and penalize him if he had to. Dey replied, "Kenny, you're doing fine. Just hold your chin up proudly and keep walking. You're about to be the US Open Champion."

Venturi sank a 15-ft par putt on the last green and put his hands to his head, exclaiming, "My God, I've won the Open." His playing partner, Raymond Floyd, retrieved the ball from the hole and brought it to Venturi. When Venturi saw him, he began to sob, for Floyd was already crying from the emotion of the moment.[12]

Later that year, the US Golf Association changed the format of the US Open to only 18 holes per day. In December 1964, *Sports Illustrated* voted Venturi its "Sportsman of the Year." In 1965, he developed the aforementioned problems with his wrists and never reached those heights again.

SUMMARY

Not only the weekend or club player is afflicted by injuries or illnesses that affect his or her golf game. Many of the world's best professionals have encountered— and often have overcome—most of the problems discussed in the remaining chapters of this book.

REFERENCES

1. Barkow, A: Golf's Golden Grind: The History of the Tour. Harcourt Brace Jovanovich, New York, 1974.
2. Beard, F and Schaap, D: Pro: My Life on the Pro Tour.
3. Flick, J and Saunders, B: The answer man fields questions. Golf World, Nov 30, 1971, p 18.
4. Graffis, H: The PGA: The Official History of the PGA of America. Crowell, New York, 1975.
5. Gregston, G: Hogan: The Man Who Played for Glory. Prentice-Hall, Englewood Cliffs, NJ, 1978.
6. Hogan, WB: An evening with Hogan. Golf World, Sept 27, 1954, p 20.
7. Jones, RT and Keeler, OB: Down the Fairway: The Golf Life and Play of Robert T. Jones, Jr. Blue Ribbon Books, New York, 1934.
8. Peery, PD: Billy Casper: Winner. Prentice-Hall, Englewood Cliffs, NJ, 1969.
9. PGA Tour: PGA Tour Senior Media Guide: 1988. PGA Tour, Ponte Vedra Beach, FL, 1988.
10. PGA Tour: PGA Tour Media Guide: 1989. PGA Tour, Ponte Vedra Beach, FL, 1989.
11. Player, GJ and Thatcher, F: Gary Player: World Golfer. Word, Waco, TX, 1974.
12. Sommers, R: The United States Open: Golf's Ultimate Challenge. Atheneum, New York, 1987.
13. Wind, HW: The Story of American Golf. Greenwood, Westport, CT, 1956.

Epidemiology of Golf Injuries

John R. McCarroll, MD
William J. Mallon, MD

ntil recently, the frequency of golf injuries had not received much attention in the literature. Many older reports consisted primarily of unusual case reports, such as fractures of the hook of the hamate,[9] or an acute comminuted, nonpathologic fracture of the tibia from a golf swing.[1] This is unfortunate, for although golf is usually considered a rather benign activity, it is now well established that golfers play despite numerous ailments, some minor, some major.[2-5,7,8]

It has been estimated that more than 50% of touring professionals have sustained some injury that required them to stop playing competitively for periods averaging 3 to 10 weeks.[4] This is not a totally unexpected statistic. As in all professional sports, the demands placed on the touring professional to remain competitive require continually pushing the body to the edge of overuse. It is not unusual for professional golfers to hit more than 300 full shots, putt for several hours, and play a full round of golf daily, requiring up to 10 hours of continuous activity.

Injuries to recreational or weekend golfers have not been studied in much detail. The innocuous appearance of the sport has probably caused most practitioners not to expect many injuries from golf. Yet they do occur in the amateur golfer.[5] A golf swing involves a significant rotary torque of the trunk and requires both shoulders to be moved through a wide, rather unusual range of motion at very high speeds. Weekend golfers do not place the same demands on their bodies while playing golf as professionals do, but their lesser demands are placed on bodies less well suited to the task. In addition, their swing techniques are less refined and efficient.

The best known epidemiologic studies of golf injuries are those of McCarroll, Rettig, and Shelbourne.[4,5] Jobe, Moynes, and Antonelli[2] and Stover[8] also have discussed their own experience with injuries among their golfing patients. Since 1985, Mallon[3] has written a column in the most widely read American golf magazine (*Golf Digest*, current circulation 1.3 million per month). During this period, more than 1400 letters concerning golf injuries and illnesses have been received for that column. These letters, which constitute a fairly large body of data concerning the injury patterns of the recreational golfer, are discussed later in this chapter.

Among professional golfers, McCarroll and Gioe[4] found the lower back to be the most commonly injured in men, followed by the left wrist and shoulder. Women profes-

TABLE 2–1. Injuries Among Professional Golfers

Site	Men (n = 192)		Women (n = 201)		Total (n = 393)	
	No.	%*	No.	%*	No.	%*
Left wrist	31	(16)	63	(31)	94	(24)
Lower back	48	(25)	45	(22)	93	(24)
Left hand	13	(7)	15	(8)	28	(7)
Left shoulder	21	(11)	6	(3)	27	(7)
Left knee	14	(7)	12	(6)	26	(7)
Left elbow	6	(3)	9	(5)	15	(4)
Left thumb	10	(5)	3	(2)	13	(3)
Feet	4	(2)	9	(5)	13	(3)
Cervical spine	9	(4)	3	(2)	12	(3)
Right wrist	3	(2)	9	(5)	12	(3)
Ribs	6	(3)	6	(3)	12	(3)
Right elbow	8	(4)	3	(2)	11	(3)
Right shoulder	1	(1)	9	(5)	10	(3)
Thoracic spine	8	(4)	0	(0)	8	(2)
Ankles	2	(1)	6	(3)	8	(2)
Groin	2	(1)	3	(2)	5	(1)
Left hip	4	(2)	0	(0)	4	(1)
Head	2	(1)	0	(0)	2	(1)

*Percentages may not total 100 as a result of rounding.
Source: Adapted from McCarroll, JR and Gioe, TJ: Professional golfers and the price they pay. Phys Sportsmed 10(7):54–70, 1982. Reproduced with permission of McGraw-Hill, Inc.

sionals most commonly injured the left wrist, followed by the lower back (Table 2–1). Overall, the left wrist was the most common site of injury, followed very closely by the lower back and, much less frequently, the left shoulder. Of approximately 300 professionals on the two tours, fewer than 5 play left-handed, so it can be seen that the lead, or target-side, arm is most frequently injured. The incidence of injuries to the right arm was quite low.[4]

In male amateur golfers, the lower back was the most commonly injured area, followed by the elbow, hand and wrist, shoulder, and knee. Among women, the elbow was the most commonly injured site, followed by the back, shoulder, hand and wrist, and knee (Table 2–2). In this study, the elbow involved was not specified. McCarroll, Rettig, and Shelbourne[5] also found that the lateral elbow was much more frequently a source of injury (by nearly 5:1) than the medial elbow among amateur golfers.

The most common cause of injury in both professional and amateur golfers was believed to be repetitive practice.[4,5] In amateur golfers, poor swing mechanics was considered the second most frequent cause of injuries. Among both professionals and ama-

teurs, most of the golfers believed that their injuries were caused by stresses occurring while nearing impact. The wrist and the hand were the most frequently injured during the impact phase.[4,5]

Among amateur golfers, there was a mildly significant increase in injuries in the low-handicap golfer ($P < 0.10$) (Table 2–3). It was also found that in 528 golfers age 50 or younger, the injury rate was 58.3%. The 616 golfers older than age 50 sustained an injury rate of 64.9%, a statistically significant difference ($P < 0.05$).[5]

In these studies of professional and amateur golfers, 54% of the professionals and 45% of the amateurs considered their injuries chronic. On the average, these injuries caused the golfers to lose 5 weeks of playing time.

Among the more interesting findings in both studies[4,5] were the various treatments that the players received and the lack of a consistent, uniform treatment program (Table 2–4). The most common treatments were rest and physical therapy. It is noteworthy that amateurs were treated with rest alone much more frequently than were professionals (31% versus 16%). This discrepancy is certainly related, at least in part, to the pressure on the professionals to continue

TABLE 2-2. Injuries Among Amateur Golfers

Site	Men (n = 584)		Women (n = 124)		Total (n = 708)	
	No.*	%†	No.*	%†	No.*	%†
Lower back	210	(36)	34	(27)	244	(35)
Elbow	190	(33)	44	(36)	234	(33)
Lateral	160	(27)	34	(27)	194	(27)
Medial	30	(5)	10	(8)	40	(6)
Hand and wrist	124	(21)	18	(15)	142	(20)
Shoulder	64	(11)	20	(16)	84	(12)
Knee	52	(9)	14	(11)	66	(9)
Neck	26	(5)	2	(2)	28	(4)
Hip	18	(3)	4	(3)	22	(3)
Ribs	16	(3)	6	(5)	22	(3)
Ankle	8	(1)	10	(8)	18	(3)
Foot	12	(2)	0	(0)	12	(2)
Head	12	(2)	0	(0)	12	(2)
Thigh	8	(1)	0	(0)	8	(1)
Face	6	(1)	0	(0)	6	(1)
Abdomen	4	(1)	0	(0)	4	(1)
Calf	4	(1)	0	(0)	4	(1)
Forearm	0	(0)	2	(2)	2	(0)

*Some subjects sustained more than one injury.
†Percentages may not total 100 as a result of rounding.
Source: Adapted from McCarroll, JR, Rettig, AC, and Shelbourne, KD: Injuries in the amateur golfer. Phys Sportsmed 18(3): 125, 1990. Reproduced with permission of McGraw-Hill, Inc.

playing as a means of earning a living. The study of professionals was carried out in the early 1980s, however, and it is possible that treatment is now more consistent and appropriate since the advent of the fitness trailer that now follows the PGA and LPGA Tour.

A detailed analysis of the *Golf Digest* letters[3] is given in Table 2-5. Much of the data agrees with the findings of McCarroll, Rettig, and Shelbourne.[5] The most frequent source of complaints among these recreational golfers was the lower back. In fact, back complaints constituted a majority (52%) of the letters received since the initiation of the column. Although analysis of pathology is not possible, a significant proportion of the letters mentioned that back pain

occurred while putting or chipping. Although these are very low-stress activities, they require the player to bend over sharply at the waist, which may increase the static stresses on the lumbosacral spine and back musculature.

The second most common complaint (24%) concerned injuries to the elbow. It appears that this injury may be even more

TABLE 2-3. Injuries by Handicap Level

Handicap	No. of Players	No. of Injured Players	Injury Rate (%)
0-9	240	162	67.5
10-17	450	278	61.8
18 or more	454	268	59.0

Source: Adapted from McCarroll, JR, Rettig, AC, and Shelbourne, KD: Injuries in the amateur golfer. Phys Sportsmed 18(3):126, 1990. Reproduced with permission of McGraw-Hill, Inc.

TABLE 2-4. Treatment of Injuries (%)

Treatment	Professionals	Amateurs
Rest	16	31
Physical therapy	17	12
Ice	6	11
Medicine	11	9
Injections	10	9
Heat	9	8
Braces	6	8
Surgery	6	4
Ultrasound	5	6
Miscellaneous (acupuncture, chiropractic, DMSO [dimethyl sulfoxide], traction)	2	2

Source: Data from McCarroll and Gioe[4] and McCarroll, Rettig, and Shelbourne.[5]

TABLE 2-5. Injury Complaints of Amateur Golfers Writing to *Golf Digest*

	Men (n = 1160)		Women (n = 249)		Total (n = 1409)	
	No.	*%*	*No.*	*%*	*No.*	*%*
Lower back	617	(53)	111	(45)	728	(52)
Left elbow	273	(24)	68	(27)	341	(24)
Lateral	131	(11)	49	(20)	180	(13)
Medial	44	(4)	19	(8)	63	(4)
Left shoulder	101	(9)	10	(4)	111	(8)
Left wrist	71	(6)	35	(14)	106	(8)
Left ankle	34	(3)	7	(3)	41	(3)
Vision problems	28	(2)	6	(2)	34	(2)
Right hip	13	(1)	4	(2)	17	(1)
Left hip	10	(<1)	4	(2)	14	(1)
Right knee	7	(<1)	3	(1)	10	(<1)
Left knee	6	(<1)	1	(<1)	7	(<1)

Source: Data from Mallon.[3]

common, as most of the writers had had elbow pain for several years and had already tried virtually every remedy described in the literature. Thus, these elbow complaints were probably from "end-stage" sufferers.

"Tennis elbow," the common name for lateral epicondylitis, is the most frequent elbow problem in athletics.[6] "Golfer's elbow" also has been described and usually refers to medial epicondylitis. (However, Nirschl[6] calls this "medial tennis elbow.") It is presumed from these definitions that medial epicondylitis is an overuse syndrome associated with golf, whereas lateral epicondylitis is more common among tennis players. Among the letter writers who described the location of their elbow pain, however, lateral elbow pain was almost three times more common than medial elbow pain. The pain was invariably in the left elbow of right-handed players. Both the side and site of pain agree with McCarroll's findings. Thus it appears that tennis elbow, or lateral epicondylitis, is more common among golfers than golfer's elbow, and occurs predominantly in the lead arm.

Shoulder and wrist complaints were about equal in number. Of the shoulder problems, most were in older players and involved pain in the left shoulder of right-handed golfers. Of those describing when the pain occurred during their golf swing, virtually all stated that the pain occurred at the top of the backswing. This is a transition period in the golf swing, when the club is changing directions and thus places significant eccentric loads on the muscles about the shoulder. This is also the position of maximum elevation of the left arm, and the pain may be related to impingement. This report contradicts McCarroll's findings that most of the golfers believed that their injury occurred near impact. McCarroll, however, did not specifically address the percentage of shoulder pain occurring during the backswing or downswing.

Wrist pain frequently occurred among low-handicap players, analogous to McCarroll's findings that wrist pain was second in incidence among professionals. It was also more common among women (14% versus 6%); wrist pain was also the most common injury among women professionals in McCarroll and Gioe's study.[4] Most of the players could remember a single traumatic event that caused the pain, often involving striking a tree root or rock. As the club nears impact, it may be traveling at speeds in excess of 100 miles/h (even with iron clubs); the sudden deceleration caused by an unexpected impact can impart a great deal of stress to the wrist. Again, as with the elbow, many of these problems were long-standing and had been resistant to multiple treatment regimens.

Stover, Wiren, and Topaz[8] discussed stress syndromes from golf but did not perform a detailed epidemiologic study. They believed that lateral epicondylitis occurred only in the right elbow from pronation, whereas medial epicondylitis occurred primarily in the left elbow. They attributed its origin to the supination required near and after impact.[8]

Jobe, Moynes, and Antonelli[2] reviewed their golf patient population. Of 412 injuries attributable to golf, they found that 85 (21%) involved the shoulder and believed that 79 of these were injuries to the rotator cuff. (They did not discuss details of the remaining 327 patients.[2]) Although this is a higher proportion of shoulder injuries than found either by McCarroll or Mallon, Jobe is renowned as a shoulder surgeon and has a specialized referral practice.

SUMMARY

Although in the past golf was not believed to be a sport associated with injuries, it is now becoming clear that golfers sustain a significant number and variety of injuries. Among professionals, it is likely that these are overuse syndromes relating to the quantity of practice and play required to perform at that level. Among amateurs, injuries have been attributed to poor conditioning and improper swing mechanics.[5]

By reviewing the epidemiologic studies discussed earlier, one can see that the low back and the left elbow are the most common sites of injuries among golfers. In ad-

dition, it seems that wrist injuries are common and increase in incidence among low-handicap and professional golfers. Women golfers also appear to be at an increased risk to develop wrist pain. It appears that the term "golfer's elbow" may not be accurate because it describes medial epicondylitis, whereas most injuries to the elbow among golfers appear to involve the lateral side of the lead arm.

REFERENCES

1. Evarard, A: Golf. J R Coll Gen Pract 3:293, 1970.
2. Jobe, FW, Moynes, DR, and Antonelli, DJ: Rotator cuff function during a golf swing. Am J Sports Med 14(5):388–392, 1986.
3. Mallon, WJ: "Ask the Doctor." Semimonthly column, Golf Digest, 1986–1991.
4. McCarroll, JR and Gioe, TJ: Professional golfers and the price they pay. Phys Sportsmed 10(7):54–70, 1982.
5. McCarroll, JR, Rettig, AC, and Shelbourne, KD: Injuries in the amateur golfer. Phys Sportsmed 18(3):122–126, 1990.
6. Nirschl, RP: Muscle and tendon trauma: Tennis elbow. In Morrey BF (ed): The Elbow and Its Disorders. WB Saunders, Philadelphia, 1985.
7. Roberts, J: Injuries, handicaps, mashies, and cleeks. Phys Sportsmed 6:121, 1978.
8. Stover, CN, Wiren, G, and Topaz, GR: The modern golf swing and stress syndromes. Phys Sportsmed 4:42–47, 1976.
9. Torisu, T: Fracture of the hook of the hamate by a golf swing. Clin Orthop 83:91, 1972.

PART
2

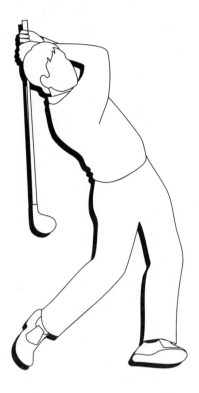

Preparation for Golf

The Biomechanics of Golf

• •

Glenn S. Fleisig, MS

THE IMPORTANCE OF PROPER MECHANICS
THE FIVE STAGES OF THE GOLF SWING
SET-UP
BACKSWING (INCLUDING TAKE-AWAY)
TRANSITION
DOWNSWING (AND IMPACT)
Upper-Pendulum Acceleration
Lower-Pendulum Acceleration
Impact
FOLLOW-THROUGH

A s shown by the dearth of books and articles dealing with golf training and injury prevention, golf has not often been considered a vigorous athletic activity, but in fact, many injuries are common to golfers. The most common injuries in professional golfers are those to the left wrist and lower back (see Table 2–1).[9,10] Most golf injuries involve overuse syndromes such as tendinitis, sprains, and strains and are the consequence of repetitive swinging.[9,10]

This chapter provides an understanding of the mechanics of a golf swing. The analysis does not focus on performance improvement but rather on golf's physical demands and pathomechanics. Both the general kinematics (range of motion) and kinetics (forces

and torques) necessary for an effective, normal swing are described. Differences in technique that may contribute to the variation of abilities among golfers are not addressed.

Data from most of the references are derived from the swings of a limited number of skilled golfers. Data given without references are based on the evaluation of 15 PGA golfers seen at the American Sports Medicine Institute during 1990. It is not reasonable to assume that all golfers do, or even should, precisely fit the biomechanical description given. As in every other sport, golf has some successful performers who appear to differ from the "ideal model." Individual physical attributes allow for individual variations on successful mechanics,[13] but all golfers should fit the general description of the model swing. Lower-level golfers, however, are often less consistent than better golfers, although the exact aspects in which they differ from the model have not yet been investigated thoroughly.

It is worth pointing out that research conducted to date has dealt almost exclusively with the swing of the driver. A study by Neal and associates[14] showed that the temporal characteristics of the swing are indeed altered with the use of a different club or with the use of submaximal effort. Body positioning and range of motion also are affected by the length of the club. Future research should be broadened to cover all aspects of golf.

THE IMPORTANCE
OF PROPER MECHANICS

Improper mechanics may result in injury. The golf swing as a whole is fairly reflexive.[16] The swing of a professional golfer is a highly efficient mechanism with excellent kinetics, requiring a small amount of activity from muscles to produce sufficient energy.[16] To compensate for improper mechanics, a less-skilled golfer may try to generate extra force from certain muscles and ligaments. Research by Hosea and colleagues,[6] for example, showed that in certain situations amateurs may develop up to 80% more peak torque about their lumbar spine than professionals (see Chapter 11). Muscles required to generate excessive force are then at a higher risk of overuse injury.

Overuse injuries also may be the result of insufficient strengthening of certain muscles. An understanding of kinematics as well as of muscle activity during a proper golf swing should help in the development of conditioning and training programs. Muscles involved in the golf swing should be strengthened, particularly through their active range of motion during the swing (see Chapter 4).

THE FIVE STAGES
OF THE GOLF SWING

An understanding of proper golf mechanics and muscle activity is therefore crucial to minimize the chance of injury. To explain the biomechanics of a golf swing, many authors have broken down the swing into three to five parts.[3,4,7,9,10,12,18] Here, the swing is broken into five stages: set-up, backswing, transition, downswing, and follow-through (Fig. 3–1). In the following description, the golfer is assumed to be a right-handed man.

SET-UP

A functional and consistent set-up is important for any golfer. The set-up is composed of the proper grip and body position. A proper grip allows the two hands to function as one unit. Specifically, the grip permits both wrists to radially deviate and ulnarly deviate in unison. The golfer should try not to let his right hand dominate; instead, the grip strength should be evenly balanced between both hands. Most people believe that the grip is the essential first step toward successful golf. Therefore, the golfer should not even go on to the next step (body position) until he has mastered the grip. A golfer who does not allow his wrists their full range of motion most likely will compensate by requiring excessive motion from other joints. This may lead to inconsistent performance, as well as to an increased chance of injury.

The angle of the club to the ground at address depends on the lie angle of the club selected. The golfer should stand with the ball approximately 80% of the distance from the back foot toward the front foot. The ball should be at this position (approximately even with the left armpit) for every club.[8] When using a driver, the golfer should have his center of weight located halfway between his left foot and his right foot. According to Leadbetter and Huggan,[8] a slight variation in weight distribution should be present when using different length clubs. When the golfer is using a driver, the distance between the lateral malleoli should be about 135% of the distance between his left and right lateral femoral condyles. For other clubs, the shorter the club, the narrower the stance.[8]

The hips should be aligned in the direction of the target, while the right shoulder should be dropped slightly. A line from the left shoulder to the right shoulder should be tilted about 15° downward and about 15° open to the target. The knees and the hips should be comfortably flexed, resulting in the right shoulder being approximately directly above the ball of the right foot.[8] For a driver, the right knee should be flexed about 45° and the trunk should be tilted about 45° down from the vertical. Figure 3–2 shows a proper set-up position.

Figure 3–1. A typical golf swing. (From Fleisig,[3] p 12.)

BACKSWING (INCLUDING TAKE-AWAY)

The purpose of the backswing is to put the golfer and the club into the optimum position from which to start the downswing.[4] Figures 3–3 and 3–4 illustrate the backswing. The backswing starts with the golfer addressing the ball. As the club starts its backswing, the right foot applies an anterior shear force, while the left foot applies a posterior shear force, producing a clockwise torque (as viewed from above).[1,18] This torque produces a rotation, which is transferred up the body. The golfer rotates, in order, the knees, hips, and the lumbar and cervical spine, while the head remains fairly stationary.[9,10] The rotation is around an approximately vertical axis through the center of the body, in a clockwise direction, as viewed from above.

As the backswing continues, the left arm forward flexes and horizontally adducts. The only substantial electromyographic (EMG) activity in the upper extremities at this time is that of the subscapularis of the left arm.[7,12] The force of the feet toward the target decreases and eventually becomes a force away from the target, which helps slow down the club near the top of its arch.[1,18] There is hyperextension of the left thumb, radial deviation of the left wrist, and dorsiflexion and radial deviation of the right wrist.[9,10]

Figure 3-2. Set-up.   (A)   (B)

Repeated stress may cause lumbar strains, tendinitis of the wrist, epicondylitis and cervical problems.[9,10] However, less than one fourth of all golf-swing injuries are believed to occur during the backswing stage.[9]

TRANSITION

The golf swing cannot be properly divided only into a backswing and a downswing be-

Figure 3-4. Mid-backswing.

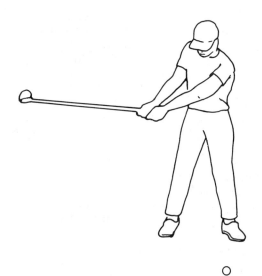

Figure 3-3. Early backswing.

cause part of the body should start its downward or forward motion while the club is still in its backswing. This brief period can be referred to as a transition stage. The transition stage can be defined as starting when the golfer begins to shift weight back onto his left foot. Figure 3-5 shows a typical

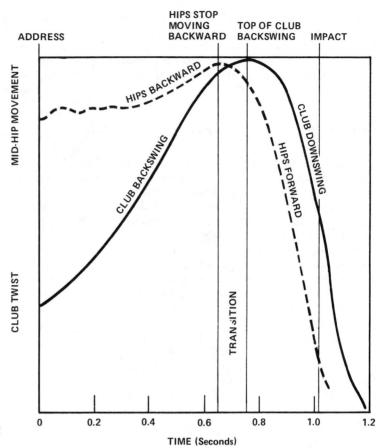

Figure 3–5. Timing of golf swing phases.

graph of the relative timing between the club swing and the hip motion for a professional golfer, although the timing varies from person to person.

By starting to shift his body forward while the club is still swinging back, a golfer can stretch out the muscles in his body. This stretching gives the golfer an added element of elastic energy to add into his downswing. Some believe that this initial weight shift is best achieved by shifting the hips linearly toward the target,[2,4,5] whereas others recommend a supination of the left foot and ankle, which moves the left knee toward the target[8] and transfers weight onto the lateral side of the left foot.

The transition stage is complete when the club (as seen when facing the golfer) has stopped moving in a clockwise direction (Fig. 3–6). At this point, the trunk has rotated so

Figure 3–6. Transition.

that the hips are closed about 45° and the shoulders are closed about 100° from the direction of the target. Also, the hands are at or slightly above head height, and the club shaft lies over and behind the head near horizontal.[4]

DOWNSWING (AND IMPACT)

McCarroll and Gioe's[9] studies have shown that there are more than twice as many downswing injuries as backswing injuries. This is easy to believe because the club during downswing covers the same range of motion as in the backswing but about three times as quickly (Table 3–1). The force of impact, transmitted up the golf club to the golfer, also can contribute to injury.

To help explain the biomechanics of the downswing, one can model the golfer as a double pendulum.[2-4,11,14] The upper pendulum represents a link between the two wrists on the club and either the left shoulder[3,11] or a point between the two shoulders.[2,4] The lower pendulum represents the club, from the wrists to the club head.[2-4,11] The downswing can then be broken into two phases: upper-pendulum (i.e., arm) acceleration and lower-pendulum (i.e., club) acceleration.

Upper-Pendulum Acceleration

As the downswing stage begins, the golfer continues to shift his weight onto his left foot[1,15,18] by moving his hips toward the hole. The golfer pushes in the anterior direction with the left foot and in the posterior direction with his right foot,[1,18] generating a

counterclockwise torque. This torque is then passed to the upper body, with additional torque and force generated by the buttocks, quadriceps, hamstrings, and lower back muscles.[10] This torque causes a counterclockwise (i.e., downswing) acceleration of the upper pendulum, through moderate levels of activity in the pectoralis major, latissimus dorsi, and rotator cuff muscles in both shoulders,[1,7,12] as well as through gravity (Fig. 3–7). These are the same muscles that were eccentrically loaded to stop the club at the end of the backswing.[1] Some believe that the downswing should be initiated by the golfer's pulling down along the shaft of the club and applying a positive (downward) torque on the club at the hands.[17]

It is important to notice that the muscles of the right shoulder are contributing, as well as those of the left. The right arm adds rigidity and speed to the upper pendulum, especially at the weak points of a left-arm-only swing.[2] During early downswing, the wrists apply a negative torque[17] by remaining radially deviated, preventing the lower pendulum from opening.[2-4,9-11] By the time the club is approximately horizontal, the right wrist is in maximum dorsiflexion, the left thumb is extended, and muscles of the left forearm are under tension (Fig. 3–8).[9,10]

TABLE 3–1. Approximate Breakdown of Timing During Swing

Stage	Approximate Length of Stage (s)
Weight shift prior to club movement	0.5
Backswing	0.7
Transition	0.1
Downswing	0.3
Follow-through	1.0

Source: Data from Carlsoo[1] and Williams and Cavanagh.[18]

Figure 3–7. Early downswing.

Figure 3-8. Mid-downswing.

Lower-Pendulum Acceleration

When the club has reached an approximately horizontal position, the wrists ulnarly deviate toward a neutral anatomic position as the left forearm supinates and the right forearm pronates. The angle between the club shaft and the left arm becomes progressively larger.[4,11] This "releasing" of the wrists starts to accelerate the lower pendulum but also decelerates the upper pendulum.[4,11] The lower pendulum is powered by

the pectoralis major, subscapularis, and latissimus dorsi of both arms.[7,12]

Maintaining an acute left arm–clubshaft angle until well into the downswing allows the upper pendulum to reach a greater velocity, due to a low moment of inertia. (This is the same physics principle that allows spinning figure skaters to spin more quickly by keeping their arms in closer to their bodies.) Increasing the left arm–clubshaft angle swings the lower pendulum (i.e., the club), adding even more velocity to the club head. This delay between the upper- and lower-pendulum swinging allows the club head to achieve the greatest total velocity (the summation of velocity generated by both the upper and lower pendulums).[11]

Impact

The downswing phase ends with impact (Fig. 3–9). The head of the club and the ball are in contact for approximately half a millisecond (0.0005 seconds). From a performance aspect, the purpose of impact is to hit the ball as far as possible in the proper direction. From a safety aspect, the purpose of impact is to have a smooth transition from pendulum acceleration to deceleration, even though contact is made with an object (usually the ball, but sometimes a divot).

Figure 3-9. Impact.   **(A)**   **(B)**

Several factors contribute to the successful performance of a swing. Equipment used is important; the choice of golf ball as well as the length, mass, and flexibility of the golf club are factors. Wind and weather also can affect the ball's flight. The distance the ball goes is also dependent on the position and orientation of the club face at impact with respect to the ball. Slight variations in the position and orientation of the club to the ball at impact can have drastic effects on the outcome. To make last-instant adjustments before impact would require large torques applied in an extremely short time, which is neurophysiologically impossible.[2] Swing imperfections must therefore be corrected earlier in the swing.

At impact, the counterclockwise torque of the feet has ended. The left foot is supporting most of the load, and both feet apply a shear force to retard foot motion toward the hole.[1,18] Richards and colleagues[15] found that at contact, the left foot is supporting 80% to 95% of the load. They found this to be true for both low-handicap and high-handicap golfers. The skilled golfers, however, had their weight supported toward the heel of the left foot, whereas the less-skilled golfers tended to be supported in the middle of the foot.[15] This finding probably implies that skilled golfers get more counterclockwise rotation during their swing (hence their weight is supported farther back, toward their heel).

Valgus stress occurs on the right knee around the time of impact.[9,10] In addition, both wrists are under compression, and the left elbow extension mass contracts.[9,10] The left wrist, hand, and elbow are often hurt due to the compression of impact.[9,10] These injuries can result from unexpected impact with a divot, as well as from the usual impact with the ball.

FOLLOW-THROUGH

The purpose of the follow-through is to decelerate the pendulums without requiring excessive effort from the muscles. About one fourth of all golf-swing injuries occur during this stage.[9]

After impact, the left forearm continues to supinate, the right forearm continues to pronate, and the lumbar and cervical spines

Figure 3–10. Early follow-through.

rotate and hyperextend (Figs. 3–10 and 3–11).[9,10] Hip rotation is also completed.[9,10] In order to decelerate the pendulums, the subscapularis continues to be active, as do the latissimus dorsi and pectoralis major of both arms, at reduced levels.[7,12]

Both legs also rotate—the right knee flexes and the left ankle supinates.[10] As the club rises, the right heel is lifted off of the ground, and almost all of the vertical load is on the left foot (Fig. 3–11).[1,10,15,18] Good

Figure 3–11. Mid–follow-through.

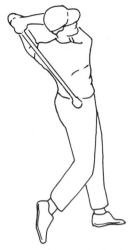

Figure 3 – 12. End of swing.

golfers seem to be a little better at transferring their vertical load as far forward as possible.[15] Shear forces retarding foot motion toward the hole are present until the club is horizontal.[1,18]

As the club decelerates, the golfer may extend his back into a reverse "C" position (Fig. 3 – 12).[10] Most injuries in this phase occur in the back (especially the lower back), due to the hyperextension.[10] This hyperextension of the spine may cause chronic back problems, especially in golfers with an excessive reverse "C."[10]

SUMMARY

Golfers, like all other athletes, must keep themselves in good physical condition. The golfer should concentrate on conditioning the muscles most used for the golf swing. It is notable that, unlike most other upper-extremity sports, the golf swing requires very little from the deltoids, possibly due to the limited elevation of the arm.[7,12] The rotator cuff of both arms must be strengthened specifically to prevent supplantation by the more dominant deltoid.[7,12] The latissimus dorsi and pectoralis major muscles of both arms, as well as the muscles of the lower back, should also be conditioned. The golfer must strengthen these muscles through the range of motion required for the golf swing. Warming up and stretching before playing is also a good idea. Endurance conditioning is also important for a golfer; a golfer tired from walking and playing stands an increased chance of becoming "lazy" and using improper mechanics to reduce the demands on certain tired muscles. These improper mechanics may result in injury. Conditioning and training for the golfer are addressed more thoroughly in Chapter 4.

REFERENCES

1. Carlsoo, S: A kinetic analysis of the golf swing. J Sports Med Phys Fitness 7:76 – 82, 1967.
2. Cochran, A and Stobbs, J: The Search for the Perfect Swing. Heinemann Educational Books, 1968.
3. Fleisig, GS: Analysis of a Mechanical Model of the Golf Swing. Unpublished B.S. thesis, M.I.T., 1984.
4. Hay, JG: The Biomechanics of Sports Techniques. Prentice-Hall, Englewood Cliffs, NJ, 1973, pp 270 – 287.
5. Hogan, B and Wind, HW: Five Lessons: The Modern Fundamentals of Golf. AS Barnes and Co, 1957.
6. Hosea, TM, et al: Biomechanical analysis of the golfer's back. In Cochran, AJ (ed): Science and Golf. E & FN Spon, London, 1990, pp 43 – 48.
7. Jobe, FW, Moynes, DR, and Antonelli, DJ: Rotator cuff function during a golf swing. Am J Sports Med 14:388 – 392, 1986.
8. Leadbetter, D and Huggan J: The Golf Swing. The Stephen Greene Press, 1990.
9. McCarroll, JR and Gioe, TJ: Professional golfers and the price they pay. Phys Sportsmed 10(7):64 – 70, 1982.
10. McCarroll, JR: Golf. In Schneider, RC, et al (eds): Sports Injuries: Mechanisms, Prevention, and Treatment. Williams & Wilkins, Baltimore, 1985, pp 290 – 294.
11. Milburn, PD: Summation of segmental velocities in the golf swing. Med Sci Sports Exerc 14(1):60 – 64, 1982.
12. Moynes, DR, et al: Electromyography and motion analysis of the upper extremity in sports. Physical Therapy 66:1905 – 1911, 1986.
13. Nagao, N and Sawada, Y: A kinematic analysis of the golf swing by means of fast motion picture in connection with racial difference. J Sport Med 14:55 – 63, 1974.
14. Neal, RJ, et al: The influence of club length and shot distance on the temporal characteristics of the swings of expert and novice golfers. In Cochran, AJ (ed): Science and Golf. E & FN Spon, London, 1990, pp 43 – 48.
15. Richards, J, et al: Weight transfer patterns during the golf swing. Res Quarterly for Ex and Sport 56(4):361 – 365, 1985.

16. Shibayama, H and Ebashi, H: Development of a motor skill using the golf swing from the viewpoint of the regulation of muscle activity. In Matsui, H and Kobayashi, K (eds): Biomechanics VIII-B. Human Kinetics Publishers, 1983, pp 895–902.

17. Vaughan, CL: A three-dimensional analysis of the forces and torques applied by a golfer during the downswing. In Morecki, A, Fidelus, K, Kedzior, K, and Wit, A (eds): Biomechanics VII-B. University Park Press, Baltimore, 1981, pp 325–331.

18. Williams, KR and Cavanagh, PR: The mechanics of foot action during the golf swing and implications for shoe design. Med Sci Sports Exerc 15(3):247–255, 1983.

Training and Conditioning

William J. Mallon, MD

Training and conditioning for golf may serve two purposes: (1) improving performance as a golfer, and (2) lessening the risk of injury from playing the sport. Although professionals currently espouse exercise as beneficial to achieving both goals, very little scientific evidence exists to support this dogma. However, a 1994 book[14] addresses the prevention of injury in sport, including a specific chapter devoted to golf,[11] and includes training and conditioning as the cornerstones of preventing injuries. Also, because of the proliferation of injuries to the back among golfers, Larkin and associates[10] have stated that the necessity for low-back conditioning programs for golfers has become apparent.

Professional golfers have not long been known as proponents of exercise as a method of improving their golf games. In the late 1940s and early 1950s, world-class amateur Frank Stranahan was known for his devotion to fitness and his use of weight lifting as a training aid.[13] It was not until the success of Gary Player in the early 1960s, however, that players became aware that off-season conditioning could improve one's golf game.[13] Prior to that time, golfers were notorious for their lack of fitness and general poor level of conditioning. Currently, most professional golfers (both PGA and LPGA) do exercise. Exercise is now popular enough among the professionals that a fitness trailer staffed by a physical therapist to help with any injuries travels along with the professional tours, providing a common site for exercise.

Although few scientific studies have analyzed the golf swing and training for improvement in golf, by applying well-known principles of athletic training one can outline a training program that should help golfers fulfill their potential and decrease the chance of overuse injuries from golf.

RELEVANT PRINCIPLES OF TRAINING

The most important principle of athletic training is probably the specificity principle. This states that training produces a beneficial effect that is specific to the type of exercise performed. For example, long-distance running does not help sprinting ability because the muscle fibers used are totally different. Performing bench presses does not help one become better at performing bicep curls, because the muscles exercised are different. Performing an isometric exercise does not necessarily increase strength when the exercise is extended over a full range of motion. Thus, the single best exercise for golf is to play golf or to hit golf balls on a practice tee, because it is the most specific.

Many professional golfers swing a heavy club in the off-season, reasoning that this will help strengthen their golf muscles, increase club head speed and thereby increase their distance. However, examining the motion reveals that the players are swinging a heavy club relatively slowly. Thus they are developing the muscles that help them swing slowly. Specifically, they are probably conditioning the slow-twitch fibers in the muscles that control the golf swing. Swinging a heavy club is a good exercise to stretch the muscles, because the extra weight puts a traction-type force on the body at the limits of the swing. The exercise does not accomplish what it is supposed to do, however.

Expanding on the principle of specificity, it is not possible to state whether any single exercise will "get one into good shape." A single exercise can only improve one's ability to perform that exercise, or exercises that use closely related muscle groups in a similar manner.

Thus, one must be very specific in designing any exercise program. Does the athlete wish to get stronger? Does he or she wish to run faster for short distances or for long distances?

For golf, the questions that need be addressed usually include: Does the golfer wish to hit the ball farther? Does the golfer wish to get into better aerobic condition so that he or she does not fatigue while playing golf? Does the golfer wish to become more flexible to increase his or her body turn?

AEROBIC CONDITIONING

Aerobic exercise is exercise performed at a low enough level that the body can use oxygen as its primary fuel source throughout the exercise. Aerobic conditioning is done below this level. It forces the heart and lungs to work at higher loads for prolonged periods of time. An excellent guideline is that the exercise is aerobic when one can talk on a conversational level during the exercise.

The benefits of aerobic conditioning are many.[1,16] It has been shown to aid in weight control, decrease hypertension, decrease the levels of cholesterol and triglycerides in the blood, improve depression, and decrease insulin demands in diabetic patients.[1,16]

Any exercise that raises the pulse to 75% of predicted maximum and maintains it there for 20 or more minutes can be classified as an aerobic exercise. The most common types of aerobic exercise practiced by the general population are running, walking, cycling, swimming, cross-country skiing, and aerobics.

It is difficult to say if any one exercise is best for the golfer. Running and aerobics both carry the risk of injury from repetitive impact. Walking, swimming, and cycling minimize this risk. Cycling, however, carries the danger of accidents. Swimming, while an excellent aerobic exercise, has not been as effective in weight control, if this is the golfer's desire.

Walking is an excellent aerobic exercise with minimal injury risks. In addition, it perfectly mimics the aerobic requirements of golf, which, admittedly, are minimal. The only real drawback to walking as an exercise is that it can be done at such low intensity that no real training effect occurs.

FLEXIBILITY TRAINING

It has never been proven scientifically that one plays better golf by becoming more flexible. It seems, however, that this would be the case because of the wide range of motion demanded of multiple joints during a golf swing.

During the backswing of a top-caliber golfer, the trunk rotates 90° or more relative to the target line. This is usually termed the "shoulder turn" and is a combination of the hip turn, which occurs via pelvic rotation, and trunk rotation, which occurs primarily in the thoracic spine.

Also during the backswing, the shoulders must move through a wide range of motion.[6] The left shoulder must flex from 50° to 80°, and then horizontally adduct almost 70°, to reach a position in which it crosses the chest. In addition, it also undergoes internal rotation. The right shoulder is abducted about 70°, and externally rotated about 90°.

In golfers with limited flexibility, the range of motion required by the shoulders and back will be near to that golfer's maximum. Two alternatives then exist: either (1) the golfer will be forced to shorten his or her swing, or (2) the golfer will still attempt a full-length swing, but with greatly increased muscle tension. There is nothing inherently wrong with a short swing, but if a golfer can increase flexibility, a swing of any length will function with decreased muscle tension because the ranges of joint motions required will be a smaller percentage of maximum. In general, most professionals believe that too much muscle tension is detrimental to the golf swing. Also, if golfers are more flexible, the swing will not stress the outer limits of their ranges of motion, which may predispose to injury.

Nicklaus has described an excellent series of exercises to increase trunk flexibility, although he mentioned using them only as a warm-up series of stretching exercises.[12] The exercises are:

1. Trunk rotation with the club placed behind the lower back.
2. Trunk rotation with the club behind the back with the arms fully extended behind the back.
3. Trunk rotation with the club in front of the body with both arms elevated to shoulder height.

Trunk rotation is probably the key element to be developed in any flexibility program for golf. Two excellent exercises for this are illustrated in Figures 4–1 and 4–2.

Both involve placing a bar of some type over the shoulders. Both exercises are performed in the seated position. In Figure 4–1, the trunk is slowly rotated side-to-side. In Figure 4–2, the trunk is leaned toward the floor, and then, after returning to the upright, the body is leaned toward the opposite side. Although the exercise can be performed with a broomstick or a golf club, a slightly weighted bar or stick, such as a barbell, will add a slight stretch at the end of the exercise because the weight will pull the body through the last few degrees of stretch. To avoid injury, this should be done very slowly and not overdone. Ten movements to each side, performed once a day, are sufficient and will greatly increase one's flexibility.

Flexibility in the shoulders, which is also very important, can be developed in several ways. One is to place a golf club overhead, then lower the club gradually behind the neck as far as it will go, keeping the arms as straight as possible. In addition, Nicklaus's exercise of performing a trunk rotation with the club behind the back with the arms fully extended will also increase the flexibility in the shoulders. Finally, simply rotating the arms individually in circles as widely as possible will increase flexibility.

Perhaps the ultimate exercise for developing flexibility for golfers is to swing a weighted club. Swinging a weighted club slowly will stretch the trunk and shoulders at the top of the back swing. The player should attempt to maintain fairly good form, by neither letting the left foot raise up too high off the ground nor rolling the weight to the outside of the right foot, and by keeping the left arm fairly straight. If these parameters are maintained, the stretch will be placed entirely on the trunk and shoulders, and flexibility will be developed in these areas. Swinging a weighted club for 5 minutes every day will aid flexibility greatly and will also strengthen the golfing muscles to some degree.

The player should perform the exercise to the limits of his or her motion, without stressing these limits on the initial sessions. Then every day the player should attempt to add just a slight amount of stretch to the motion by going a bit farther. When doing this, however, it is important to maintain good form and keep the movements slow. One should not "bounce" into the stretch, which can lead to injuries.

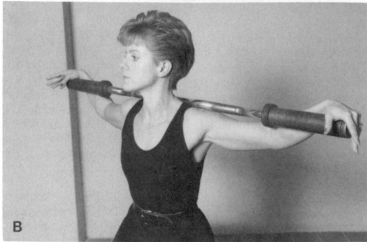

Figure 4–1. Trunk rotation (*A*) to the left; (*B*) to the right.

DISTANCE AND STRENGTH TRAINING

The distance a ball travels depends on many factors, but if swing mechanics do not change, increasing club head speed at impact will always increase distance. Many players state that length comes from the legs, but it is necessary that the arms swing at a very high velocity to generate club head speed. The muscles of the upper back help swing the arms through impact, especially the left arm.

Developing the ability to swing the arms more quickly would then increase club head speed and impart greater velocity to the ball at impact. Using the specificity principle, the best way to train the arms to swing quickly is

not to swing a heavy club, as many golfers believe. This increases flexibility but must be done at a slow speed, thereby training the muscle fibers responsible for swinging the club slowly. Instead, by swinging faster than maximum speeds, it should be possible to train the muscle fibers responsible for high-speed movement of the golf club. Although one may wonder if it is possible to swing faster than maximum, this can be done by swinging a lighter club. This principle is used by the Eastern Europeans in field events.[3,9] Rather than training with heavier shots or javelins, they use lightweight shots and javelins to increase arm speed, attempting to develop the "quick arm." A similar method is used to train sprinters who are

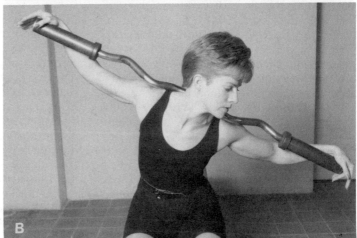

Figure 4–2. Side bends (*A*) to the right; (*B*) to the left.

also faced with the difficult problem of finding a way to train at supramaximal speeds. This is accomplished either by running downhill or by being towed behind a motorcycle, which decreases wind resistance and pulls the runner just above his or her maximum for short bursts.

An excellent drill to increase arm and club head speed is to turn the club upside-down, holding the shaft just above the head, swing the club back slowly, and then attempt to make the loudest "whoosh" possible on the forward swing. It is possible to use a relatively normal club and still perform a similar drill. By removing the sole plate of a driver

and taking all the lead out of the club, a very lightweight club can be created, weighing less than a C-0 swingweight. Swinging this 10 to 20 times a day will train arm speed.

A second method used to increase speed by many of the European sports programs involves the principle of plyometric training.[2] This principle concerns prestretching the muscles prior to their use in an explosive contracture. To train jumping ability, one method used is to jump off boxes 2 or 3 ft in height and then spring up as high as possible. The jump from this height causes a prestretch in the quadriceps and gastrosoleus groups. By then immediately jumping as high as possible, the prestretched muscles are able to exert a greater force.

Plyometrics could be extended to golf to help increase the speed and force developed during the swing. The drill should be performed as follows:

1. From a normal address position, take a full backswing to the maximum turn possible.
2. At the top of the swing, stop and hold the position for 2 to 3 seconds at full stretch.
3. At the end of the pause, force the trunk and arms to turn just slightly further and take the club back a few inches farther. Then immediately begin a full-speed forward swing.

Performing this drill 10 to 20 times a day will help develop flexibility as well as increase the force that the golf muscles can generate.

It should be cautioned that plyometrics and supramaximal velocity training are very strenuous exercises—much more than simply swinging a heavy club. They probably should be attempted only by tournament players or young players in fairly good condition. They should not be attempted until the player has fully warmed up by swinging a regular club or a heavy club at normal speeds for 5 to 10 minutes. Golfers attempting these exercises will be astonished at the amount of muscle soreness they will feel the next day, and they should be cautioned to begin these exercises slowly with only two or three repetitions of each at first.

In a discussion of training to increase distance and strength in the golf swing, it may seem that weight training has been overlooked. This has been popularized by Gary Player and is a valuable adjunct to any complete golf training program.[13] Unfortunately, most people who want to begin weight training for golf get their advice from bodybuilders or weight lifters, who have little conception of the muscles used in a golf swing. Consequently, the program often includes a lot of bench presses or other exercises that are not believed to be helpful to the golf swing and may even be detrimental. A properly designed weight-training program should be able to help one's golf game.

As mentioned earlier, club head speed is determined to a large extent by how quickly the arms are swung on the forward swing. For right-handed golfers, the arms are led by the left arm and thus the speed of the swing of the left arm will help determine the distance one can hit a golf ball. If the golfer cannot swing the left arm quickly, it will become the rate-limiting factor and the entire swing will slow down.

The left arm is swung across the chest by the muscles of the upper back. Two standard exercises to help develop these muscles are chin-ups (Fig. 4–3) and lat pull-downs (Fig. 4–4) (lat is short for latissimus dorsi, the large muscle of the upper back that assists the left arm swing). Jobe, Moynes, and Antonelli[6] also have discussed the importance of the latissimus muscle during the golf swing.

Two exercises specific to the golf swing are demonstrated in Figures 4–5 and 4–6. The first exercise (Fig. 4–5) requires access to pulley weights. The player holds the pulley rope attachment in a position similar to that reached at the top of the backswing. Both arms are then swung across the chest, pulling down the pulley. In the second exercise (Fig. 4–6), the player leans over with a dumbbell in the left arm and swings forward from that position, to imitate the golf swing from impact through the follow-through.

The lower back, of critical importance to all golfers, is a common source of pain in many. It can be exercised by the two stretching exercises illustrated in Figures 4–1 and 4–2 (trunk rotations and side bends), but using a light barbell.

To support the lower back, it is quite important to keep the abdominal muscles strong. The best exercise for this is termed a "crunch" by bodybuilders. It is actually an abdominal curl, in which, rather than doing a full sit-up, only the head and shoulders are curled up off the floor, while keeping the small of the back pressed firmly against the floor. This should be done with the feet elevated and not held down, the hip and knees flexed, and with the arms folded across the chest rather than behind the neck. The beginning and ending movements are shown in Figure 4–7.

Two other muscle groups that should be stressed in weight training for golf are the forearms and the legs. The forearm muscles maintain the grip on the club. If not strong

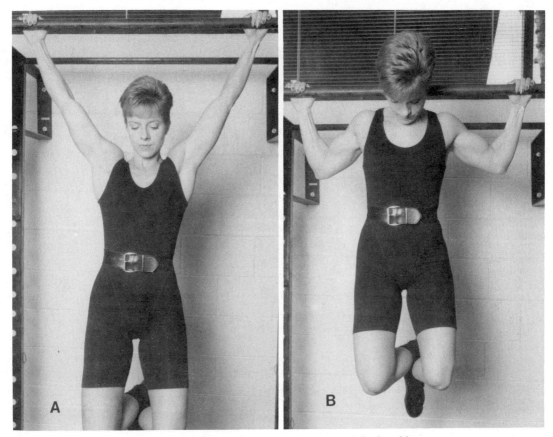

Figure 4–3. Chin-up. (A) Starting position; (B) final position.

enough, they will be unable to maintain a firm grip as club head speed is increased. During the first part of the downswing, maintaining a torque on the grip by the wrists can increase club head speed.[7] Even if the forearms are strong enough to maintain a firm grip, increasing forearm strength will allow the use of a smaller percentage of grip strength.[4] This will then increase flexibility in the wrists during the golf swing.

An excellent exercise to develop the forearms is simply to squeeze a rubber ball, performing many repetitions, up to 100 per set. Although in a different sport, this was the method used by Rod Laver to develop his left forearm so that he was able to play tennis at championship levels.

Three weight exercises to develop the forearm are the wrist curl (Fig. 4–8), the reverse wrist curl (Fig. 4–9), and the wrist roller (Fig. 4–10). In the first two, the barbell is lowered to the end of the fingertips and then the fingers curl the weight back into the palm, after which the wrists volar-flex (wrist curl) or dorsi-flex (reverse wrist curl) to lift the weight another inch or two. The wrist roller is performed by rolling the weight up until the rope is fully wound around the bar (Fig. 4–10).

The legs can be developed by running, cycling, or several of the other aerobic exercises already mentioned. These are excellent for training the legs for the walking necessary for 18 holes of golf. For the golf swing, however, the legs need to be trained for a slightly more explosive-type movement. No other exercise for the legs is similar to the golf swing, so simply hitting practice balls may be the best exercise for the purpose. However, other explosive-type training exercises for the legs may have some crossover benefit. These include rope jumping or running sprints uphill (or up steps). These are both very strenuous exercises that probably

Figure 4–4. Lat pulldown. (*A*) Starting position; (*B*) final position.

should be reserved for young players, tournament players in good shape, or recreational golfers in very good shape who work up to this exercise.

DESIGNING A FITNESS PROGRAM

As shown earlier, various types of fitness can be developed to improve one's golf game, but the many types of exercises need to be organized into a concise fitness program. Large numbers of variables can be adjusted to design an individual fitness program. How often should it be done? Should something be done in every workout for all three types of fitness (aerobic, flexibility, strength) every day or just for one or two types per workout day? Should one rest a day between workouts? When working out, how many repetitions should one do, how many sets, how far should one run/walk/cycle?

Should workouts be performed year-round or only in the off season?

Definitive answers cannot be given to these questions because programs should be developed on an individual basis. The physician should evaluate the risk of participating; consultation should probably include a golf professional, to evaluate the individual's goals, and a fitness trainer, to guide the choice of exercises and routines that will help to accomplish those goals.

No two people, or golfers, are alike in their body habitus. The program should be aimed at improving any weaknesses in the player's golf game or body structure. In addition, the player's initial level of aerobic and strength fitness should be considered.

Some guidelines can be given, however. For example, it takes several hours to work on each of the three types of fitness effectively and still recover from each section. For those who cannot afford this time com-

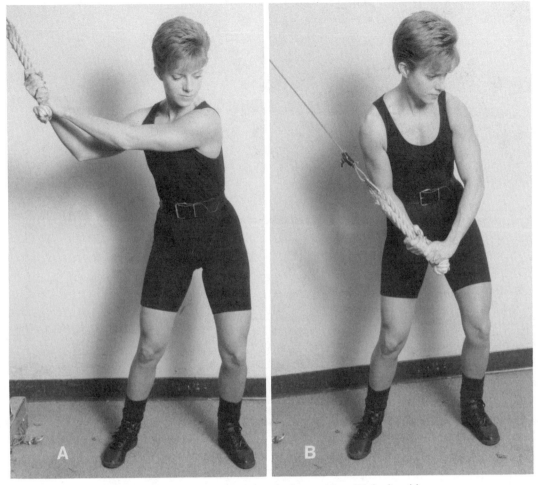

Figure 4–5. Pulley golf swing. (*A*) Starting position; (*B*) final position.

mitment, I recommend exercising daily, but only for one or two of the three main types of fitness.

This pattern avoids another problem — overwork. It is possible to exercise too much. Specifically, many recommend that weight-lifting or strength-building exercises should not be done every day because the muscles need a day to recover from hard exercise.[1] This theory has been challenged and is probably not correct for people already in excellent condition or for competitive athletes accustomed to weight lifting.[1,16] For the average golfer, however, strength training every other day, or every third day, avoids

overtraining the muscles, which can lead to muscle or tendon injuries.

Aerobic exercise also can be overdone, especially those exercises with high repetitive impact, such as running and high-impact aerobics. Performing these exercises every other day will avoid this problem, but they should be performed for a minimum of 20 minutes to achieve a training effect for the cardiovascular system.

In strength training, the number of sets and repetitions can be adjusted *ad infinitum.* Because the golf swing is a low-repetition, high-speed exercise, and because high weights can cause muscle or tendon injuries,

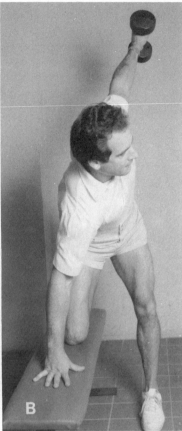

Figure 4–6. Dumbbell follow-through. (*A*) Starting position; (*B*) final position.

it would be ideal to perform the strength exercises with low repetitions and very high speed, while imitating the motion of the golf swing. The best way to do this is to swing a lighter club very quickly, as mentioned earlier. Swinging a lightweight club at high speed is much more difficult than it sounds; many muscles are being used and being stretched. I recommend doing this only about 5 times the first day, building up to no more than 10 to 15 per day.

All the above recommendations must be individualized. A club golfer with a 15 handicap who is not in very good condition should not try even this much until he or she has built up some muscle slowly with weight training using lower weights and higher repetitions. Although they definitely should be adapted to individual needs, a set of suggested workout programs for golfers of varying abilities (and with varying time available) is shown in Table 4–1.

Flexibility training need be done for only a few minutes and can be performed daily. The key point in flexibility training is to stretch to the point of a slight muscle pull and then gently go just a bit further. The amount of stretching varies with each person. By gently going just beyond the point of comfort — but not to the point of pain — the individual will gradually become a bit more flexible each day.

Because muscle soreness may hamper their swing, competitive golfers probably should not do any significant strength training during the competitive season. That should be reserved for the 2 to 3 months off-season each winter. Club golfers who play only on weekends can probably work out during the week, but they should avoid

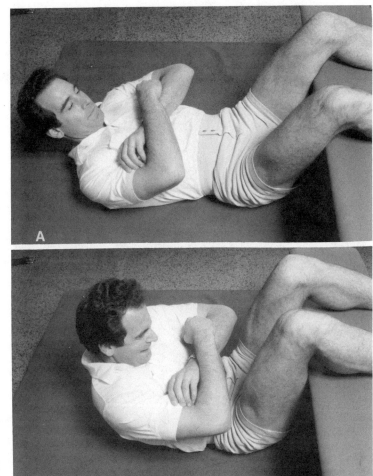

Figure 4-7. Abdominal curl. (*A*) Starting position; (*B*) final position.

weights on the day before playing. Aerobic conditioning should be performed even throughout a competitive season. It may be good to decrease the time spent on aerobics, however, to avoid feeling overly fatigued while playing.

Flexibility not only can be done year-round but it probably should be done almost daily to help prevent injuries and muscle soreness. Contrary to previous beliefs, the best time to stretch is after an aerobic or strength training workout, not before it.[5] At this time the muscles are thoroughly warmed up but have a build-up of lactic acid. Stretching then accomplishes two things: (1) it has been shown to promote the break-

down of lactic acid, decreasing subsequent muscle soreness, and (2) with the muscles already warmed up, it is possible to stretch more, with less risk of injury.[1] Stretching without any previous gentle warm-up can cause muscle injuries. It is possible to stretch too much.

Warm-up should be performed before an exercise session of any type.[8] This is best accomplished simply by performing the exercises at half-speed and through a smaller range of motion, then gradually building up to full speed and full motion. It is similar to beginning a practice session on the tee by hitting only a few half-wedge pitches.

Cool-down should also be performed after

Figure 4–8. Wrist curl. (*A*) Starting position; (*B*) final position.

any exercise session. Again, the best method is simply to gear back and perform the exercises slowly and with less amplitude. As mentioned earlier, this is also an excellent time to perform flexibility training. Most of the flexibility exercise should be done at the end of the workout as part of the cool-down.[5]

OFF-SEASON TRAINING

Any off-season program for a competitive golfer should at least include hitting balls into a net, if possible. Such nets are usually available at most college golf programs. If a net is not available, swinging both a heavy club slowly (for flexibility) and a light club quickly (for strength) will keep the muscles loose. The off-season also is the time when competitive golfers who have shunned intensive strength training (especially with weights) to avoid muscle soreness can step up the level of that part of their conditioning program.

Competitive high school or college golfers often ask what sports are good for the off-season, should they desire to engage in some other competitive sport. (This is often important in northern areas, where the off-season is longer.) Probably the best sport to

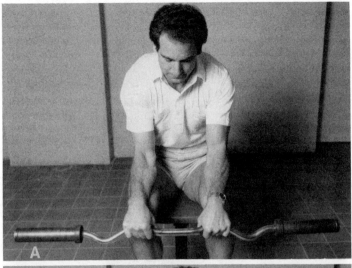

Figure 4-9. Reverse wrist curl. (*A*) Starting position; (*B*) final position.

develop strength and flexibility in the upper body and trunk is gymnastics, although it is not very popular in the United States.

Other sports have some things to recommend them for the golfer. Basketball, for example, is excellent for aerobic conditioning and good for flexibility and explosive power in the legs. It is not very helpful in developing strength, however, and presents a high injury risk.

Volleyball is excellent for developing explosive power in the legs, and is good for aerobic conditioning, flexibility, and arm strength. There is less risk of injury than in basketball.

Skiing is excellent for leg strength. Cross-country skiing is particularly good for aerobic conditioning, and downhill skiing is also helpful (though less so) in that regard. Downhill skiing presents a very high risk of injury for all except the most skilled, however.

Racquetball is excellent for aerobic conditioning. It also promotes flexibility and strength in one arm, but this may be a detriment in a two-sided sport like golf.

Figure 4–10. Wrist roller.

TABLE 4–1. Suggested Exercise Program

Most of the specific exercises within each category are described in the body of the chapter. Which specific exercises to perform each day must be decided based on the golfer's priorities and other time commitments.

Young Player, Tournament Caliber, Lots of Time to Devote to Training

OFF-SEASON (WINTER) (AVERAGE DAILY TIME COMMITMENT: 2–4 H)

Daily	Stretching and flexibility exercises (15–30 min)
4–5 d/wk	Aerobic exercise (run, walk, cycling, etc.) (30–60 min)
2–3 d/wk	Weight training (60 min)
Daily	Hit balls into a net (if possible) (60–90 min)
Daily	Putt indoors on a carpet (60–90 min)

IN-SEASON (AVERAGE DAILY TIME COMMITMENT: 5–6 H)

Daily	Stretching and flexibility exercises (10 min)
2–3 d/wk	Aerobic exercise (20–30 min)
1–2 d/wk	Weight training (forearms and sit-ups for back) (20 min)
Daily	Play and practice (most of sunlight hours)

TABLE 4–1. Suggested Exercise Program
(*Continued*)

Good Player, Low-to-Middle Handicap, Some Time Available, Reasonable Condition

OFF-SEASON (WINTER) (AVERAGE DAILY TIME COMMITMENT: 1–2 H)

Daily	Stretching and flexibility exercises (10–15 min)
3–4 d/wk	Aerobic exercise (run, walk, cycling, etc.) (20–30 min)
1–2 d/wk	Weight training (30 min)
2–3 d/wk	Hit balls into a net (if possible) (30 min)
2–3 d/wk	Putt indoors on a carpet (30 min)

IN-SEASON (AVERAGE DAILY TIME COMMITMENT: 2–3 H)

Daily	Stretching and flexibility exercises (10 min)
2–3 d/wk	Aerobic exercise (20–30 min)
1–2 d/wk	Weight training (forearms and sit-ups for back) (20 min)
2–4 d/wk	Play and practice (2–5 h)

Weekend Player, Minimal Time Available, Less Than Top Condition

OFF-SEASON (WINTER) (AVERAGE DAILY TIME COMMITMENT: 1–1½ H)

Daily	Stretching and flexibility exercises (10–15 min)
3–4 d/wk	Aerobic exercise (run, walk, cycling, etc.) (20–30 min)
1–2 d/wk	Weight training (forearms and sit-ups for back) (15 min)
2–3 d/wk	Putt indoors on a carpet (30 min)

IN-SEASON (DAILY TIME COMMITMENT: 1–2 H)

Daily	Stretching and flexibility exercises (10 min)
2–3 d/wk	Aerobic exercise (20–30 min)
1–2 d/wk	Play and practice (2–5 h)

SUMMARY

Training and conditioning have historically been neglected in the sport of golf, but today's touring professional is much more conscious of the need to maintain an adequate level of fitness. Although the aerobic demands of golf are low, a good level of aerobic fitness will help the golfer to avoid fatigue late in the round. A high amount of flexibility is required, and many average golfers may find that flexibility training will help them to play better. Although golf's strength requirements are not great, proper strength training may help in increasing the club head speed at impact (and thereby the distance the ball travels). The development of stronger muscles also will allow the player to remain more flexible during the swing, since a smaller proportion of maximum effort will be needed. An adequate level of fitness of all kinds also should help the golfer to avoid injury.

Golfers at all levels will benefit from a conditioning program to improve their individual weaknesses and to maintain fitness in the off-season. The program should be carefully planned to achieve their personal goals while avoiding overtraining.

ACKNOWLEDGMENTS

I express my appreciation to Ms. Fran Butler (Instructor, Nautilus Fitness Center, Durham, North Carolina) and Mr. Sonny Falcone (Strength Coach, Duke University Department of Athletics, Durham, North Carolina) for their assistance as models for the exercises.

REFERENCES

1. Åstrand, P-O and Rodahl, K: Textbook of Work Physiology: Physiological Bases of Exercise, 2nd ed. McGraw-Hill, New York, 1977.
2. Bobbert, MF, Huijing, PA, and Van Ingen Schenau, GJ: Drop jump. I: The influence of jumping technique on the biomechanics of jumping. Med Sci Sports Exerc 19:332–338, 1987.
3. Brokhin, Y: The Big Red Machine. Random House, New York, 1978.
4. Cochran, AJ and Stobbs, J: The Search for the Perfect Swing. JB Lippincott, Philadelphia, 1968.
5. George, F: Discussion. Year Book of Sports Medicine, 1987, p 391.
6. Jobe, FW, Moynes, DR, and Antonelli, DJ: Rotator cuff functions during a golf swing. Am J Sports Med 14:388–392, 1986.
7. Jorgensen, T: On the dynamics of the swing of a golf club. Am J Physics 38(5):644–651, 1970.
8. Joy, M, Cairns, AW, and Spriging, D: Observations on the warm-up phenomenon in angina pectoris. Br Heart J 58:116–121, 1987.
9. Gilbert, D: The Miracle Machine. Coward, McCann & Geoghegan, New York, 1980.
10. Larkin, AF, et al: Annual torso specific conditioning program for golfers. In Cochran, AJ (ed): Science and Golf. E & FN Spon, London, 1990.
11. Mallon, WJ: Injury prevention among golfers. In Renström, P (ed): Prevention of Injuries in Sport. International Olympic Committee, Lausanne, 1994.
12. Nicklaus, JW: My 55 Ways to Lower Your Golf Score. Simon & Schuster, New York, 1968.
13. Player, G: Gary Player's Positive Golf. McGraw-Hill, New York, 1967.
14. Renström, P (ed): Prevention of Injuries in Sport. International Olympic Committee, Lausanne, 1994.
15. Shephard, RJ: Discussion. Year Book of Sports Medicine 1988, p 20.
16. Strauss, RH: Sports Medicine. WB Saunders, Philadelphia, 1984.

5

The Psychology of Golf

· ·

Robert J. Rotella, PhD

For years, golfers have marveled at the role of psychology in playing their beloved game effectively. The impact of the mind on golf play has been described and discussed for decades, beginning in 1908 with Arnold Haultain's *The Mysteries of Golf* [2] and continuing with other books in almost every decade since. [1,3-10] There is little doubt that the play of the game is at least 50% mental, and each of these books delivers one consistent message: The mind is a powerful asset that is malleable and capable of being used in such a manner that even individuals with limited physical abilities are capable of outplaying those with far more impressive-looking physical attributes. Indeed, the ability to control one's mind is an often overlooked but most powerful ability available to everyone.

This chapter presents *basics* to help golfers use their minds to the fullest while playing golf. The following analyses, recommendations, and suggestions are based on years of playing and studying the game of golf and advising and counseling players of both amateur and professional ranks. Even though the demands and requirements of the game are much greater for professionals than for amateurs, the approach to mastering the mental aspects of golf are fundamentally the same. Golfers must learn how to win the battle with themselves—perhaps the ultimate human and sporting challenge. It is an inner game.

43

TWO ESSENTIAL RULES

All golfers must understand two basic rules if they wish to learn the mental game for improving their golf performance:

1. Golfers cannot control all of the events that will happen to them, but they can control their response to them.
2. Golfers cannot control performance until they learn to control their minds and emotions.

The Need for a Simple, Quiet Mind

Most intelligent people have spent a significant part of their lives becoming adept at making the simple things in life highly complicated. This is a skill learned through education and socialization. To achieve a mindset that is effective for golf, it is crucial to develop the skill of making and keeping the potentially complicated things in golf *simple*.

The mechanics of the golf swing and the employment of strategic thinking must be made extremely basic and simple in order to do them repeatedly shot after shot, day after day, week after week. What this means is that the mental game of golf demands the self-discipline to *stay totally attentive to doing the same old simple and potentially boring thing constantly*. This is a difficult challenge for people who have mastered the ability to analyze, evaluate, criticize, and judge almost everything they do. It took many years of diligent study to learn how to think in this style (often described as left-brain dominant), in which the mind is constantly active. It will in turn take disciplined and persistent attention before one is able to spend 4 to 5 hours playing golf in a passive, quiet, simple, and nonjudgmental mindset.

Two Kinds of Self-Discipline—Two Different Mindsets

Success in golf requires two somewhat similar, yet different forms of self-discipline. To advance from beginner level to a level halfway or two thirds of the way to the best of one's ability requires the self-discipline to work physically on the technical fundamentals of the game. A few golfers will be able to trust and score without persistent efforts at ingraining these fundamentals, but such individuals are exceptions.

Whether self-taught or learned with the help of a professional teacher, the technical fundamentals seem boring and mundane to many golfers. Yet the self-discipline to work diligently and persistently on the practice range is usually essential. To develop the technical efficiency that allows the golfer to trust his or her swing, most players must spend countless hours ingraining these fundamentals, often on hot and humid summer days. The mindset necessary for this part of the game, requiring the physical exertion kind of self-discipline, may be called the "training mindset."

The Training Mindset

The majority of golfers who truly dream of becoming successful in the game have this kind of self-discipline and as a result develop technical proficiency that allows them at least to repeat their swing on the driving range.

This training mindset is extremely comfortable for most adults, who spend their lives trying hard to get better and working both at work and at life. It is easy to feel secure applying this same mindset to golf. It is a conscious mindset involving attempts to take control over one's life and one's golf game. It is characterized by trying harder, forcing it to happen, making it happen, being certain to be ready, and constantly analyzing, evaluating, judging, and criticizing. The training mindset is an active mindset dominated by working on weaknesses, analyzing and evaluating past mistakes, and preparing for future challenges. It is frequently influenced by fear, guilt, and worry.

This mindset is great in the early stages of development. Later, it is useful some of the time on the driving range. Helpful for preparation, it is an essential building block. On the downside, though, many people fall in love with this mindset because they have seen themselves improve because of this kind of thinking. It causes many golfers to prefer "trying their hardest" to "trying their best." Many get stuck on being perfectionistic and self-critical in a way that motivates but destroys confidence and trust. In this mindset, spontaneity, playing, feeling, and instincts are diminished; attitudes become increasingly serious. Eventually, as more time is spent practicing than playing, the training mindset becomes the dominant and most comfortable mindset, so that even when playing in tournament competition, these golfers practice and consciously work on their swing or stroke. *In reality, golf is never played.*

Golfers with this kind of discipline and this mindset are often technically solid enough to shoot between 70 and 80 most of the time. Such golfers would willingly stay up all night three or four nights a week hitting balls if that was necessary for them to break through to the next level. This type of discipline and the willingness to do physical work will not take them to the next level, however.

How easy it would be if this were the kind of discipline and mindset required for success! It is ever so easy to get dedicated golfers to care more, try harder, and want it more. Perhaps it is unfortunate that this is not where the answer is to be found. A different kind of discipline and a different mindset are required for the desired breakthrough to the next level.

The Trusting Mindset

In the *trusting mindset*, the discipline to focus the mind takes priority over the willingness to put forth physical effort. Now the self-discipline that allows one to control the mind becomes crucial. It involves focusing attention and freeing up the body simply to react to the input from the mind and the eyes. It demands trusting one's training. It requires that the fear of failure, the fear of making mistakes, the fear of embarrassment, and the guilt associated with feeling as if you are not trying your hardest be thrown away. This is the mindset necessary for taking one's golf game to the golf course, to tournament competition, to shooting low numbers, to playing consistently well, to playing well when in position to win, and to learning to score better than you hit the ball. This is the mindset that allows golfers to get the rest of the way to the best of their ability.

Most golfers get stuck on the training mindset. They fall in love with working harder than others, but never seem to understand that to get the rest of the way is more of an inner battle than an outer (physical/technical) battle. This willingness to look on the inside and trust is a key ingredient

that separates top golfers. It requires an understanding of the trusting mindset and the *mental discipline to lock the eyes and mind into doing the same thing on every shot.*

The trusting mindset involves playing, spontaneity, creativity, and feel. It requires letting go of conscious effort and allowing your swing or stroke to flow. When trusting, golfers wait and let it happen. It is a passive mindset dominated by patience, acceptance, and a nonjudgmental attitude. For most golfers to think in this manner is a tremendous test of their mental discipline. It is simple to do but not necessarily easy to do, given dominant habits of thinking found useful in other parts of life. Disciplined people know, however, that habits can be changed and often must be changed.

Blending the Two Necessary Mindsets

It will take time and understanding to learn how to blend these two different mindsets and to use the appropriate mindset for the time and place, but it must be learned. Table 5–1 compares terms descriptive of each mindset.

ACCEPTANCE OF THE GAME

Many golfers who say they love golf walk off the course day after day frustrated, in a foul mood, filled with tension, tired and worn out as if they have just survived fighting the toughest battle of their life. In many cases, they have fought a tough battle, but have failed to survive. During their round,

TABLE 5–1. The Two Mindsets of Golf

Training	Trusting
Active	Passive
Inquisitive thinking	Quiet Mind
Evaluate	Accept
Judgmental	Nonjudgmental
Critical	Waiting
Force it to happen	Let it happen
Make it happen	Wait for it to happen
Impatience	Patience
Work on technique	Play
Look good	Just score and get the ball in the hole
Set expectations and standards	Throw away expectations

these golfers have tried to fight their nature, a fight that cannot be won.

Golf is a game. It is not a war or a battle. Because it is a game, *it must be played.* Those who do not accept that golf is a game have no chance. They will only get more and more serious as they work more and more diligently at golf and gradually get worse and worse. Doing so will only add to their frustration. Eventually, instead of being a recreational activity filled with enjoyment, golf becomes more tiring and irritating than work. These golfers can't wait for the weekend to end so that they can recover during the week at their real job, to get ready for the next weekend and the torture they are sure to face until they change their mental approach to the game and start to *play* golf.

Golfers must honestly come to grips with the reality that *golf is a game of mistakes* played by human beings who are *prone to error.* Golfers who spend their time and energy fighting the game and who think they must hit every shot perfectly to play the game successfully do not have a chance from the outset. Golf is not a game of perfection. *The idea of the game is to see who can score the lowest despite making errors.* This is the way it always has been and the way it always will be.

Many golfers go to their club professional to learn how to perfect their swing. When years of effort directed at this quest fail, they turn to a sport psychologist to help them perfect their play. But it can't be done. *Golfers with great minds give themselves a chance to hit every shot to the best of their ability.* There is a big difference between giving yourself a chance to hit each shot perfectly and doing it, however. Golfers can have total control over their mind but only limited control over whether the ball goes where they thought it would go. The idea of the mental game is to think in a way that gives you your best chance on every shot, and then to accept wherever the ball goes because you know that you did all that you could do.

Gaining Confidence

Because golf is a game of mistakes, and because mistakes in golf may miss the target by a much wider margin than in other sports, it has often been called a "humbling game." What does this mean to the mental game? It means that every time you play golf, it is easy to have your confidence destroyed. It means that most golfers become more cautious, tentative, doubtful, indecisive, and fearful as they advance from their first tee shot to their last putt. It means that most golfers lose confidence as they have more years of experience playing golf. As their physical skills improve, their confidence in those skills deteriorates. Their scores stay the same or get worse, and they leave the course feeling humbled and frustrated.

Any golfer wishing to improve must constantly face this challenge. To succeed, golfers must consciously pay attention to becoming more confident, more decisive, more trusting, and looser and freer as they move from the first tee to the last green and from the first time they play golf to the present. Doing so is an absolute necessity. Most golfers let their self-confidence depend on how well they hit their first few shots and how well they stroked their first few putts. With the exception of those days on which everything goes in the desired manner over the first few holes, the typical tendency for most golfers is to let their thoughts simply respond to their experience. If their experiences with the ball are negative, negative thoughts will follow. This is a self-defeating approach to the game, which leaves golfers as victims of how the first few holes are played. It works fine when the first few holes are played successfully, but leaves golfers devastated and out of control when the holes are not. Instead, between shots, golfers must consciously think in a way that keeps them growing in confidence, trust, and decisiveness. It is fine, however, to play totally unconsciously on those days when everything is going right. Doing so allows the golfer to slip into the so-called "zone" where so many great rounds occur, as he or she performs on "automatic pilot."

Throwing Away Fear

It is inevitable that golf will create fear. When the game is made even more difficult by weather conditions, long roughs, lightning-quick greens, or golf courses designed by architects striving to scare and distract players, it is not surprising that fear can show up at any time. In addition, the results become public information because golf is a social game played with friends; in tournaments, scores will be posted on a scoreboard and perhaps in the local paper.

To succeed at the mental game of golf, it is crucial that the golfer *throw away the fear of making mistakes* and the *fear of what other people may think*. The mind must be disciplined to be free of such concerns, which, if present, will distract the best of players and thus destroy their play.

Golfers must learn that they make a choice on each shot. They may choose *to fear making a mistake*, such as hitting out of bounds or into a hazard, or they may choose *to think about the ball going where they want it to go*. This is indeed a challenge, considering that the ball may not have gone to the intended target on the previous few shots, and that good thinking is not a guarantee that the ball will go to the desired target. Playing a shot while afraid or even slightly tentative or indecisive often does guarantee that the shot will not be the best possible, however.

Similar thoughts pertain to social anxieties. Golfers must focus their minds on the task at hand rather than on what others are thinking of them. Social anxieties are quite common for "nice" people, who by definition care about what others think of them. While playing golf, however, it is important to get lost in one's own little world. Golf must be played with a single-minded focus in which there is a total lack of concern about anyone else's judgment of you as a golfer or as a person. The mind must be totally absorbed in the ball and the target. There really is no other option. For "nice" people, this is a challenge that must be faced every day.

Taking Less Time over the Ball

It is often stated that golf is more difficult than other sports because (1) it is not a reactive sport, and (2) the golfer has so much time to think. What is so intriguing about these points is that most people who make such remarks tend to play as slowly as humanly possible. They stand over their shots and putts for a long time so as to make sure they have thought of everything. Given their statements about what makes the game so difficult, this makes no sense.

Athletes in every sport make the game more difficult when they take time to think about being careful and getting ready just prior to the moving of their bodies, with the mistaken belief that doing so will help their performance. In golf, unlike basketball, however, the opponent cannot steal your ball or block your shot if you take too much time to pull the trigger and swing. Golfers must listen to their own statements and learn to take less time over the ball. Doing so makes it easier to focus the mind and keep the body relaxed, so they have a chance to play to the best of their ability.

FOCUSING THE MIND AND EYES

Golf ultimately comes down to picking a small, precise target that is where you *want* the ball to go on every shot. While standing behind or next to the ball, golfers must look at the small target and "lock" their mind and eyes onto the ball going to the target. It doesn't matter if the golfer visualizes the ball going to the target or simply thinks about the ball going to the target. The eyes and mind must be totally decisive. In other words, a precise target must be selected and the golfer must *know* the ball is going to go there. When moving up to the ball, the golfer must stay totally committed to this decision. If there is any fear, doubt, or indecision, the golfer must walk away from the ball and start over again.

Once over the ball, the golfer must have systematic, simple, and short physical and mental routines. These routines must be programmed in practice. Nothing should ever interfere with this routine. Golfers must be totally absorbed, as if in their own private cocoon, containing only the golfer, the ball, and the target. Golfers must train themselves in daily practice to approach each shot from this level of focused attention.

The Role of Positive Thinking

It is certainly important to think positively when playing golf; doing so is a significant challenge, which never ends. Every shot, every hole, every day, year after year, the golfer must *choose* to think positively.

All golfers realize when sitting at home that it is logical to think positively rather than negatively. Remembering to think positively on the golf course is the challenge.

At its most basic level, what is positive thinking? Positive thinking means *focusing your attention on what you want.* You want to play great. You want to play to win. You want to hit shots to your targets. You want to make putts. You want to enjoy playing a game you love. If your mind is focused on what you want, you will be thinking positively. Negative thinking occurs when you let your thoughts wander to what you don't want to happen or to what you fear might happen. As long as your thoughts are consistent with what you want, you will be thinking positively.

Sometimes in the course of a round, however, golfers make the mistake of changing what they want. They decide that what they want is *not* to play poorly or *not* to shoot over 80, 90, or 100. Sometimes golfers decide that they don't want to miss right, or they don't want to three-putt. Such thinking is negative and counterproductive. To succeed in golf, *golfers must discipline themselves to focus their minds on what they want and refuse ever to play a shot while thinking in any other manner.*

Doing so shot after shot, day after day, demands a tremendous commitment. Many golfers talk about committing themselves to thinking positively but do not consistently act on these commitments while on the golf course. A true commitment renewed every day is necessary.

During a round of golf, emotions challenge the will. The golfer will be tempted to get lost in self-pity. When bad bounces or missed shots occur, it is possible to get angry, frustrated, or discouraged. When such temptations occur, the golfer may choose to focus the mind on justifiable reasons for playing poorly, as if this was what he or she wanted. Golf presents a constant challenge either to meet the demands of the game or to appease the needs of the ego. The demands of the game must remain at the forefront of the mind, or the golfer will not have much of a chance to play to the best of his or her ability.

Using Imagery Effectively

Images are the golfer's interpretation of the world past, present, and future. For years, psychologists, sport psychologists, and great athletes have emphasized the powerful role played by regular, positive mental imagery in attaining success and enhancing performance. Today, the power of imagery is used to improve personal happiness, increase self-esteem, enhance various cancer treatments, and aid in injury rehabilitation for athletes. The noted psychologist William James once went so far as to state, "In a contest between imagination and the will, the imagination will win every time." It is also quite true, though, that a focused mind and willpower are necessary to use the imagination effectively on a day-to-day basis.

Although the idea that golfers can lower their golf scores while reclining in air-conditioned comfort is viewed as outrageous by many, it is a widely supported view with both anecdotal and research validation. Whether consciously aware of it or not, virtually all successful golfers use imagery to help them in a variety of ways. Golfers use imagery to prepare themselves mentally and emotionally for virtually every situation they might face during a round of golf: (1) how to respond effectively to playing great and making a string of birdies; (2) how to react effectively to a double bogey on the second hole, or a string of bogeys; (3) how to stay mentally tough when the breaks are going against them; (4) how to deal with being in position to win or having a chance to break 60, 70, 80, 90, or 100 for the first time; (5) how to cope with changing weather and course conditions, including slow play; (6) how to be prepared to play with potentially intimidating playing partners; and (7) how to facilitate ball striking and putting effectiveness.

All that is required is to sit back, relax, go over situations in one's mind, and prepare effective responses. For imagery to be effective, however, the golfer must be completely absorbed, as if the experience were actually happening at the present moment. The imagined experience must be happening at a personal level, and the thought and emotional sensations of competition must be felt as if real. Simply going through the motions of imagery as if it were a required and mundane task usually will not suffice. The ideal is to create in the mind a real competitive situation, so that the actual competition is a déjà vu experience. It is through this power of imagination that athletes gain years of competitive experience without actually competing. Golfers who are focused and effective at using their imagination create a situation inside themselves in which the mind cannot distinguish between real and imagined experience. When used correctly, imagery is a powerful tool.

Perhaps the most common misconceptions regarding imagery and its use on the golf course during play is that it must be *visual*. Visualization is simply one form of imagery. Some golfers, such as Jack Nicklaus, are visually dominant. Jack Nicklaus wrote about his visual imagery in great detail in *Golf My Way*,[7] when he stated:

> I never hit a shot, even in practice, without having a very sharp, in-focus picture of it in my head. It's like a color movie. First I "see" the ball where I want it to finish, nice and white and setting up high on the bright green grass. Then the scene quickly changes and I "see" the ball going there: its path, trajectory, and shape, even its behavior on landing. Then there's a sort of fade-out, and the next scene shows me making the kind of swing that will turn the previous images into reality. Only at the end of this short, private, Hollywood spectacular do I select a club and set up to the ball.
>
> It may be that handicap golfers also "go to the movies" like this before most of their shots, but somehow I doubt it. Frequently, those I play with in pro-ams seem to have the club at the ball and their feet planted before they start "seeing" pictures of the shot in their mind's eye. Maybe even then, they see only pictures of the swing, rather than of what it's supposed to achieve. If that's true in your case, then I believe a few moments of movie-making might work some small miracles in your game. Just make sure your movies show a perfect shot. We don't want any horror films of shots flying into sand or water or out of bounds.

His comments are of crucial importance, but many golfers who are not naturally visually dominant have become quite confused trying to image visually like Nicklaus. Everyone has a dominant sense for imagery, but probably only about half of the golfers in the world are visual imagers. Some are dominated by *kinesthetic* senses, and their most effective images will be feelings. Others will be *auditory*, dominated by sounds, rhythms, and balance. Other athletes simply pick a target and know the ball is going to it. This is the point to which everyone must arrive before hitting every shot. Some get to this state by visually seeing the ball going to the target, but others create a sound, or sense a rhythm or balance, and this tells them that their ball will go to the target.

Because there is no valid test to determine a golfer's dominant source of imagery, all golfers must develop enough awareness from experience and trial and error to figure out what is best for them. Whichever happens most naturally is always best. Attempting to play in a nondominant modality almost always will cause problems and create confusion. It will cause most golfers to start trying rather than trusting and doing, and it will create tension and a distracted mind, rather than relaxation and a quiet, calm, focused mind. Understanding these key points will allow imagery to be a helpful tool for enhancing golf performance and enjoyment.

A FEW BASICS FOR PRACTICE

Golf is perhaps the only sport commonly practiced in an environment totally different from the one in which competition occurs, so golfers must be extremely disciplined in the way in which they practice, especially because they usually must do so on their own, without a teacher, pro, or sport psychologist watching over them. The following four points are crucial to effective practice:

1. At all times, specific plans should be established before beginning a practice session. Stay committed to this plan and objective for the entire practice session; do not let friends at the practice area distract you from your prepared plan.
2. At least 60% of all practice time must be spent in the *trusting* mindset. Golf requires good habits, and because this

is the kind of thinking required in competition, it is important that this mindset be the dominant habit. This is of utmost necessity under competitive pressure.

3. Shots 120 yards or closer to the hole should account for 70 to 80% of all practice time. Far too many players spend most of their practice time working on their full swing despite the fact that 65 to 75% of all shots during a round of golf occur within 120 yards of the hole. It takes discipline to practice the short game, but it is crucial to golfing success. Many golfers have the discipline to practice the full swing, but those who develop into highly successful players learn to enjoy hours of practicing their short game.

4. Short-game practice is most useful if it includes competitive games. Be sure to play competitive contests when practicing.

PUTTING AND "THE YIPS"

The Problem

Putting is perhaps the least understood part of the game of golf. It is probably best to look at putting as an art form. Attempts to approach putting from a purely scientific or technical perspective are sure to fall short, so that in a culture that emphasizes knowledge and understanding as a basis for control, putting inevitably becomes a problem to many golfers.

Every hole and every round is finished with a putt, and for even the best players approximately 40% of all shots each round are putts. In other words, putting is a very important influence on total score. Although it is possible with strategy to avoid using a driver, three wood, or wedge, everyone must putt. The ball has to be putted into the hole.

As a result, it is common for confidence in putting to wane. As short putts that "anyone ought to make" are missed in front of others sure to be critical, the ego is bruised. Golfers feel embarrassed, wishing for a place to hide and wondering why they have even placed themselves in such a threatening situation. For players who are serious about their

game and who have invested great amounts of time and energy, this is a most frustrating and demeaning experience. The usual response is to try harder to take control of putting. When this response not only fails to help but makes the situation worse, the golfer grows increasingly concerned, anxious, and scared.

Most dedicated golfers respond by looking to problems in their technique rather than by honestly appraising their confidence and concentration. Then golfers think more about their stroke than about the hole. Soon their eyes start watching the backstroke, out of a concern that if it is not perfect, the putt will be missed. Eventually, with negative experience and increased doubt and tentativeness, their eyes quickly look up to see if the putt is missed before the stroke is even half finished. As others tell the players they are moving their head and looking up, they are again distracted. Attention is again diverted from making the putt to focusing on keeping the head still. As more putts are missed, confusion sets in, and the mind runs wild with anxiety. Pride is hurt, and the fear of putting poorly forever dominates the mind. What often follows is "the yips" (Fig. 5–1). As serious golfers know all too well, "the yips" have ended the careers of many talented players prematurely, including the likes of Ben Hogan and Sam Snead. A frightening possibility, this may cause putting to be

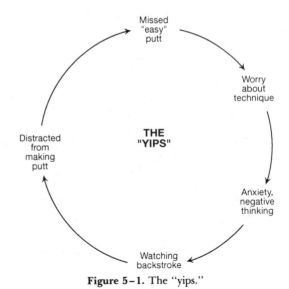

Figure 5–1. The "yips."

viewed as a hated demon that could destroy an otherwise beloved game.

At this point, not only do golfers complain constantly about their terrible putting, but all of their playing companions enjoy discussing it with them. Such discussions are filled with complaints about the unfairness of putting and disgust that something as trivial as putting could possibly be more important than ball-striking.

Psychologically, the result is late-night talks about missed putts that ruined otherwise great rounds, and sleepless nights spent worrying about missing more tomorrow. Putting becomes a nightmare. Bad experiences are relived over and over as if the objective were to ingrain every missed putt and dwell on it as much as possible.

"The yips" then increase in both frequency and severity. The result is a diabolical affliction. Many golfers describe "the yips" as an involuntary twitching of the right hand while attempting to make a relatively short putt. Most describe watching for their right hand to jump while standing over a putt. Typically, the golfer describes being unable to resist the temptation to look at what is happening to the hands and/or the blade on the backstroke. In anticipation of the twitch at the ball, the player makes a quick move at the ball in a desperate attempt to stroke the putt before the involuntary twitch occurs. The head and body pop up, and the ball shoots off in the wrong direction at the wrong speed.

The Solution

The good news is that "the yips" are curable (Fig. 5–2). They are a breakdown in confidence and concentration. "The yips" are not caused by nerve damage if there is any part of the game in which the nerves function effectively. "The yips" are simple to cure, but doing so requires consistent commitment to the following principles:

1. Anytime you think about putting, think about putting *successfully.*
2. Accept that the best putters in the world sometimes miss short putts and three-putt, but they do not let doing so bother them, because a missed putt will not prevent one from playing great. Only overreacting to missed putts can cause a problem.

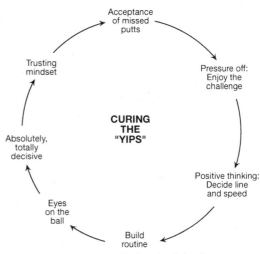

Figure 5–2. Curing the "yips."

3. Refuse to stroke a putt without being totally and completely decisive that the putt is going in the hole. If any doubt or hesitancy occurs over the putt, walk away from the ball and start over again.
4. Accept that it is easier to putt effectively by taking the pressure off rather than by putting the pressure on.
5. Eliminate terms such as "I must," "I should," or "I ought to" make this putt. Instead, use terms such as "I *will* make this putt" and let nothing deter you from this conviction.
6. Do not hang around with "friends" who want to talk about poor putting, missed putts, the lousy greens, or the unfairness of putting.
7. Accept that it took a while to let putting deteriorate and it may take a while to build confidence.
8. Build a mental and physical routine that will be used on each and every putt. Once a solid habit is developed, monitor the mental and physical routine regularly to make certain it is maintained.
9. Focus the eyes on the ball or on a spot on the ball; never watch the backstroke.
10. Practice making putts rather than practicing missing. This typically means that the golfer will spend the

majority of practice time making short putts.

11. Develop an attitude of enjoying putting and the challenge of putting.
12. Accept that great putters do not need to have perfect and technically "correct" strokes. There is no such thing. There are strokes that work and those that don't, and any way that works is great.
13. Accept that putting successfully involves paying attention to doing the same old, potentially boring thing putt after putt, regardless of whether or not they are all going in the hole.
14. Accept that a casual approach to putting is better than an even slightly too-serious approach.
15. Accept that anyone willing to be disciplined, decisive, and trusting is capable of becoming a very successful putter.

AMATEURS VERSUS PROFESSIONALS

Each of the mental fundamentals presented in this chapter applies to golfers of all ability levels. The fundamentals do not change, but professional golfers must adhere to them better and more consistently to compete at a professional level, where reporters' questions may tempt them to think about things better not considered, and where victory may mean the fulfillment of a lifelong dream. Nevertheless, at every level, the competition in golf is primarily oneself and the golf course.

SUMMARY

Golf is a most challenging game. It is usually not easy, and anyone can make it confusing and complicated. Still, golf is a game, which should be enjoyed and played. Keeping the game simple is a major challenge, facilitated by a quiet, passive, trusting mind. The golfer must constantly pay attention to focusing the mind on the desired target and on what is wanted. Every time they play, golfers must choose whether to use the mind as a helpful friend or as a destructive enemy. It is important to choose wisely.

REFERENCES

1. Gallwey, WT: The Inner Game of Golf. Random House, New York, 1979.
2. Haultain, A: The Mysteries of Golf. The Serendipity Press, Houghton Mifflin, Boston, 1908.
3. Heise, J: How You Can Play Better Golf Using Self-Hypnosis. Hal Leighton, Beverly Hills, CA, 1961.
4. Kemp, CF: They Played with a Quiet Mind. CBP Press, St Louis, 1991.
5. Morley, DC: The Missing Links: Golf and the Mind. Atheneum, New York, 1976.
6. Murphy, M: Golf in the Kingdom. Dell, New York, 1972.
7. Nicklaus, J: Golf My Way. Simon & Schuster, New York, 1974, pp 79–80.
8. Rotella, RJ and Bunker, LK: Mind Mastery for Winning Golf. Prentice-Hall, Englewood Cliffs, NJ, 1985.
9. Thompson, KR: The Mental Side of Golf. Funk and Wagnalls, New York 1947.
10. Wiren, G and Coop, R: The New Golf Mind. Simon & Schuster, New York, 1978.

ADDITIONAL READING

Cranford, PG: The Winning Touch in Golf. A Psychological. Prentice-Hall, Englewood Cliffs, NJ, 1961.
Harper, R and Kemp, CF: How to Improve Your Golf Game. Chisum Publishing, St Louis, 1986.
Hogan, C: 5 Days to Golfing Excellence. Merl Miller and Associates, Lake Oswego, OR, 1986.
Kite, T and Dennis, L: How to Play Consistent Golf. Pocket Books, New York, 1990.
Locke, B: Bobby Locke on Golf. Simon & Schuster, New York, 1954.
Mackenzie, MM: Golf: The Mind Game. Dell, New York, 1990.
Toski, B and Love, D: How to Feel the Golf Swing. Random House, New York, 1988.

Nutrition

· ·

Susan W. King, MS, RD

Recommending a diet to improve performance for a golfer still remains a riddle. Although many golfers have good nutritional habits and maintain an ideal weight for height, some golfers who are overweight and overfat, with low cardiovascular fitness levels, win many of their matches. It seems as though their added weight gives length to their drives and stability to their putting stroke. As sports consultants, we are at fault if we advise these players to lose weight to improve their game. In "the game of life," however, they are at risk, so as health care providers we owe them and all other golfers nutritional advice for the maintenance of a healthy lifestyle. Fortu-nately, most golfers will also improve their score by improving their nutrition.[14]

The golfing population includes men and women, lean and heavy, young and old, fit and unfit, well and chronically diseased, and dedicated and casual athletes. It may be helpful to divide golfers into four groups regarding nutritional recommendations:

- Elite athletes[21] younger than 50 years of age
- The general playing public younger than 50 years of age
- Senior players older than 50 years of age, including both elite and casual competitors
- Players with a chronic illness

For all these groups, nutrition and exercise are two critical factors influencing health and fitness, for it is well documented[7,8,18] that physical fitness can reduce risk factors for cardiovascular disease. Such fitness can result from moderate exercise modalities such as walking,[4,19] both on the golf course and as a separate activity. In addition, Yerg and associates[27] found that the decrease in pulmonary function that was thought to be a natural consequence of aging can be reduced by endurance exercise. Nutritional factors can contribute to health both directly and by facilitating participation in exercise activities such as golf. The golfer can learn to control such factors, including adequate hydration, following recommended dietary guidelines,[3] and optimally timing food and fluid intake.[11]

IDEAL BODY WEIGHT AND PERCENTAGE OF BODY FAT

Maintaining an ideal weight for height and achieving a healthy percentage of body fat are important fitness factors in which nutrition is critical. An ideal body weight (IBW) is always determined as weight for height and includes a variable for gender. Body mass index (BMI), a ratio of weight to height, with weight expressed in kilograms and height in meters squared (BMI = kg/m²), is currently the measurement of choice for adults older than 18 years of age in sports medicine literature. A BMI of 19 to 26 for men and 18 to 24 for women has been recommended.[14] The IBW of children, younger than 19 years of age, is evaluated as a percentage of the norm, including age, sex, and height as variables.

The "gold standard" to determine the percentage of body fat is underwater weighing, and very expensive body impedance machines are also available. Most practitioners find, however, that measurements made with skin calipers are very accurate if the person taking the measurements is proficient. As stated by Cooper,[5] the maximum percentage of body fat for men should be 19% and for women, 22%. Both the BMI and the percentage of body fat are valuable measurements for all golfers, because IBW does not correlate with lean body mass or with any other body compartments, and both measurements influence health and fitness.

NUTRIENTS AND FOOD

There are six basic nutrients: water, protein, carbohydrate, fat, vitamins, and minerals. Contrary to popular belief, the nutrient needs of athletes are very similar to those of the general population. A diet composed of 10% to 15% protein, 55% to 70% carbohydrate, and 20% to 30% fat (with saturated fat contributing only 10%) is recommended.[1,3] Athletes who exercise vigorously do need more calories for energy than the sedentary population, so the elite and competitive amateur golfer or the golfer who exercises aerobically will require increased calories. Because increased amounts of the other nutrients are not needed, these extra calories should be derived from carbohydrates,[23] thus increasing the percentage of carbohydrate in the diet of these golfers.

Golfers' ideas about nutrition are susceptible to fraud and quackery,[24] and even health care providers and coaches may be at fault in their dietary recommendations to athletes.[20] A golfer's needs for nutrients should be met by consuming a wide variety of foods and drinks, so he or she should be aware of which foods are good sources of the various nutrients. Table 6–1 lists 50 popular American foods, with their caloric, protein, carbohydrate, and fat content. Notice how the nutrient content may vary within groups of similar foods.

Hydration

Water is an often-neglected nutrient; dehydration not only puts the golfer at risk of heat injury but also has a negative impact on performance. Although significant fluid losses through sweat occur primarily during extreme conditions,[10] many golfers do lose large amounts of sweat. If the humidity is high, the body's cooling efficiency is reduced so that sweating is increased and fluid needs will be even higher.[15] Golfers who are not well conditioned,[26] who are overweight, or who have not acclimated to the heat are at increased risk of heat injury.

Golfers should be advised to begin a training session or round of golf well hydrated.[16] According to Dr. Robert Laird, adequate hydration can be recognized by urine that is "copious and clear." The golfer should be aware that thirst is not a good indicator of fluid need. By the time an athlete is thirsty, it is difficult to replace depleted fluid stores adequately during activity. Golfers can be taught to estimate their fluid requirements during a round of golf in the heat by record-

TABLE 6–1. Nutritional Content of 50 Popular Foods

Amount	Food	Calories	Protein (g)	Carbohydrate (g)	Total Fat (g)
4 oz	Beef hamburger	328	27.2	0.0	23.6
4 oz	Beef filet mignon	244	32.0	0.0	11.6
4 oz	Beef flank steak	276	31.6	0.0	15.6
4 oz	Veal roast	268	31.6	0.0	14.4
4 oz	Chicken, fried (with batter)	316	26.8	10.8	17.6
4 oz	Chicken, baked	252	32.8	0.0	12.4
6 pieces	Chicken McNuggets (McDonald's)	384	22.8	16.2	25.2
½ cup	Tuna in water (canned)	105	23.7	0.0	0.4
4 oz	Flounder, baked	132	27.2	0.0	1.6
4 oz	Salmon	208	30.8	0.0	8.4
6 medium	Scallops, steamed	162	33.6	4.8	1.8
4 inches	Italian sausage	388	24.0	2.0	30.8
2 slices	Pizza with cheese	280	10.8	40.4	8.0
8 oz	Lasagna	285	14.0	27.0	14.0
4 oz	Bologna	360	13.2	3.2	32.0
4 oz	Boiled ham	208	20.0	3.6	12.0
1 oz	Cheddar cheese	114	7.1	0.4	9.4
1 oz	Brie cheese	95	5.9	0.1	7.9
1 medium	Potato, baked	145	3.1	33.6	0.2
15	French fries	220	3.0	26.1	11.5
1 cup	Spaghetti (no sauce)	155	4.8	32.2	0.6
1 cup	Rice (cooked)	223	4.1	49.6	0.2
2 slices	Bread, whole wheat	112	4.8	22.0	1.4
½ medium	Avocado	162	2.0	7.5	15.4
8 stalks	Asparagus	32	3.2	5.6	0.0
1 cup	Corn, whole kernel (canned)	133	4.3	30.5	1.6
1 cup	Kidney beans (canned)	218	13.4	40.0	1.0
1 medium	Tomato (raw)	23	1.1	5.3	0.3
1 cup	Broccoli	37	3.6	6.4	0.0
1 cup	Green beans (fresh/frozen)	35	1.8	8.3	0.2
1 medium	Orange	62	1.2	15.4	0.2
1 medium	Banana	105	1.2	26.7	0.5
⅛ pie (9″)	Blueberry pie	286	2.8	41.2	12.8
1 piece	Angel food cake	137	3.0	31.4	0.1
½ cup	Ice cream, extra rich	175	2.1	16.0	11.9
½ cup	Ice milk	92	2.6	14.5	2.8
½ cup	Fruit ice	132	0.1	32.8	0.0
¼ cup	Peanuts, dry roasted	217	9.1	6.9	17.0
1 cup	Potato chips	84	1.0	8.3	5.7
1 cup	Corn chips	224	2.7	20.9	14.8
2 tsp	Butter	68	0.0	0.0	7.6
2 tsp	Margarine	66	0.0	0.0	7.4
1 medium	Doughnut, glazed	184	2.6	26.4	7.9
1 medium	Sweet roll	154	2.6	21.4	6.8
1 large	Egg, poached	79	6.0	0.6	5.6
1 cup	Milk, skim	86	8.4	11.9	0.4
1 cup	Milk, whole	150	8.0	11.4	8.1
1 cup	Oatmeal	145	6.1	25.3	2.3
1 cup	Total (cereal)	80	2.0	18.4	0.4
2 oz	Granola coconut cereal	260	6.0	36.0	10.0

Source: Adapted from Nutritional Data Resources.[17]

ing their naked weight (after voiding) before and immediately after the round, and calculating all fluid intake during the round. Any body weight loss (all of which can be presumed to be fluid loss) equals fluid replacement needs. That is, a loss of 2 lb would equal 1 more quart of fluid needed during the round. A fluid loss that exceeds 2.5% of total body weight can have a negative impact on performance; a loss of more than 4% is considered thermal dehydration,[6] which can lead to heat stroke and all its sequelae.

The golfer should find out ahead of time on which holes water or other fluids will be available. If the course is limited in its facilities, or if the player has a preference for a certain sports drink, he or she should carry water or the preferred drink on the course.

The diuretic effects of caffeine and alcohol will negatively impact on hydration.[25] Golfers may drink the equivalent of two cups of coffee before exercise but should not ingest any caffeine for up to 6 hours after their round. Alcohol never enhances performance, and its diuretic effect is a strong reason for limiting intake both before and after exercise.

Water is the primary fluid need for golfers, but it has been shown[2] that drinks containing glucose polymers maintain fluid volume better than water during prolonged exercise in the heat. Sports drinks such as Exceed, which contain glucose polymers, are therefore acceptable and often preferable. The golfers who would benefit most from sports drinks are elite competitors who usually play 5 or 6 days in a row, often in very hot climates during the middle of the day, or amateurs who are playing in a weekend tournament in the middle of the day, often playing 36 holes. The added carbohydrate also will maintain a higher energy level in these players. Research[9] indicates that for a low-intensity exercise such as golf, the concentration of sugars need not exceed 5%.

Many elite golfers include aerobic workouts in their exercise schedule. Adequate hydration and glucose supplementation are especially important for these golfers during both their golfing (play or practice) and the aerobic workout, because of their increased need for energy and fluid replacement.

Persons with chronic illnesses who wish to play golf also must be especially aware of the dangers of dehydration. For example, insulin-dependent diabetics habitually carry a ready glucose source, but they also should carry their own fluids and drink often while exercising, even at low intensity, so that no thermal injury can occur. Patients with chronic renal failure and other conditions that require fluid restriction should be advised not to exercise in extreme heat.

Carbohydrates

Complex carbohydrates (e.g., cereal, bread, pasta, and rice) are the dynamic central core of an athlete's diet. These foods supply glucose in long chains, for both short-term and long-term energy requirements. They also provide a little protein, very small amounts of fat, and the B complex vitamins that help use carbohydrate energy. Other carbohydrates are simple sugars, which are an excellent source of quick energy but should be eaten in smaller quantities. Table 6–2 identifies some popular foods that are good sources of carbohydrate.

Golfers who exercise aerobically should learn to replenish their carbohydrate stores immediately following their workout[13,22] to maximize their glycogen reserves.

Protein

Protein foods supply amino acids, which, when metabolized, promote growth and maintain structure and provide the nec-

TABLE 6–2. Some Popular Foods with ≥15 g Carbohydrate in a Usual Serving*

Serving Size	Food	Carbohydrate (g)
1 cup	Rice	49.6
1 slice	Blueberry pie	41.2
2 slices	Pizza with cheese	40.4
1 cup	Kidney beans	39.9
2 oz	Granola cereal	36.0
1 medium	Baked potato	33.6
½ cup	Fruit ice	32.8
1 cup	Spaghetti	32.2
1 piece	Angel food cake	31.4
1 cup	Whole kernel corn	30.5
8 oz	Lasagna with meat	27.0
1 medium	Banana	26.7
1 medium	Glazed donut	26.4
15	French fries	26.1
1 cup	Oatmeal	25.3
2 slices	Whole wheat bread	22.0
1 medium	Sweet roll	21.4
1 cup	Corn chips	20.9
1 cup	Total (cereal)	18.4
6	Chicken nuggets	16.2
½ cup	Ice cream	16.0
1 medium	Orange	15.4

*Listed in order from highest to lowest. A minimum carbohydrate intake for golfers is 250 g/day.
Source: Adapted from Nutritional Data Resources.[17]

TABLE 6-3. Some Popular Foods with ≥6 g Protein per Serving*

Serving Size	Food	Protein (g)
6 medium	Scallops	33.6
4 oz	Baked chicken	32.8
4 oz	Veal roast	31.6
4 oz	Beef flank steak	31.6
4 oz	Broiled salmon	30.8
4 oz	Baked flounder	27.2
4 oz	Beef hamburger	27.2
4 oz	Fried chicken	26.8
4 inches	Italian sausage	24.0
4 oz	Tuna canned in water	23.7
6	Chicken nuggets	22.8
4 oz	Boiled ham	20.0
8 oz	Lasagna with meat	14.0
1 cup	Kidney beans	13.4
4 oz	Bologna	13.2
2 slices	Pizza with cheese	10.8
¼ cup	Peanuts, dry roasted	9.1
1 cup	Skim milk	8.4
1 cup	Whole milk	8.0
1 oz	Cheddar cheese	7.1
1 cup	Oatmeal	6.1
1 large	Poached egg	6.0
2 oz	Granola	6.0

*Listed in order from highest to lowest. RDA[3] (with a variance for weight) for women, 50 g; for men, 70 g.
Source: Adapted from Nutritional Data Resources.[17]

TABLE 6-4. Some Popular Foods with ≥8 g Fat in a Serving*

Serving Size	Food	Fat (g)
4 oz	Bologna	32.0
4 in	Italian sausage	30.8
6	Chicken nuggets	25.2
4 oz	Beef hamburger	23.6
4 oz	Fried chicken	17.6
¼ cup	Peanuts, dry roasted	17.0
4 oz	Beef flank steak	15.6
½ medium	Avocado	15.4
1 cup	Corn chips	14.8
4 oz	Veal roast	14.4
8 oz	Lasagna	14.0
1 slice	Blueberry pie	12.8
4 oz	Baked chicken	12.4
4 oz	Boiled ham	12.0
½ cup	Extra rich ice cream	11.9
4 oz	Beef filet mignon	11.6
15	French fries	11.5
2 oz	Granola cereal	10.0
1 oz	Cheddar cheese	9.4
4 oz	Salmon	8.4
1 cup	Whole milk	8.1
2 slices	Pizza with cheese	8.0
1 oz	Brie cheese	8.0

*Listed in order from highest to lowest. A diet with 50-80 g of fat meets minimum requirements.
Source: Adapted from Nutritional Data Resources.[17]

essary components for many systems. High-protein foods include all meats, fish, and poultry, dairy products, and legumes. Smaller amounts of protein are found in nuts, complex carbohydrate foods, and other vegetables (Table 6-3).

Athletic endeavor does not stress the protein requirements of golfers.[12] A diet too high in protein is simply less efficiently digested than one that provides the needed energy from carbohydrates.

Fat

Fat is essential because it carries fat-soluble vitamins and provides linoleic and linolenic acids.[3] However, these needs can be met in the diet by polyunsaturated fats, so a diet very low in saturated fat is acceptable. Current recommendations that limit saturated fat[1,3] are derived from research indicating that serum cholesterol levels are adversely influenced by high intakes. Table 6-4 lists some popular foods with a high total fat content.

Vitamins and Minerals

Vitamins and minerals are noncaloric essential nutrients that have many functions. Vitamins primarily help us use caloric foods, by acting as components of enzymes. By themselves, vitamins do not "energize," but simply help the golfer to use food for energy. Minerals are often an integral part of functional proteins; for example, iron is part of heme, a molecule found in hemoglobin (Table 6-5).

Overdosing of any vitamin or mineral is unnecessary and may even be highly dangerous; overdoses of the fat-soluble vitamins A and D, for example, can cause death. In most circumstances, the necessary vitamins and minerals will be obtained from the diet if a wide variety of foods are eaten. For example, Table 6-6 lists some common foods that are good sources of vitamin C. However, vitamin C is one of the vitamins that may be lost in long storage or overcooking of food, so attention should be paid to methods of food preparation.

TABLE 6–5. Some Popular Foods with ≥1.5 mg Iron in a Usual Serving*

Serving Size	Food	Iron (mg)
1 cup	Total (cereal)	7.99
6 medium	Scallops	4.32
4 oz	Veal roast	3.96
4 oz	Beef flank steak	3.92
4 oz	Beef filet mignon	3.40
1 cup	Kidney beans	3.23
4 oz	Beef hamburger	2.76
4 oz	Tuna (canned in water)	2.56
8 oz	Lasagna with meat	2.50
2 oz	Granola cereal	2.16
1 cup	Rice	1.84
4 in	Italian sausage	1.80
4 oz	Bologna	1.72
1 cup	Oatmeal	1.59
6	Chicken nuggets	1.50

*The RDA[3] for iron = 15 mg.
Source: Adapted from Nutritional Data Resources.[17]

COMPOSITION AND TIMING OF MEALS AND SNACKS

Because their tee times are not consistent, many golfers cannot follow a scheduled pattern for meals and snacks. If a golfer is scheduled for an early tee time, for instance, it may be difficult to eat a large breakfast (such as the one shown in Table 6–7), even though breakfast is important because it breaks the nighttime fast. It should contain carbohydrate, protein, and fat to replenish the body's stores. Before an early round, a small glass of juice with a bagel and cream cheese or a muffin with a small glass of skim

TABLE 6–6. Some Popular Foods with ≥8 mg vitamin C in a Usual Serving

Serving Size	Food	Vitamin C (mg)
1 cup	Broccoli	89.0
1 medium	Orange	69.7
8 stalks	Asparagus	32.6
1 cup	Total (cereal)	24.0
1 medium	Tomato	21.7
1 average	Baked potato	20.0
1 cup	Whole kernel corn	13.9
15	French fries	12.5
1 cup	Green beans	11.1
1 medium	Banana	10.4
½	Avocado	7.9

*RDA[3] for vitamin C = 60 mg.
Source: Adapted from Nutritional Data Resources.[17]

milk could be eaten an hour or so before play in place of a large breakfast.

Lunch should be high in carbohydrate foods, following the theory that during the day it is advisable to eat foods high in readily available energy, to meet the energy requirements of daily activities. Unfortunately, a tee time of 11 AM will preclude lunch, increasing the importance of hearty snacks (see below).

Dinner can be higher in protein and fat than breakfast or lunch, because these nutrients are slower to digest than carbohydrate. Energy needs are reduced during sleep, so evening becomes the appropriate time to eat larger quantities of protein foods and enough fat to meet essential requirements.

Snacks are very important for all athletes. Carbohydrate foods tend to be bulky, so it is difficult to meet all one's needs at two or three sittings. In addition, because all golfers desire to maintain a high energy level throughout the whole competition, the entire golfing population should be encouraged to incorporate snacks into their training sessions and competitions; golfers will find that they are "energized" if they eat the right food when they need it.[14]

Table 6–7 provides a suggested menu for vigorously exercising men, with comments on how to adjust it for women and for those who are less active. Before prescribing a menu, however, a nutrition counselor should listen to the athletes' preferences and needs, and then try to help them to design a sports menu that will both improve the quality of their life and very likely improve their golfing performance.

SUMMARY

The nutritional needs of the golfer are similar to those of the general population. Even very active golfers should not consume excess amounts of protein or fat, but rather should regulate their diet to meet their caloric needs by adjusting their consumption of carbohydrate-rich foods, especially those that are good sources of complex carbohydrates. Both quality of life and golfing performance are likely to be improved by maintaining an ideal body weight and appropriate percentage of

TABLE 6–7. High-Carbohydrate Menu

This menu is for men who are exercising quite vigorously. Women golfers and men who do not add a component of aerobic exercise to their daily activities should select smaller servings of the foods that are italicized and should choose fewer snacks. However, it is important to eat at least five times per day, so not all snacks should be eliminated.

Meal/Foods	Protein (g)	Carbohydrate (g)	Fat (g)	Calories
Breakfast				
1 banana	1.2	26.7	0.5	105
1½ cups whole grain cereal	6.8	49.3	1.1	248
2 cups 1% milk	16.0	23.4	5.2	204
3 slices whole wheat bread	7.2	33.0	2.1	168
3 tsp margarine	0.0	0.0	11.1	99
3 tsp jam	0.0	14.1	0.0	54
1 cup fruit juice	1.3	22.1	0.2	94
Snack				
Lunch				
2½ cups pasta salad with mayonnaise	14.3	93.1	20.4	607
½ cup peas	4.1	11.4	0.2	63
2 bran muffins	6.2	34.4	7.8	208
½ cantaloupe	2.4	22.4	0.8	92
Snack				
Dinner				
4 oz salmon	30.8	0.0	8.4	208
3 boiled potatoes	6.9	81.0	0.3	348
3 tsp margarine	0.0	0.0	11.1	99
1 cup green beans	1.8	8.3	0.3	35
1 cup broccoli	3.6	6.4	0.1	37
2 dinner rolls	4.6	29.6	3.2	166
1 cup lemonade	0.2	26.0	0.0	99
½ cup ice cream	2.4	15.9	7.2	135
Snack				
Totals (without snacks)	110 g	497 g	78 g	3067 kcal
% of calories	14%	63%	23%	

Snack foods: dried and fresh fruits, fruit ices, bread, muffins, bagels, crackers, cereals, water, juice, sports drinks, and occasionally soda pop.

body fat. Energy for play can be maintained by snacking often on foods containing complex and simple carbohydrate. Finally, it is most important for the golfer to begin each round adequately hydrated, especially in hot weather, and to consume adequate fluids during play to avoid dehydration.

REFERENCES

1. American Heart Association, Nutrition Committee: Circulation 74:1465A, 1986.
2. Carter, JE and Gisolfi, CV: Fluid replacement during and after exercise in the heat. Med Sci Sports Exerc 21:532, 1989.
3. Committee on Dietary Allowances, Food and Nutrition Board, National Research Council: Recommended Dietary Allowances. National Academy Press, Washington, DC, 1980.
4. Cook, TC, et al: Chronic low level physical activity as a determinant of high density lipoprotein cholesterol and subfractions. Med Sci Sports Exerc 20: 455, 1988.
5. Cooper, KH: The Aerobics Program for Total Well-Being. M Evans & Co, New York, 1982, pp 11 and 13.
6. Costill, DL and Sparks, KE: Rapid fluid replacement following thermal dehydration. J Appl Physiol 50:123, 1973.

7. Ekelund, LG, et al: Physical fitness as a predictor of cardiovascular mortality in asymptomatic North American men. N Engl J Med 319:1379, 1988.
8. Fang, CL, et al: Exercise modality and selected coronary risk factors: A multivariate approach. Med Sci Sports Exerc 20:455, 1988.
9. Foster, C, et al: Gastric emptying characteristics of glucose and glucose polymer solutions. Res Q 51:299, 1980.
10. Gisolfi, CV: Electrolyte supplementation. In Grandjean, AC and Storlie J (eds): Bridging the Gap, Report of the Ross Symposium. Ross Laboratories, Columbus, OH, 1989, p 11.
11. Grandjean, AC: Elite Athletes. In Grandjean, AC and Storlie, J (eds): Bridging the Gap, Report of the Ross Symposium. Ross Laboratories, Columbus, OH, 1989, p 102.
12. Hecker, AL and Wheeler, KB: Protein: A misunderstood nutrient for the athlete. NSCA J 7:28, 1985.
13. Ivy, JL: Effect of amount of a carbohydrate supplement on rapid glycogen resynthesis post-exercise. J Appl Physiol, in press, 1988.
14. King, SW and Chandler, B: Nutrition counseling for recreational athletes. Topics Clin Nutr 4:3, 1989.
15. Knochel, JP, Ditin, LN, and Hamburger, RJ: Pathophysiology of intense physical conditioning in a hot climate. J Clin Invest 51:242, 1972.
16. Laird, R: Medical Advice for the Ironman Triathlon. Unpublished report. Burlington, VT, 1988.

17. Nutritional Data Resources, Willoughby, OH.
18. Paffenbarger, RS, et al: Physical activity, all-cause mortality, and longevity of college alumni. N Engl J Med 314:605, 1986.
19. Palank, EA and Hargreaves EH, Jr: The benefits of walking the golf course. Phys Sportsmed 18:77, 1990.
20. Parr, RB: Nutrition knowledge and practices of coaches, trainers, and athletes. Phys Sportsmed 12:126, 1984.
21. Parsons, TW, et al: Profile of the elite athlete. Coaching Review 9:62, 1986.
22. Reed, MJ, et al: Muscle glycogen storage postexercise: Effect of mode of carbohydrate administration. Am Physiol Soc 161:7567, 1989.
23. Sherman, WM: Carbohydrate, muscle glycogen and muscle glycogen supercompensation. In Williams, MD (ed): Ergogenic Aids in Sport. Human Kinetics, Champaign, IL, 1983.
24. Smith, NJ: Food Fraud and the Athlete. Report of Symposium on Nutrient Utilization During Exercise. Ross Laboratories, Columbus, OH, 1983.
25. Stamford, B: How to avoid dehydration. Phys Sportsmed 18(7):135, 1990.
26. Wyndham, CH and Strydom, NB: The danger of inadequate water intake during marathon running. S Afr Med J 43:893, 1969.
27. Yerg, YE, et al: Effect of endurance exercise training on ventilatory function in older individuals. J Appl Physiol 58:791, 1985.

Vision and Golf

David Robinson, MD, FACS

L ike many other sports, golf is a game of accuracy. The golfer must be able to repeat a swing and send the ball to a distinct target area. Unlike many other sports, however, golf often calls for decisions to be based on visual information that may be gained from hundreds of yards away. Also, reading breaks on a green requires sophisticated stereoscopic visual information that most of us take for granted. Virtually all golfers, if they are fortunate enough to play golf throughout their lifetime, eventually will have to deal with some changes in visual acuity, whether from myopia or astigmatism in youth, presbyopia in adulthood, or other medical or pathologic problems commonly seen with older golfers. Fortunately, most of these problems are correctable if diagnosed. This chapter discusses the most common visual problems with which all medical personnel dealing with the golfing athlete should become familiar.

REFRACTIVE ERRORS

The most common visual problem for any athlete is a simple refractive error in the eye. This is easily corrected with spectacles or contact lenses. Many golfers who are able to function normally in daily activities without glasses find that a correction of refractive error may be necessary to refine stereopsis or improve distance vision and their ability to judge subtle changes in undulating terrain. One important thing to remember is that these refractive errors may change dramatically through the lifetime of a golfer. For this reason, routine eye exams are important. Below are brief descriptions of the most common types of refractive errors.

Myopia (Nearsightedness)

Myopia means that the refractive power of the cornea and lens is too strong for the eye. This puts the object of regard in focus in front of the retina and thereby leaves a blurred image on the retina. Although these patients can see near objects clearly, objects at a distance are blurred. This very common problem may not be recognized by the patient but is easily corrected when found.

Hyperopia (Farsightedness)

Hyperopia means that the refractive power of the cornea and lens is too weak for the eye. This puts the object of regard in focus behind the retina and thereby also leaves a blurred image on the retina. Younger golfers usually can overcome this type of refractive error because of the accommodative ability of the lens of the eye. However, in cases of severe hyperopia, correction may be necessary. As a golfer ages, the ability of the eye to accommodate decreases (presbyopia), and a latent hyperope may start to develop symptoms.

Astigmatism

Astigmatism means that the cornea or lens of the eye does not have a spherical shape, and instead has an irregular shape with one radius of curvature different from another. This shape causes the object of regard to be focused on the retina as a blurred line rather than a focused point. This also can be overcome with corrective lenses. Of course, it is possible for someone to have myopia or hyperopia also associated with astigmatism. This extremely common combination requires a more sophisticated lens to correct, but it is easily done. Recent advances in contact lens design and materials allow many people with astigmatism who previously could not be helped by contact lenses now to be fitted with them.

Presbyopia

"Presbyopia" describes the natural process whereby the human lens loses its ability to accommodate on close objects. For the average person, this usually becomes significant at about 40 to 45 years of age. Although the only real problem presbyopia may cause a golfer is difficulty reading the scorecard, he or she may have a tremendous amount of difficulty adjusting to the bifocal lenses used to correct these problems. The problem results from the different focal lengths of the distance and reading segments of the glasses, which may cause a disturbance when the golfer focuses on the ball on the set-up and backswing. This is an extremely common problem, and many different solutions have been tried. Because the approach must be individualized for each patient's stance and habitus, the golfer complaining of this problem should be asked to discuss it with his or her ophthalmologist.

CORRECTIVE LENSES

Spectacles

Spectacle correction is the most common and simple form of treating a refractive error. The frame should fit properly and be comfortable. Choosing one with minimal obstruction of peripheral vision is important, and fortunately many frame styles are available that achieve this. If a person is severely myopic or hyperopic, however, the peripheral distortion from the lenses can be great; these golfers may enjoy the improved peripheral vision gained with contact lenses.

Contact Lenses

Contact lenses are an excellent way to treat refractive errors in many patients. There are many different types, including hard, soft, gas-permeable, daily-wear, and extended-wear contact lenses. The decision about which lens is best for each individual should be made by the patient and his or her ophthalmologist. Although contact lenses can improve peripheral vision and reduce distortion, they do not protect the eye from trauma, or usually from ultraviolet light.

They also are a possible source of severe infection and should always be removed immediately if there are any problems of the eye. This aspect is discussed later, in the section on eye injuries.

Bifocals, Trifocals, and Progressive Lenses

As discussed earlier, presbyopia (the loss of accommodation) can be a significant problem for the older golfer. Bifocal lenses have a small area located inferiorly on the lens for reading vision (Fig. 7–1A), usually with a focal length of approximately 13 to 17 in. Unfortunately, this is usually also the area of the lens through which the golfer views the ball during the set-up and backswing. Because the ball is 5 to 6 ft away from the eye, it appears blurred and also can be displaced in the golfer's field of view because of the prismatic effect of the bifocal.

One possible solution for this blurred image is trifocal lenses (Fig. 7–1B). Trifocals have an intermediate segment between the distance and reading segments, which allows the ball to be in focus during the set-up and backswing. Unfortunately, the disturbing image jump or displacement seen with bifocals also can be a problem with trifocals.

Progressive lenses (Fig. 7–1C) are blended such that there are no distinct areas of different focal lengths but rather a gradual progression of increasing refractive error as one looks farther down the lens. The golfer can bring the ball (or the scorecard or distance vision) into focus by simply tilting his or her head until the appropriate area of the lens is found. Although an excellent solution for many people, some golfers find these glasses to have too much peripheral distortion in the area where the progressive lens is blended.

Overall, presbyopia can be a difficult problem for the golfer to solve. Many players choose to wear glasses without a bifocal or have special glasses made specifically for golf, with a small bifocal segment placed up in one corner of one lens, used just to read the scorecard. These types of special circumstances should again be discussed with the eye doctor.

PROTECTIVE EYE WEAR FOR GOLF

Ultraviolet Light Protection

As underscored by a large amount of recent medical literature, chronic ultraviolet

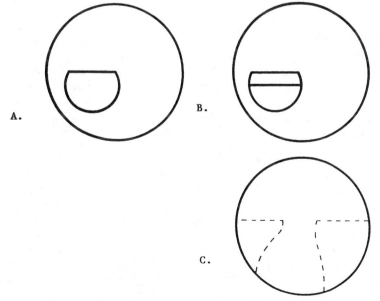

Figure 7–1. (A) A standard flat-top bifocal commonly used for presbyopia. (B) A trifocal with the smaller intermediate segment used for intermediate distances. (C) The dotted lines demonstrate the areas of a progressive blended bifocal. The lines are not seen on the glasses but can cause distortion in these areas.

exposure can have negative effects on the eye. Actinic keratosis of the conjunctiva can lead to chronic inflammatory disorders of the eye and the growth of a pterygium over the cornea. Pterygia are fibrovascular growths of bulbar conjunctivae onto the cornea, which, in severe cases, may require surgical intervention if vision becomes affected. Ultraviolet light also has been reported to have progressive effects on cataract formation in the lens and macular degeneration of the retina.[1,5-7]

Golfers are particularly at risk because of the long hours spent outdoors. They should be encouraged to wear glasses with an ultraviolet light filter. It is important to recognize that an ultraviolet filter is a clear coating and can be put on clear lenses as well as tinted lenses. In fact, a darkly tinted lens does not necessarily filter ultraviolet light. If it does not, such a lens may actually be more harmful to the eye than no glasses at all because a dark lens will allow the pupil to enlarge and therefore will actually let more dangerous ultraviolet light enter the eye. As information about ultraviolet damage has become more widely known, some professional golfers now use protective sunglasses.

A hat or visor also acts to decrease the amount of direct sunlight exposure and decreases overall exposure to ultraviolet light.

Polycarbonate Lenses

Although traumatic injury to the eye is fortunately rare in golf, a word should be said about protective lenses for ocular trauma. Polycarbonate lenses offer distinct advantages over "shatterproof" glass lenses.[2] Shatterproof lenses are designed to crumble into thousands of tiny pieces on impact. These sharp pieces of glass, however, can still enter the eye and cause serious ocular damage. Polycarbonate lenses are designed to withstand tremendous impact forces without shattering and, in some instances, can withstand a shotgun blast without shattering. For the golfer concerned about optimal protection, polycarbonate should be recommended. It is also possible to tint polycarbonate lenses and apply an ultraviolet light filter.

EYE INJURIES IN GOLF

The Hazards of Hazards

A foreign body in the eye is probably the most common acute eye injury on the golf course. Although such injuries are usually self-limiting, a high-speed projectile from the club head striking the ground or sand in a hazard can cause serious damage in some cases. If the foreign body can be seen, it can be removed with a clean, cotton-tip applicator, or simply irrigated out of the eye with an eye wash solution. All medical personnel should be familiar with the technique of everting the upper lid to locate and dislodge a foreign body. This is an extremely common place to find a foreign body, which can cause a serious corneal abrasion if not removed.

Sand in the eye can be a particularly difficult problem for the contact lens wearer because sand under a lens can quickly abrade the cornea. The contact lens or lenses should be removed immediately and cleaned and the eye irrigated before replacing the lens on the eye. All golfers who wear contacts should carry in their bag the equipment necessary to remove and store their lenses and should have eyeglasses available to wear if needed. Continuing to wear contact lenses when a foreign body is suspected can put the golfer at high risk for a serious corneal infection.

Corneal Abrasions

Corneal abrasions of the eye can be caused by foreign bodies and contact lenses, as discussed earlier, but also commonly occur by accidentally being struck by tree limbs or bushes around the golf course. Any significant injury of this sort should be evaluated as soon as possible by an ophthalmologist because an occult corneal perforation may otherwise go unrecognized. The golfer is at particularly high risk for infection because of bacteria and fungi commonly found on plant matter. A pressure patch on the eye can help the golfer remain comfortable until medical help is available.

However, if a penetrating or perforating injury to the eye is suspected, an eye shield —not a pressure patch—should be used because any pressure on an open globe can cause further herniation of intraocular contents through the wound.

Blunt Trauma

Fortunately, blunt trauma to the eye is rare on the golf course, but when these injuries do occur from the ball or club they are usually very serious.[3] Golf accounted for 11 (14%) of 80 sports-related injuries that resulted in eye enucleations at the Massachusetts Eye and Ear Infirmary from 1960 to 1980.[4] If a golfer is struck directly in the eye with either a golf club or a golf ball, the eye should be evaluated immediately. This type of blunt trauma can severely damage the eye internally even though the external appearance of the eye may be unremarkable. When an eye is struck by a blunt object, expansion of the vitreous base can result in retinal tears, retinal hemorrhages, and retinal dialysis. Some trauma victims note immediate visual disturbances, but many who report no significant changes in their vision have severe retinal pathology on dilated retinal exam. Once again, if a rupture of the globe is suspected in a case like this, an eye shield and not a pressure patch should be used until the patient can obtain medical help.

THE ALLERGIC EYE

Allergic symptoms of the eye are common on the golf course. The pollens of hay fever season, freshly cut grass, and some chemicals and pesticides used to treat grasses on the course are common allergens. Contact lens wearers are often particularly susceptible to these allergic stimuli. Antihistamines, used both orally and in the form of eye drops, can be prescribed for these types of acute problems. Topical nonsteroidal anti-inflammatory medications also are available now and have been reported to be effective for allergic eye symptoms. These are prescription medications that are taken three to four times per day as needed. In severe cases, topical steroids can be given, but this should only be done under the direction of an ophthalmologist.

THE AGING GOLFER

Many aging golfers will experience visual problems no more serious than advancing presbyopia and the need for bifocals. However, as golf becomes increasingly popular with athletes of retirement age, sports medicine practitioners should be aware of the more common visual diseases that can severely affect vision and the player's ability to participate in golf.

Cataracts

As the eye ages, the crystalline lens gradually becomes sclerotic and develops a haziness that can cause dramatic visual changes. The earliest symptom is often glare and inability to follow the flight of the ball. These symptoms commonly develop after 65 to 70 years of age, but may appear earlier in some people. Sunglasses often can help in the early stages, but eventually the problem may require surgical removal of the cataract, with an intraocular lens implant.

Macular Degeneration

Macular degeneration is an extremely common disease of the retinal pigment epithelium and is the second-leading cause of vision loss in the older population. It is usually a slowly progressive disease that can dramatically affect reading and fine distance vision, while leaving the peripheral vision intact. This disease also can progress to an exudative form that can affect the vision acutely, and may require urgent laser treatment.

Glaucoma

Glaucoma is a disease of elevated intraocular pressure that can cause progressive damage to the optic nerve. It initially may have no symptoms but gradually can cause loss of peripheral vision and eventually lead to blindness if not treated. Because of the complete lack of symptoms, all patients more than 40 years old should have routine eye exams to check for glaucoma.

SUMMARY

· Any complete evaluation of a golfer should always include a visual acuity check and review of any visual symptoms. The patient should be referred for a more complete evaluation if any problems are identified. Some very simple solutions to problems, such as correction of a refractive error with glasses or contact lenses, can have a dramatic effect on a golfer's self-confidence and result in a more positive attitude and improved performance.

REFERENCES

1. Bochow, TW, et al: Ultraviolet light exposure and risk of posterior subcapsular cataracts. Arch Ophthalmol 107:369–372, 1989.
2. Galic, GJ: Polycarbonate lenses: New technology in eye protection. National Safety News, July 1981.
3. Millan, GT: Golfing eye injuries. Am J Ophthalmol 64:741, 1967.
4. Portis, JM, et al: Ocular sports injuries: A review of cases on file in the Massachusetts Eye and Ear Infirmary Pathology Laboratory. International Ophthalmology Clinic 21(4), 1981.
5. Rosenthal, FS: The ocular dose of ultraviolet radiation to outdoor workers. Invest Ophthalmol Vis Sci 29:649–656, 1988.
6. Taylor, HR: The biological effects of UV-B on the eye. Photochemistry and Photobiology 50(4):488–492, 1989.
7. Werner, JS, et al: Loss of human photoreceptor sensitivity associated with chronic exposure to ultraviolet radiation. Ophthalmology 96:1152–1158, 1989.

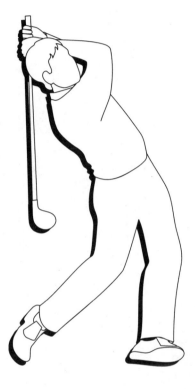

Special Populations

8

The Cardiovascular System

Edward A. Palank, MD, FACC

Cardiovascular disease is extremely prevalent in our society, accounting annually for nearly 50% of all deaths.[12] In 1991, an estimated 1.5 million individuals in the United States had a heart attack and more than 500,000 died. Myocardial infarction is not confined to the elderly; nearly 50% afflict those between ages 40 and 65.[14]

According to the National Golf Foundation, half of the more than 25 million individuals who play golf are older than 35.[8] Golfers older than 60 account for one third of all rounds played. Given the incidence of coronary disease in the population and the age of those who play the game, it can be reasoned that many golfers may have or develop this disease. This chapter addresses the potential cardiovascular benefits of playing golf, the risk of playing golf in the presence of cardiovascular disease, and the implications of various treatment modalities for golf participation and performance.

THE CARDIOVASCULAR BENEFITS OF GOLF

Improved Lipid Profile

Golf has been found to have potential benefit as an exercise.[24] A number of studies have demonstrated that regular physical activity is associated with a decreased incidence of coronary heart disease[3,21,22] and increased longevity.[23] The specific association of leisure-time physical activity with reduced incidence of coronary heart disease also has been described.[21,23] Physical activity may reduce the likelihood of developing coronary disease by altering plasma lipid and lipoprotein levels. High-density lipoprotein cholesterol (HDL-C) has been shown to have an inverse effect on the development of coronary heart disease.[9] Although most studies[11] have suggested that vigorous exercise is required to elevate HDL-C, Cook and associates[4] demonstrated elevated levels of HDL-C in postal carriers who did not engage in other physical activity.

Because walking is the most common form of leisure-time physical activity, Palank and Hargreaves[24] evaluated the effect of walking the golf course on 28 previously sedentary male golfers (aged 48 to 80, median age 61), comparing them with 16 other men who did not engage in any regular exercise. The golfers walked the course about three times per week (approximately 15 miles per week) for 4 months. The study demonstrated that walking the golf course significantly reduced low-density lipoprotein cholesterol (LDL-C) levels and improved the ratio of total cholesterol to HDL-C, which has been suggested[9] to be a more important indicator of coronary heart disease risk than total cholesterol or HDL-C alone. In a practical sense, more individuals may benefit from participation in golf than from other forms of prescribed exercise because its attractiveness may improve compliance.

Energy Expenditure

The American Heart Association has endorsed a regular program of dynamic physical activity as a means to improve cardiovascular functional capacity.[18] Exercise intensity is measured as a percentage of the body's maximal ability to use oxygen (VO_2max), a well-defined and reproducible physiologic endpoint that is widely accepted as the best criterion for cardiorespiratory endurance capacity or physical fitness.[1] There is no evidence that regular golfing, either walking or riding a cart, will increase one's VO_2max. Murase, Kameis, and Hoshikawat[19] estimated that the mean oxygen uptake during 18 holes of golf while walking and using caddies was 1.17 L/min. The heart rate after nine holes of golf has been reported to be 108 beats per minute for men[19] and 102 beats per minute for women.[30]

Even though golf has not been demonstrated to improve fitness, it does involve an energy expenditure that yields benefits, including weight loss and improved cholesterol metabolism. The golfers in Palank and Hargreaves' study[24] lost 1.4 kg, while non-golfers gained 1.6. A universal method of defining energy expenditure has been to classify the energy cost of exercise in METs. One MET is the equivalent of resting oxygen consumption measured in a sitting position, approximately 3.5 mL/kg per minute. Playing golf while using a power cart uses a low energy range, about 2 to 3 METs. If one walks and carries a bag, a level of 4 to 5 METs may be achieved.

The caloric expenditure of an activity can be directly computed using MET levels. Getchell[6] reported the caloric cost of playing golf to be 3.7 kcal/min. Table 8–1 lists the estimated energy expenditure when playing golf under various conditions. The golfer's body weight will affect the total number of calories consumed during a round, as shown in Table 8–2. For example, a 190-lb golfer who walks a 7000-yard course, estimating an extra 1000 yards from straying from the midline and walking between greens and tees, could expect to expend 486 kcal[13] — more if the course is hilly or if a bag is carried.

Body Composition

Few data are available on the body composition of amateur golfers. A study[13] of 38 male professional golfers (mean age 32) found that their body fat averaged 17.5% over a 2-year period. The average 30- to 35-year-old man exceeds 20% body fat.[17] A study[5] of women on the professional tour reported 24% body fat.

TABLE 8–1. Energy Expenditure During Golf

Activity	Energy Range
Using power cart	2–3 METs
Using pull cart	3–4 METs
Carrying clubs	4–6 METs

Source: Data from Guidelines for Gradual Exercise Testing and Exercise Prescription.[10]

TABLE 8-2. Effect of Body Weight and Golf Bag on Caloric Expenditure

| Weight (lb) | Energy Expenditure | |
	Without Bag	With Bag
130	332 kcal	385 kcal
160	409 kcal	459 kcal
190	486 kcal	537 kcal
210	537 kcal	587 kcal

Source: Data from Jackson and North.[13]

THE RISKS OF CORONARY ARTERY DISEASE IN THE GOLFER

Myocardial Ischemia

The fundamental effect of coronary artery disease is inadequate delivery of oxygen to the myocardium, which results in alteration of metabolic processes and is accompanied by clinical signs and symptoms. When a fixed obstruction or spasm reduces the diameter of the arterial lumen, myocardial ischemia can result.[20,27] The pain of angina is a symptom of cardiac ischemia, the result of imbalance between myocardial oxygen supply and demand. Although angina is generally described as a chest tightness and presents as a retrosternal discomfort, it may present in an atypical fashion (Table 8-3). It may radiate to the right or left arm, neck, jaw, and back, or even the midepigastric area. Shortness of breath may be an anginal equivalent.

TABLE 8-3. Site of Anginal Pain: % Involvement at Any Given Time

Site	Involvement (%)
Anterior chest	96
Left arm (upper)	31
Left arm (lower)	29
Right arm (upper)	10
Right arm (lower)	13
Back	17
Epigastrium	3
Forehead	6
Neck	22
Chin and perioral area	8

Source: Data from Sampson and Cheitlin.[28]

Chest discomfort in golfers is sometimes mistakenly attributed to musculoskeletal problems by teaching professionals and even by physicians. Chest discomfort late in a round, "golfer's rib," a chest discomfort occurring while walking the fairway, may in fact be angina rather than a musculoskeletal problem.

Particular situations on the course increase myocardial oxygen demand. For example, anxiety and stress activate the autonomic nervous system, resulting in the release of epinephrine and norepinephrine, and epinephrine raises oxygen demand by increasing blood pressure, heart rate, and myocardial contractility. Thus golfers with coronary disease may have angina only in stressful tournament conditions and not during routine play. It is not uncommon for angina to occur on the first tee, primarily precipitated by anxiety; first-tee angina also may follow a spasm resulting from higher coronary tone in the early morning hours. Finally, the onset of fatigue late in a round may be associated with angina. It is appropriate, therefore, for the golfer with coronary artery disease to avoid activities that increase myocardial oxygen consumption, such as climbing hills; playing in hot, humid weather; and participating in stressful tournaments.

Sudden Death During Golf

A study[25] of the incidence of death during recreational exercise in Rhode Island reported that the highest number of deaths (19 during an 88-month period) occurred in golfers. This finding may reflect a higher incidence of underlying coronary disease (especially considering that one third of all rounds of golf are played by those more than age 60), but it also is possible that more time was spent participating in golf than in other sports because playing golf may take several hours.

Death during vigorous exercise primarily has been associated with coronary artery disease in athletes more than 30 years of age and with hypertrophic cardiomyopathy and congenital anomalies in those who are younger.[16] The overall incidence of death during exercise has been well described,[7, 29] but the actual number of deaths or coronary events that occur on golf courses is unknown. Certainly, though, studies such as that in Rhode Island suggest that educational programs and cardiopulmonary resuscitation (CPR) training should be available to golf professionals and golf course personnel.

GOLF AND THE TREATMENT OF CARDIOVASCULAR DISEASE

Medication

The golfer with angina should be compliant with medication and not delay its consumption until after the round is completed. The prophylactic use of nitroglycerin may be warranted if the golfer is faced with a situation, either mental or physical, that is likely to produce angina.

Beta blockers are commonly used to control angina and hypertension. In addition to lowering heart rate, blood pressure, and myocardial contractility, however, they also improve steadiness and therefore are banned in sports such as archery. The Sports Council, a governmental body in England, includes beta blockers on a list of drugs that may enhance athletic performance, and their use may result in disqualification from tournaments such as the British Open.

Diuretics are sometimes employed in the treatment of hypertension and congestive heart failure. Their dosage may need to be altered for golfers playing on hot and humid days in order to avoid problems with dehydration.

The Post-Myocardial Infarction Patient

Individuals who have sustained a myocardial infarction may return to limited golf activities in their convalescent period, especially chipping and putting. Uncomplicated postinfarction patients have a functional capacity equivalent to 4 to 6 METs.[2,26] Walking the golf course requires an energy expenditure of 3 to 4 METs (see Table 8–1). Prior to returning to the full play of 18 holes, however, the patient should undergo a near-maximal or maximal multilevel stress test because the physician's recommendations concerning the amount of golf to be played and whether the golfer should walk or ride will depend not only on the degree of coronary disease but also on the patient's individual body energy requirements and myocardial oxygen demands. Other factors to consider are the golfer's skill level and competitiveness, and playing conditions such as temperature and altitude.

The Coronary Bypass Patient

Coronary bypass surgery has enabled many individuals with coronary artery disease to return to an active lifestyle. Julius Boros and Bob Rosburg are two professionals who have undergone coronary bypass surgery and returned to the professional tour. Following surgery, these patients should be able to return to playing golf within 1 month if the cardiac condition is stable. The only limiting factor will be chest wall discomfort resulting from the sternal incision.

Pacemakers in Golfers

Advancements in pacemaker technology have had positive implications for the golfer, resulting in improved hemodynamic function for these active individuals.[15] The pacemaker is generally implanted in the left precordial region, in order not to interfere with the swing of the right-handed golfer. The use of a bipolar pacemaker should be considered, to avoid possible electrical interference from muscle potentials.

SUMMARY

Recent data have confirmed that walking the golf course has beneficial effects on the golfer's lipid profile and may aid in weight control and improve body composition.

The presence of cardiovascular disease is not a reason to discontinue golf, which can be used to complement the exercise program for the cardiac patient. Adherence to medication, avoidance of extremes of temperature, and limitation of severe physical and emotional stress are warranted.

REFERENCES

1. Åstrand, PO and Rodahl, K: Textbook of Work Physiology. McGraw-Hill, New York, 1971.
2. Bergstrom, K, Bjernut, A, and Erickson, O: Work capacity and heart blood volume before and after physical training in male patients after myocardial infarction. Scand J Rehab Med 5:51–64, 1974.
3. Blair, S, et al: Physical fitness and all-cause mortality. JAMA 262:2395–2401, 1989.
4. Cook, T, et al: Chronic low level physical activity as a determinant of high density lipoprotein cholesterol and subfraction. Med Sci Sports Exerc 18:653–657, 1986.
5. Crews, D, et al: A physiologic profile of Ladies Professional Golf Association tour players. Phys Sportsmed 12:69–76, 1984.
6. Getchell, LH: Energy cost of playing golf. Arch Phys Med Rehab 49:31–35, 1968.
7. Gibbons, LW, et al: The acute cardiac risk of strenuous exercise. JAMA 244:1799–1801, 1980.
8. Golf participation in the United States. National Golf Foundation, Jupiter, FL, 1990.
9. Gordon, T, et al: High density lipoproteins as a protective factor against coronary heart disease: The Framingham Study. Am J Med 62:707–714, 1977.
10. Guidelines for Gradual Exercise Testing and Exercise Prescription, American College of Sports Medicine. Lea & Febiger, Philadelphia, 1980.
11. Hartung, GH, et al: Relationship of diet to HDL-cholesterol in middle-aged marathon runners. N Engl J Med 302:357–362, 1980.
12. Heart Facts 1988. American Heart Association, Dallas, TX, 1987.
13. Jackson, A and North, S: Golf for Fitness and Health. National Golf Foundation, Jupiter, FL, 1985, p 40.
14. Kannel, WB: Some lessons in cardiovascular epidemiology from Framingham. Am J Card 37:269–289, 1976.
15. Levine, PA and Mace, RC: Pacing therapy. Futura Publishing, Mount Kisco, NY, 1983.
16. Maron, BJ, Epstein SE, and Roberts, WC: Causes of sudden death in competitive athletes. J Am Coll Cardiol 7:204, 1986.
17. McArdle, W, Katch, F, and Katch, V: Exercise Physiology. Lea & Febiger, Philadelphia, 1991.
18. McHenry, PL, et al: Statements on exercise. Circulation 81:396–397, 1990.
19. Murase, Y, Kameis, S, and Hoshikawat, T: Heart rate and metabolic responses to participation in golf. J Sports Med Phys Fitness 29:269, 1989.
20. Oliva, SB, Potts, DE, and Ploss, RA: Coronary arterial spasm in Prinzmetal's angina: Documentation by coronary arteriography. N Engl J Med 288: 788–789, 1973.
21. Paffenbarger, RS and Hale, WE: Work activity and coronary heart mortality. N Engl J Med 292:545–550, 1975.
22. Paffenbarger, RS, et al: A natural history of athleticism and cardiovascular health. JAMA 252:491–495, 1984.
23. Paffenbarger, RS, et al: Physical activity, all-cause mortality and longevity of college alumni. N Engl J Med 314:605–613, 1986.
24. Palank, EA and Hargreaves, EH: The benefits of walking the golf course. Phys Sportsmed 18: 77–80, 1990.
25. Ragosta, M, et al: Death during recreational exercise in the state of Rhode Island. Med Sci Sports Exerc 16:339–349, 1984.
26. Rousseau, MF, et al: Hemodynamic effects of early physical training after acute myocardial infarction: Comparison with a control untrained group. Eur J Cardiol 2:39–45, 1974.
27. Rubio, R and Berne, RM: Regulation of coronary blood flow. Prog Cardiovasc Dis 18:105, 1975.
28. Sampson, JJ and Cheitlin, MD: Pathophysiology and differential diagnosis of cardiac pain. Prog Cardiovasc Dis 13:507, 1971.
29. Siscovick, DS, et al: The incidence of primary cardiac arrest during vigorous exercise. N Engl J Med 311:874, 1984.
30. Skubic, V and Hodgkins, J: Relative strenuousness of selected sport as performed by women. Res Quart 38:305–313, 1967.
31. Wood, PD, et al: The distribution of plasma lipoproteins in middle aged runners. Metabolism 25:1249–1257, 1976.

9

Golf Participation by the Physically Challenged

Cornelius N. Stover, MD
DeDe Owens, EdD
Robert C. Wilson
Kathy Corbin

AMPUTEE GOLF
Lower-Extremity Amputees
Upper-Extremity Amputees
Multiple Amputees
CHAIR GOLF
GOLF FOR THE BLIND
OSTEOARTHRITIS
CONDITIONING
SPECIAL EQUIPMENT
SPECIAL INSTRUCTION
PSYCHOLOGICAL VALUE

olf, more than most other sports or recreational activities, lends itself to participation by individuals who are physically challenged. Adjustments in equipment and technique make the game suitable to individuals with the most disabling conditions. Where necessary, even the rules of the game can and have been changed to accommodate the needs of the individual with a permanent medical handicap.

A stimulus to participation by the physically challenged was provided by the Golf Writers Association of America when they established the Ben Hogan Award. This award is symbolic of Hogan's great determination to return to competitive golf after a near-fatal automobile accident in 1949, and it is given annually to an individual who has continued to be active in golf despite a physical handicap. Among the early recipients of this award were Dale Bourisseau, founder of the National Amputee Golf Association, and Ernest Jones, who lost a leg in World War I but returned to become one of the game's great teaching professionals. Other recipients have included blind golfers Charles Boswell and Joe Lazaro. Ed Furgol received the award after winning the National Open despite a left arm that had been badly crippled in a childhood accident. Another recipient, Larry Hinson, a touring professional, had overcome poliomyelitis that left him with a very atrophied left arm. Dennis Walters received the Hogan Award in recognition of his persistence at mastering golf from a wheelchair after an accident left him paralyzed below the waist.

In the past, golf instruction for individuals with disabling conditions has been limited. Teachers were interested, but felt inept. In some instances, individuals reported greater discouragement following a lesson than before. These golfers learned through trial and error, with help from friends. The Professional Golfers' Association of America (PGA) recognized this void in instruction and the desire of many individuals with disabling conditions to participate in golf. They established a Committee for the Physically Challenged[1] to develop instructional strategies and to train PGA professionals. Now, individuals seeking golf professionals knowledgeable in this area may contact the PGA in North Palm Beach, Florida.

AMPUTEE GOLF

Golf is of immense value both physically and psychologically to amputees. The number of amputees in the United States is approximately 2.2 million and is increasing by about 170,000 a year. Amputees have pursued athletic activities for many years, but among the first to participate in golf was Ernest Jones, a British teaching professional. He developed his famous theories of the golf swing after losing his own leg in World War I. The physical challenge he faced as an amputee contributed to his concepts of balance and swinging the club head rather than simply hitting the ball. Golf for amputees received its formal start after World War II, when Dale Bourisseau, a below-the-knee (B/K) amputee, along with others, conceived and organized the National Amputee Golf Association (NAGA) and conducted its first tournament in 1949. Since that time, the organization has grown to more than 3000 members, and the annual tournament now attracts more than 100 participants. The organization is further divided into three regional and seven state associations. Tournaments and "Learn to Golf" clinics are conducted on a regular basis.

To provide equity and competition, multiple divisions have been established according to the type of handicap: above knee, below knee, above elbow, below elbow, and double, triple, and quadruple amputees. There are also divisions for juniors and ladies. The International Senior Amputee Golf Society holds a separate tournament annually. At tournaments, flights are established within divisions and no handicaps are used, allowing those without an established United States Golf Association (USGA) handicap to compete. Golf events are conducted according to the USGA rules with certain exceptions. In 1981, the NAGA became aware that USGA Rule #14 concerning artificial devices required the Tournament Committee to disqualify entrants if they used an artificial prosthetic device. The rule further stated that the use of such devices modified in any way to enable a person to play golf is a definite breach of the rules. The NAGA took exception to this position and in January of 1984, Rule #14 was changed to permit modified prosthetic devices in NAGA-sponsored and -sanctioned competition. Later, the USGA was approached to permit the use of motorized carts by the amputee. This request was rejected, and to date, neither artificial devices nor motorized carts are permitted in USGA competition. The USGA commitment to preserve the game of golf and protect its heritage according to established standards is readily understandable as it is applied to able-bodied individuals. On the other hand, strict adherence to the established rules deprives many individuals of the opportunity to participate, and reduces the stimulus to innovation.

Women amputees have not commonly participated in these events. This is definitely changing, as exemplified by Blanche Shapiro,[11] a quadruple amputee (Fig. 9–1). Due to a rare blood disorder, disseminated intravascular coagulation, her extremities were amputated below the elbows and below the knees.

Lower-Extremity Amputees

The primary goal of the lower-extremity amputee is functional and pain-free ambulation. For those who desire to carry their rehabilitation one step further and participate in golf, however, a more versatile prosthesis may be required. Modifications and adjustments can be made to allow the prosthesis to adapt more easily to changes in terrain, including walking slight inclines and going from grass to pavement. The needs and

Figure 9–1. Quadruple amputee fitted with upper- and lower-bilateral prosthetic devices. (From Hodgson, M: Not an exception. Amputee Golfer Magazine, 1989, p 43, with permission.)

ideas of amputee golfers have been invaluable to prosthetists and limb makers on the leading edge of technical advancement. New plastics that are tough and flexible and will stand up to sports applications have been developed for use in prosthetics. The use of these plastics in flexible sockets provides firm support where needed but enough flexibility to function and move. The Cat-Cam socket for above-the-knee (A/K) amputees is an excellent example. This socket is a contoured, adducted trochanter with controlled alignment method. The intimate fit of this technique is made possible by the use of a flexible thermoplastic socket, which allows smooth transition of movements during the golf swing.

The newest technology available in prosthetic componentry was introduced to this country with the carbon-fiber, titanium, and aluminum prosthesis from Endolite[4] (Fig. 9–2). This prosthesis is very durable and yet very lightweight. Recent models weigh 50% less than earlier models. The socket is made of polyethylene and the retainer, polypropylene. The multiflex ankle is ideally suited for golf. It allows full range of motion with con-

trolled inversion and eversion in addition to plantar and dorsiflexion. This is particularly helpful on uneven terrain.

Swing instruction for lower-limb amputees centers on their ability to maintain balance while maximizing their arm swing and upper body rotation. A/K amputees may have a stability problem in weight bearing, but this can be addressed in their set-up position. B/K amputees should experience fewer stability problems than A/K amputees. Lower-limb amputees may be limited in their lower-body motion, but they are free in their arm swing to create good club head speed for distance and accuracy. With the available lower-limb prosthetic designs for golf, however, even these amputees can be free to develop good lower-body motion. There have been many low-handicap golfers who were A/K and B/K amputees.

Upper-Extremity Amputees

It has long been noted that loss of an arm is a greater problem for the golfer than loss of a lower leg. The one-armed player has to

Figure 9–2. Extremely lightweight and durable, the modern prosthesis permits near-physiologic ankle motion. Newer models provide controlled rotation.

Figure 9-3. Upper-extremity amputee playing forehanded.

consider which way to swing, with the remaining arm used in either a forehand or a backhand manner (Figs. 9-3 and 9-4). For individuals who are just learning to play golf, it is recommended that they learn the golf swing in a backhand manner, which provides greater control, although it sacrifices some distance. The forehand swing has greater potential distance because the backswing arc is larger, but the advantage is reduced by the lack of control it imposes.

New amputees with former golf experience should be encouraged to experiment (with supervision) with both forehand and backhand styles because of their previous established movement patterns. An understanding of the advantages of both styles should be communicated to the golfer. The forehand swing will take longer to learn and will present the greatest initial frustrations. The final decision should always take into consideration the individual's present and potential ability and interest.

Various prosthetic devices have been adapted for attachment to the club or the involved extremity.[2] The golf club may be held and swung successfully with a single extremity, but greater action and power are obtained by holding with both hands and arms. Earl Puhl, himself an amputee, has developed a device that can be fitted onto the club to permit an upper-extremity amputee to play golf (shown in Fig. 9-1).[2] The device is interchangeable with a prosthetic club or prosthetic hand (Fig. 9-5). It fits readily into the standard prosthetic arm and can be used by right- or left-handed golfers. One of the most important features of the device is that the wrist unit, made of polyurethane and rubber tubing with steel rods separated by a slight gap, is flexible enough to allow the necessary wrist action and rotation during backswing and follow-through (Fig. 9-6). A similar device (Figs. 9-7 and 9-8) was designed by F. B. Goldman of Dallas for players missing the left-upper extremity and is another example of innovation resulting from a particular physical handicap.

A variety of similar units with special variations to meet individual requirements have been developed and are generally in use at the National Tournament. The innovators are usually more than willing to share information regarding the manufacturer and the cost.

Figure 9-4. Upper-extremity amputee playing backhanded.

Figure 9–5. The prosthetic device facilitates use of the trunk in both backswing and downswing.

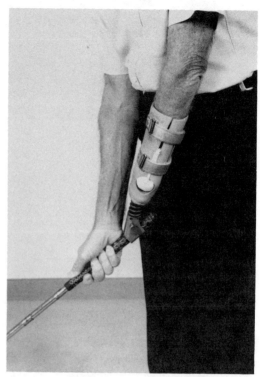

Figure 9–7. Prosthetic device designed for left below-elbow amputee.

Multiple Amputees

Multiple amputees present special additional problems and are by necessity some of the most creative of the physically challenged golfers. For example, some double-arm amputees play without prostheses; others use club-holding devices attached to both prostheses. Either way, remarkable skills have been developed.[8]

CHAIR GOLF

People who cannot use their legs for support may play golf from a seated position (Fig. 9–9).[7] Amputees and other physically challenged golfers are frequently aided by the use of the golf cart. Because of restrictions about carts on greens, however, they either have avoided putting or have gone onto the putting surface on their torso (Fig. 9–10), propelled by their hands. Although they feel awkward at first, many chair players have developed workable swings with a minimal amount of practice and have

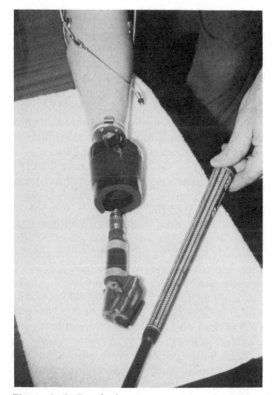

Figure 9–6. Prosthetic components permit necessary wrist motion.

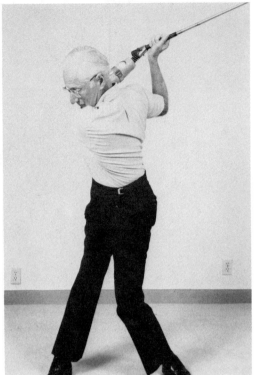

Figure 9–8. The prosthetic device aids extension during backswing and contributes to stability at the top of the swing.

Figure 9–10. The restriction preventing carts or chairs on greens can be overcome by using the hands to propel the torso over short distances.

Figure 9–9. Golf from a wheelchair is quite feasible. The chair arms have been removed to permit a free swing.

enjoyed hours of fun and recreation with the game. Whereas paraplegics and some other wheelchair users must play the game from a seated position, others, such as double-leg amputees and people who have had strokes, are sometimes capable of leaning against a stool or portable support or even against the golf cart while swinging. New innovations in wheelchairs may even permit individuals to stand rather than sit while swinging.

A number of variations in standard wheelchairs are available. For the low-level paraplegic, with no upper-body balance problems, removing the sidearms is helpful. A more sophisticated version is a golf cart with a swivel seat that turns 90°, allowing the golfer to play the course from the motorized cart. Unfortunately, a specialized cart is expensive and not currently available to the public. The Edwin Shaw Hospital in Akron, Ohio, is building a practice range and golf course designed to be fully accessible for the disabled golfer.

The swing motion from a wheelchair is a flatter motion than that used when standing. The individual needs to experiment to find the best position from which to swing. For example, some individuals find hitting their irons is easier when the ball is positioned to the side of the chair. This allows them to create a more upright swing arc for the irons, which is desirable. The woods require a flatter angle of ball contact and are easier for some when the ball is positioned in front of the chair. This preference may vary, so allow experimentation.

GOLF FOR THE BLIND

Golf for the blind has gained momentum in recent years and is now participated in by individuals from all over the country. Like amputees, blind golfers have their own organization and tournament schedules. A significant difference, of course, is the need for a coach for each blind player, who serves as the player's "eyes." The coach lines up the shot and provides information on distance, direction, the contours and terrain of the course, and additional data necessary for low scoring. The golfer, however, still hits the ball and is capable of a sound and functional golf swing.

The swing mechanics for the visually impaired golfer are the same as for the sighted golfer. The emphasis in the instruction of the visually impaired, however, must be both verbal and tactile-kinesthetic. Clarity of explanation, coupled with purposeful and directed manipulation, is critical in the initial stage of learning the swing. Feedback related to movement expectancy and outcome is likewise crucial between the teacher and golfer.

A golf course scale model is an excellent teaching aid, especially if labeled in braille. The different aspects of the course such as the rough, fairway, greens, and traps are made of different textured materials. The holes can be laid out to indicate doglegs, different length holes, and hazards. A smaller model can be taken to the course so the golfer can "feel" the course as it is being played.

OSTEOARTHRITIS

Progressive osteoarthritis, especially when it involves the hips and knees, has forced many individuals to give up the game. The advent of total replacement, along with other improvements in recent years, has permitted many golfers to return to the game.[10] (see Chapter 10).

In the early stages of osteoarthritis, individuals with knee or hip problems can be taught as if they were limited in lower-body motion, similar to lower-limb amputees. Pressure can be taken off the joints through various swing adjustments, and the swing emphasis is placed on the use of the arms and upper body, with the pivot or turning motion centered around the nonaffected leg.

CONDITIONING

Conditioning is needed for all golfers. It not only enhances the individual's mobility in the swinging motion but also reduces the chances for injury due to muscle pulls, strains, and general muscle imbalances. Individuals with any disabling condition increase their chances for injury because of the already existing tendencies for movement compensation in their everyday life. With golf, they are adding the high degree of twisting and torquing of the upper body in the lumbar and pelvic areas induced during the swing.

Steven Fleischer-Curtain,[5] a physical therapist who works with professional athletes and several noted golfers, has given these recommendations:

▶ Specific muscles in the shoulder complex and arms should be strengthened. This can be done through the following exercises:
  ▶ Seated rowing (latissimus dorsi, middle and lower trapezius)
  ▶ Lat pull-down (latissimus dorsi)
  ▶ Upright rowing (upper trapezius and deltoid)
  ▶ Curl-ups (rectus abdominis)
  ▶ Curl-ups with a twist (obliques and rectus abdominis)
  ▶ Arm curls (triceps and biceps)
  ▶ Arm/hand pronation and supination (brachioradialis, supinator, pronator, quadratus, pronator teres)
▶ Muscles in the pelvic and hip area are key components in stabilizing the hip area during the swing. These muscles can be strengthened through the following exercises:
  ▶ Leg extensors (quadriceps)

- ▶ Leg curls (hamstrings)
- ▶ Hip adduction (pectineus, biceps, femoris)
- ▶ Hip abduction (sartorius, gluteals)
- ▶ Leg press (gluteus maximus and hip extensors)
- ▶ External rotators (piriformis, gluteus medius)

Upper-body, single-limb amputees need to follow the suggested exercises with attention to the shoulder complex. The exercises will provide the needed strength to improve club control and increase stamina to sustain 18 holes.

Lower-limb amputees need upper-body as well as lower-body strength to maintain stability. The hip region will fatigue quickly during a round because of the twisting the area sustains, plus the constant need for stability, with or without a prosthesis.

Wheelchair amputees need to follow the conditioning program suggested for a stronger shoulder complex because the ball is positioned farther away than normal. Additionally, stronger obliques and abdominals are needed because of the excessive torque around the lumbar area that results from stabilization of the pelvis while sitting.

Conditioning for golfers with osteoarthritis is needed to maintain as much range of motion as possible in the joints. Exercises to strengthen the muscles around the joints are important. As with the lower-limb amputee, the gluteals on the side opposite the affected joints should be strengthened to provide greater stability during the swing.

Before beginning a conditioning program, individuals must obtain medical clearance. Then the program should be set up by a *qualified professional*, with initial and periodic supervision advised.

SPECIAL EQUIPMENT

In addition to prosthetic devices and motorized carts, specialized clubs are available. Club head speed is often difficult for amputees to generate and can be enhanced greatly by the use of clubs that permit high shaft flex with fast recovery. The resulting increased club head speed may potentially add as much as 15 to 20 yards to the drive.

SPECIAL INSTRUCTION

A number of centers around the country provide customized instruction tailored to individual needs. The Never Say Never Clinic in Phoenix is such a clinic that is well known for its success in teaching the golf swing to physically challenged individuals. Since 1981, the NAGA has received growing numbers of requests from recreational physical therapists throughout the world for information to help establish golf as an integral part of their rehabilitation programs.

The Professional Golfers' Association of America and the Junior Golf Foundation published the "First Swing Program" in 1986. The program was designed to introduce and prepare teachers to conduct basic golf instruction. These seminars and learn-to-golf clinics for the physically challenged are regularly held at numerous sites around the country.

The National Golf Foundation, based in Palm Beach, Florida, also conducts golf clinics and workshops for teachers in the summers. Special sessions have been conducted on teaching those with various disabilities. Emphasis is on indications and contraindications for the disabilities related to movement potential, while focusing on the individual, not the condition.

To date, few books have addressed golf instruction and the specific needs of individuals with disabling conditions. One, *Teaching Golf to Special Populations*, edited by DeDe Owens, EdD,[9] deals specifically with the needs related to teaching golf and the learning characteristics of such population groups as the visually, mentally, or physically impaired.

PSYCHOLOGICAL VALUE

The psychological value of golf for the physically challenged is undoubtedly considerable. One need only to ask the participants or observe them in action to appreciate golf's benefits. The progressive skill opportunities that can be established, based on individual needs, foster success and challenges with minimal frustration and can aid in the personal progress of each individual. These individuals want to challenge themselves and want to be challenged by others. In addition, tournaments may reduce feelings of isolation by allowing these golfers to meet others with similar disabilities.[11]

The impact of golf can extend beyond the course and is perhaps best reflected in the following two quotes by amputee golfers.[6]

An amputee, after the 1982 International Senior Amputee Golf Society tournament:

After losing a leg, my walking was limited to no more than a few city blocks and left me suffering from pain and blisters for several days afterwards. My first contact with golf was as an observer at an NAGA Championship. This brought new life to me. Just watching amputees play golf inspired me to do the same. During my association with others with the same physical condition as mine, and participating as a golfer, I found my physical condition improved almost 100% overnight. With help from other amputees, within a year I was walking 18 holes with a freedom that I had never imagined was possible before meeting them. I am now an able person instead of disabled.

Another amputee, previously a champion at tennis and handball:

Time caught up with me and I lost my left leg and some strength in my arm. No more tennis or handball. I could not compete again. . . . I "suffered" for 10 years. Then someone suggested golf. To make a point — nothing could have been more important. If ever the situation would arise for anyone who, as a senior, needed physical activity for morale as well as for fitness, I would suggest that he/she be made aware of the benefits of our sport, golf. I know it helped me. I have played for a year and a half now and hit in the 90s, but more than my score — my morale, it couldn't be better!

SUMMARY

The benefits of golf are often missed by the casual observer. For the participant, however, they are limitless and differ with each individual. The setting is right for individuals with disabling conditions to learn and enjoy the game. Far greater opportunities are available to foster success with the equipment advances, instructional formats, educated professionals, and the inherent nature of the game for meeting the individual needs of the participants. Corbin Cherry,[3] a B/K amputee and former National Amputee Champion, summed up the game when he said, "Golf has allowed me the greatest of gifts: freedom of body, mind, and above all, spirit. I could ask no more."

REFERENCES

1. Addis, T: Personal communication, Dec 4, 1987. (Chairman, PGA Committee for the Physically Challenged).
2. Bhala, RP and Schultz, CF: Golf club holder for upper-extremity amputee golfers. Arch Phys Med Rehabil 63:339–341, 1982.
3. Cherry, C, quoted by Owens, ND (ed): Teaching Golf to Special Populations. Leisure Press, Champaign, IL, 1984, p 15.
4. Finnigston, AR: Technical update. Amputee Golfer Magazine, 1989, pp 26–30.
5. Fleisher-Curtain, S: Personal communication, Charlottesville, VA, April 25, 1991.
6. International Senior Amputee Golf Society (brochure), Tampa, FL, 1983.
7. Longo, P: Chair golf. Sports N Spokes 15(2):35–38, 1989.
8. Owens, ND: An Analysis of Amputee Golf Swings. EdD dissertation, University of Virginia, Charlottesville, 1980.
9. Owens, ND (ed): Teaching Golf to Special Populations. Leisure Press, Champaign, IL, 1984.
10. Ritter, MA and Meding, JB: Total hip arthroplasty. Can the patient play sports again? Orthopaedics 10:1447–1452, 1987.
11. Shapiro, B: Awakening one day to a nightmare, a young mother turns the loss of her limbs into a triumph of will. People, Nov 19, 1990, pp 146–150.

10

The Golfer with a Total Joint Replacement

William J. Mallon, MD

TOTAL HIP REPLACEMENTS
TOTAL KNEE REPLACEMENTS
OTHER TOTAL JOINT REPLACEMENTS
Shoulder
Elbow
Wrist and Ankle
LONG-TERM EFFECTS
RECOMMENDATIONS

Total joint replacements are usually performed in an elderly population. Age and the underlying disease often preclude active involvement in sports. However, many older patients desire to play golf after a total hip replacement and, in fact, often seek the operation with this in mind. Sledge,[25] a top expert in the field, has commented, "Return to golf is probably the most often cited *functional* goal for hip/knee replacement in my patient population."

No specific studies, however, have been done of golfers who have undergone total joint replacement. Several studies* have examined the effects of exercise after total hip replacement, but only the study by Ritter

---
*References 3,12,15,17,22–24,27,30.

and Meding[23] discussed golf as one of the modes of exercise. Even that study did not examine golf separately but grouped it with several other sports.

Unfortunately, it is difficult to study a population of golfers with total joint replacements retrospectively. The playing of golf is not often mentioned in the history database during the work-up for total joint replacement. Thus it is difficult to define the cohort of golfers among all total joint recipients.

To study this problem, a survey was undertaken of all members of The Hip Society and The Knee Society, groups of orthopedic surgeons who specialize in joint replacement surgery. They were asked questions concerning advice they give their patients and whether they have noticed any specific problems in patients who play golf after total hip or knee replacement. The questionnaire is shown in Table 10–1.

Two groups of active golfers were also studied. The first group consisted of all known golf professionals or professional golfers who have had either total hip or total knee replacement. The members of this group were found by contacting the 48 sectional chapters of the PGA of America.

The second group consisted of golfers

TABLE 10–1. Questionnaire Concerning Total Hip/Knee Replacements in Golfers

1. Do you discourage your total hip/knee recipients from playing golf? If so, why?
2. Do you give your total hip/knee recipients any special instructions if they choose to play golf? If so, what are they?
3. Would you recommend any swing modifications to a golfer receiving a total hip/knee replacement?
4. Do you recommend that your total hip/knee recipients use a golf cart if they plan on playing golf?
5. Among total hip/knee recipients who have continued to play golf, have you noticed any increased complication rates, notably early loosening?
6. Can you estimate what percentage of your total hip/knee recipients have been able to continue playing golf, if they desired to do so?
7. When do you recommend that your total hip/knee recipients return to playing golf?
8. Do you have any thoughts on cemented versus bone-ingrowth hip/knee prostheses in a patient who wishes to play golf frequently?
9. Would you discourage a patient with a hip/knee revision from attempting to play golf?
10. Do you believe wear will be a bigger problem in total hip/knee recipients who play golf frequently?
11. Do you have any other comments concerning total hip/knee replacements in golfers?

who responded to a request in the author's column in *Golf Digest* magazine.[16] The column requested correspondence with all golfers who had either total hip or knee replacements and continued to play golf actively. A subgroup of these patients was formed by including only those who played golf at least three times per week.

Both the golf professionals and the active amateur golfers were sent questionnaires concerning their golfing habits preoperatively and postoperatively. This questionnaire is shown in Table 10–2.

TOTAL HIP REPLACEMENTS

Twenty-six replies (26/41, 64%) were received from the members of The Hip Society. The study groups consisted of (1) 14 PGA golf professionals who had undergone 16 total hip replacements and continued to play golf and (2) 78 amateur golfers who had had 98 total hip replacements and continued to play golf at least three times a week.

All members of The Hip Society believed that a total hip replacement was not a contraindication to playing golf. Most (69%) requested that their patients use a cart; some members[6,29] stated that they advised this only for the first year. All the responding physicians stated that all patients who desired to play golf after total hip replacement were able to do so. No physicians believed that the desire to play golf would influence choice of components or fixation method, and none believed that active golfers had more problems or higher revision rates than their other patients.

Of the 14 golf professionals, 2 of whom had had bilateral total hip replacements, all were able to continue teaching and playing golf with no difficulty. The average age at time of hip replacements was 54 years (26 to

TABLE 10–2. Questionnaire for Total Joint Replacements in Golfers

TJR = total joint replacement; ATJR = at time of joint replacement

Type of joint replacement	R HIP	L HIP	R KNEE	L KNEE
Current age _____				
Age ATJR R HIP _____	L HIP _____	R KNEE _____	L KNEE _____	
Has your TJR been redone	R HIP	L HIP	R KNEE	L KNEE
Why and when was it redone?				

Do you currently have a cemented or uncemented joint replacement (circle all):

Cemented	R HIP	L HIP	R KNEE	L KNEE
Uncemented	R HIP	L HIP	R KNEE	L KNEE

Times playing golf per week	Currently	_____
	Prior to TJR	_____

Handicap: Best _____   ATJR _____   Current _____

TABLE 10–2. Questionnaire for Total Joint Replacements in Golfers (*Continued*)

Change in length of average drive since TJR
  No change   _____
  Longer since TJR by   _____ yds
  Shorter since TJR by   _____ yds

Transport during golf ATJR
  Walk, carry bag _____
  Walk, pull cart _____
  Walk, caddy _____
  Golf cart _____

Transport during golf currently
  Walk, carry bag _____
  Walk, pull cart _____
  Walk, caddy _____
  Golf cart _____

Did your surgeon recommend that you ride a cart while playing?
  Yes   No

Did your surgeon advise you not to play golf after your TJR?
  Yes   No

Did your surgeon recommend modifying your swing in any way (if so, please describe:)

When did you start playing after your TJR:
  R HIP _____ mo   L HIP _____ mo   R KNEE _____ mo   L KNEE _____ mo

Pain status in TJR joint while playing golf
  No pain   _____
  Mild ache   _____
  Continuous pain _____

Pain status in TJR joint after playing 18 holes
  No pain   _____
  Mild ache   _____
  Continuous pain for several hours   _____
  Cannot walk or play golf for several days _____

Where is the pain?
  Thigh   _____
  Buttock   _____
  Groin   _____

Since your joint replacement, do you have difficulty with hilly lies:
  Yes   _____
  No   _____

What strokes are harder for you since your TJR (circle all):
  Driving   Fairway woods   Irons   Short game   Putting

What strokes are easier for you since your TJR (circle all):
  Driving   Fairway woods   Irons   Short game   Putting

68), and the average follow-up at the time of the survey was 4 years (6 months to 12 years). Two professionals had formerly made their living as tournament players, but both had stopped playing competitively long before their hip replacements. No golf pro-fessionals had required revisions at the time of the survey.

Among the 78 active amateurs, 20 of whom had had bilateral total hip replacements, the average age at time of hip replacements was 59 (43 to 76), and the average follow-up at the time of the survey was 5 years (6 months to 15 years). Of these 78 golfers, 92% had no discomfort while playing golf. Of the six who did experience pain while playing, all stated that it was less than preoperatively. Seven of the amateurs (9%) had required revision at the time of the survey. The average golf handicap preoperatively and postoperatively showed no statistically significant difference. Several of this group were active enough to play in local amateur tournaments.

Only one patient in the study sustained a severe injury from playing golf. While playing, he slipped and fell, sustaining an open femur fracture at the tip of the prosthesis. This was treated with irrigation and débridement, followed by traction and then cast bracing. He healed uneventfully and continues to play golf. Amstutz[2] mentions a patient who had a similar problem, but gives no other data.

Sledge[25] reported that he found no difference between patients with cemented prostheses and those with bone-ingrowth prostheses regarding symptoms while playing golf; both groups of patients were allowed to participate. Some other members of The Hip Society[7,29] reported advising golfers with uncemented total hip replacements to decrease their golfing activity for up to 6 to 8 months if they developed any thigh pain while playing.

The time when patients could return to golf was usually about 3 to 4 months after total hip replacement. Borden[6] advised beginning only with chipping and putting and lengthening the swing gradually. He also reported that a few of his patients have played golf only 4 weeks after their total hip replacement. This was against his advice, but no patient developed any problems. Borden's recommendations about beginning slowly were voiced by most of the surgeons.

TOTAL KNEE REPLACEMENTS

All members of The Knee Society were asked about instructions and contraindications given to patients who desire to play golf after a total knee replacement (see Table 10–1), and 27 replied (27/43, 63%). In addition, two groups of very active golfers

were evaluated. One consisted of three PGA golf professionals who had undergone three total knee replacements and continued to play golf. The other group consisted of 39 amateurs who had had 54 total knee replacements and continued to play golf at least three times per week.

Of the responding surgeons, 93% believed that a total knee replacement was not a contraindication to playing golf; two (7%) did request that these patients not play golf. Most (77%) requested that their patients use a cart. All respondents found that all patients who desired to play golf after total knee replacement were able to do so. No surgeon indicated that the desire to play golf would influence choice of components or fixation method, and none believed that active golfers had more problems or higher revision rates than other patients.

Among the golf professionals, all were able to continue teaching and playing golf with no difficulty. The average age at time of knee replacement was 58 years (52 to 65), and the average follow-up at the time of the survey was 4 years (2 years to 8 years). None had required revisions at the time of the survey.

Among the 39 amateur golfers, 15 of whom had had bilateral total knee replacements, the average age at time of knee replacement was 63 (49 to 78), and the average follow-up at the time of the survey was 5 years (6 months to 11 years). Ninety percent had no discomfort while playing golf. Of the four golfers who did experience pain while playing, all stated that it was less than preoperatively. One amateur (3%) had required revision at the time of the survey. The average golf handicap preoperatively and postoperatively showed no statistically significant difference, and no disastrous complications from accidents while playing golf were mentioned by these respondents.

One of the surgeons[13] reported that he discourages his patients with total knee replacements from playing golf because he believes the terminal torque would be detrimental, specifically affecting the left knee of a right-handed golfer. Another[14] reported allowing his patients to play golf and allowing them to walk if they so desire. He reported that patients tell him their swing is "normal."

Questions concerning the time when patients with knee replacements could begin playing golf elicited similar answers to those given concerning patients with total hip replacements. Most of the surgeons believed that patients should not start playing golf for about 3 months after surgery and then should begin slowly, mostly chipping and putting at first. Thornhill[29] gave the guideline that he allows them to begin chipping and putting when they are weaned from assistive aids such as canes or crutches.

Our knowledge of the effects of high-stress activity after total knee replacement is quite limited. A few studies have been performed on the effect of various forms of exercise after total hip replacement,* but similar studies have not been done after total knee replacements. Good estimates of the torques and forces around the knee during a golf swing do not exist, as most studies of the kinematics and biomechanics of the golf swing have dealt with the upper extremity.

OTHER TOTAL JOINT REPLACEMENTS

Shoulder

Total shoulder replacements are usually performed for painful shoulders and are quite successful in relieving the pain of glenohumeral motion.[20] Improvement in range of motion after total shoulder replacement is, however, variable, and it usually does not occur to any significant degree.

Total shoulder replacements are usually performed either for secondary degenerative arthritis in patients with rheumatoid arthritis or for posttraumatic arthritis.[20] Rheumatoid patients with involvement of the glenohumeral joint are often too severely affected by their disease to still be active golfers, either before or after total shoulder replacement. However, many patients with posttraumatic arthritis of the glenohumeral joint desire to play golf after total shoulder replacement.

Neer, Watson, and Stanton,[20] the foremost proponents of total shoulder replacement, have indicated in their articles that they allow their patients to play golf if they so desire. In fact, they state that they allow them to play tennis, which most orthopedists specializing in shoulder reconstruction do not allow. In a recent review of 273 total shoulder replacements, Neer and colleagues[20] mentioned 23 avid golfers and tennis players who showed no radiographic evidence of loosening. Five of these patients played low-handicap golf, and one patient with the implant in his dominant shoulder was a top-ranking tennis player in the eastern United States.

Cofield[9] and Post[21] also have indicated that they allow their patients with a total shoulder replacement to play golf. Cofield[9] also mentioned that he is frequently asked by prospective total–shoulder-replacement patients if it will be possible for them to play golf.

Post[21] has designed a model that is the most commonly used in the United States for constrained total shoulder replacement. He specifically tells the patient not to play golf or tennis after a constrained total shoulder replacement. Use of constrained models of total shoulder replacement is becoming rare, however, because of the multiple complications that have occurred with their use.

Both Cofield[9] and Post[21] advise their total–shoulder-replacement patients to play "winter rules" (i.e., to improve the lie of their ball) if they continue to play golf. This would make sense because better lies can decrease the shock transmitted at impact to the arms and shoulders. If patients have difficulty even with improved lies, it might be advisable for them to tee up the ball on all lies — even in the fairway and rough. This would prevent the patient from playing in competition, however, and may even require explanation in friendly matches.

Paradoxically, recommending that the golfer employ a large shoulder turn would probably be the best way to advise patients to take stress off their shoulders. The "shoulder turn" is a misnomer because it actually involves trunk rotation. When the golfer makes the backswing with a large shoulder turn, the stress of the swing is taken up by the trunk muscles, rather than the muscles of the shoulders and arms. Shortening the swing is probably also advisable.

---

*References 3,12,15,17,22–24,27,30.

How long a patient should wait to play golf after a total shoulder replacement has never been fully addressed and remains a matter of clinical judgment. Waiting at least 12 weeks or until the patient has regained preoperative range of motion would seem to be advisable. At that point, the patient should begin with putting and chipping and advance to longer shots only if he or she remains asymptomatic while playing.

Elbow

Elbows are most often replaced for rheumatoid arthritis or posttraumatic arthritis.[19] Primary degenerative arthritis of the elbow is extremely rare. Total elbow replacement usually provides good pain relief and often will allow an improvement in range of motion to make the extremity functional. Full range of motion is rarely regained, however, and the implants themselves are not able to withstand high stresses. Both of these factors make it difficult to play golf after total elbow replacement.

The two foremost exponents of total elbow replacement are probably Morrey[18] and Coonrad.[10] Both have stated that they do not allow their patients with total elbow replacements to play golf because they prohibit any activities with greater than 5 to 10 lb of force across the elbow joint. Morrey[18] would allow a truly avid golfer to try chipping and putting, but no more.

Wrist and Ankle

Total wrist replacement and total ankle replacement are rarely performed outside of major medical centers. Both procedures probably should still be considered experimental inasmuch as results have not been good and complication rates have been extremely high in both cases.[4,26,31] Because of the risk of complications, including early loosening, even in unstressed replacement of these joints, total joint replacement of either the wrist or ankle should be considered an absolute contraindication to playing golf. Patients with total ankle replacement would probably have no difficulty with chipping and putting, but even chipping may place too much stress on a total wrist replacement.

LONG-TERM EFFECTS

As mentioned in the introduction, no previous studies have been done of the results of total hip replacements in a population of active golfers. Several European studies, however, have addressed the larger subject of sport and exercise after total hip arthroplasty.* Most of these studies have evaluated walking, swimming, rowing, and cycling. Although golf was not mentioned in any of the articles, the results are revealing for comparison. In addition, no studies have been published evaluating postoperative exercise in the patient with a total knee replacement.

Rütten[24] studied rowing as an exercise after total hip replacement. He concluded that it entailed all the advantages beneficial to patients with a hip endoprosthesis and should generally be adopted as an appropriate rehabilitation measure. Steinbrück and Gärtner[27] were less dogmatic, but they did state that swimming, cycling, gymnastics, walking, and rowing seemed suitable after total hip replacement.

Dubs and colleagues[12] made a comparison between two groups of patients after total hip arthroplasty. From a study group of 110 patients, 56% were found to engage in intense sporting activity after hip replacement. When comparing this subset with those who did not engage in intense sporting activity, they found that the incidence of revision due to loosening was much higher in the group who engaged in no sporting activity (14.3% vs. 1.6%).

This study correlates well with the study by Black and associates,[5] which evaluated bone density after total hip replacement in relation to patients' activity levels. They found that after hip replacement, significant loss of bone density occurred secondary to disuse if the patient was not active. Bone density was preserved after total hip arthroplasty if activity levels remained high. Aldinger and Gekeler[1] reached opposite conclusions, however, noting that the patient's lifestyle must be adjusted because external weight-bearing stress affects the durability of the prosthesis.

---

*References 1,3,12,15,17,22,24,27,29.

A study evaluating the ability to exercise after total hip replacement[30] found that patients who had had total hip replacement were able to cycle or swim more frequently after surgery than preoperatively. This result probably relates to decreased pain levels.

Ritter and Meding's[23] study of the effects of exercise after total hip replacement is the only one to mention the effects of golf. They concluded that there seemed to be no detrimental effect from active exercise at a follow-up period of 5.8 years (minimum 3 years). They evaluated walking, swimming, golf, biking, and bowling. Unfortunately, they did not specifically study each sport. In addition, only 10 (4%) of the patients were playing golf actively after their operation. They did conclude that intelligent participation in the activities they studied had no influence on the outcome of a total hip replacement.

Most of the members of The Hip Society and The Knee Society surveyed reported that their patients commonly asked about the ability to play golf after joint replacement. It did not appear that their joint replacement patients had more difficulty if they elected to play golf actively. This would correlate with the European studies, most of which found exercise after total hip replacement to be beneficial. In patients with bone-ingrowth prostheses, it may be that exercise will encourage the ingrowth of bone by stimulation, in correlation with Wolff's law.

The cohort of golfers studied compares well with other active groups cited in the literature[8] in terms of pain and rates of revision. Although it can be argued that a rather diverse group was evaluated (different surgeons, ages, types of prostheses, methods of fixation, lengths of follow-up, etc.), in general the two groups of active golfers did as well as most groups studied in the literature with regard to the above two factors. These golfers, however, may not be indicative of all people who attempt to play golf after total joint replacement. Only golfers who continued to play actively were studied. It could be argued that these patients did well because their joint arthroplasties were successful enough to allow them to play golf.

The question of whether golf after total joint replacement would be beneficial or detrimental to the lifespan of a prosthesis must be evaluated both on clinical studies and on biomechanical studies of the stresses placed on the protheses by golf swings. Chandler and associates[8] noted that one factor that often adversely affects the result after total hip replacement is heavy activity on the part of the patient. Crowninshield and colleagues[11] noted that the predicted levels of stress in cement surrounding a hip prosthesis are often close to the critical levels for failure.

Torques and forces about the hip joint during a golf swing have never been studied in detail. By analyzing shaft bend during the swing, Stover, Wiren, and Topaz[28] were able to estimate that the torque around the hip reaches 300 to 400 in-lb. They also postulated that the torque around the left hip (for a right-handed player) was greater than that for the right hip. Among the active golfers who were surveyed, there was no statistical difference between golfers who had a left or right hip replaced in terms of pain while playing or after playing golf.

Coonrad's[10] point about total elbow replacements is quite relevant, however, inasmuch as it is known that they tolerate only minimal stresses. Although the stress across the elbow during a golf swing has not been measured, it can be estimated to be far more than that which would be tolerated by a total elbow replacement. Thus patients with total elbow replacements should be discouraged from playing golf.

Similar dogmatic statements for or against golf after total joint replacement cannot be made for other joints. Biomechanical studies of the golf swing have been rarely published until recently, and none deal specifically with the stresses across joints during a golf swing—much less across joints that have been replaced by a prosthesis. Amstutz[2] has studied some aspects of stresses across total hip replacements with activity and has classified golf as a low-impact activity. It is not possible, however, to say at this point exactly how much stress is placed on a total joint replacement during a golf swing.

Laskin has stated that it is difficult to tell what will happen in the long run to total hip recipients who remain very active.[17] He believes that repetitive impact loading tends to loosen the femoral component of total hip replacements and thus advises his patients to refrain from impact activities such as jogging, tennis, basketball, and volleyball. He does allow them to play golf, however, as well as swim, cycle, and ski cross-country, activities he classifies as low-impact.

RECOMMENDATIONS

Methods do exist to take stress off a joint prosthesis by altering one's swing mechanics. Definitive answers to this problem should be discussed in some detail with a patient's orthopedic surgeon and golf professional. As an example, Hungerford's[13] comment that the terminal torque in the left knee (for right-handed players) would be detrimental to the total knee replacement has never been proven in any study and may not be correct. In a proper golf swing, the right knee is probably under a great deal of stress at the top of the backswing. By making swing adjustments, however, such as playing with spikeless shoes, playing with an open stance, and rolling over onto the left ankle a bit more, one may be able to take stress off the left knee during the downswing and follow-through.

Because of my background as a professional golfer prior to becoming an orthopedic surgeon, I have been placed in a unique position to evaluate this problem from both sides. I would make the following recommendations to any patient with a total joint replacement who wishes to continue playing golf. (It should be noted that these recommendations are for right-handed golfers and the terms left and right need to be reversed for left-handed players.)

1. Do not play golf in wet weather—slipping and falling during a golf swing could be disastrous.
2. The golfer/patient may be able to play better without golf spikes because if the feet are not quite as stationary, they can turn a bit during the swing and take the stress off the knee and/or hip. The patient/golfer must be cautioned to be careful, however, because the chance of slipping and falling without spikes is slightly increased.
3. Golfers with a joint replacement should learn to play more "on their toes." Patients/golfers should not listen to the articles and lessons from golf pros who tell them not to raise up much on their toes. This is for young, very flexible golfers with normal joints. Swinging flat-footed requires that a lot of stress be placed on the joint replacement. On the backswing, the left heel should come off the ground, and on the downswing, the right heel should come off the ground.
4. Golfers with total hip replacements should learn to play with a bigger hip turn, although this sounds paradoxical. However, the hip turn is really done by the lower back — by the trunk muscles. By turning the trunk more, the muscles about the hip are stretched less and take stress off the hip replacement. This must be accompanied by playing "on their toes" (Fig. 10–1), however, or the stress of the trunk rotation will be transmitted to either the hip or knee.
5. Right-handed golfers with *right* total knee replacements may benefit from "stepping through" their shots with their right leg. This is similar to what Gary Player does frequently, in which the right leg comes off the ground during the downswing and follow-through and actually steps toward the target. This helps the weight shift and takes some stress off the right knee. No right-handed golfer with a *left* total

Figure 10–1. This golfer is playing "on his toes" during his backswing and follow-through.

knee replacement should attempt this — it will not help and may be dangerous.

6. Right-handed golfers with a *left* total knee replacement will probably benefit from a fairly open stance. This will make the backswing a bit more difficult, but if the left heel is allowed to come up, a full turn should be possible. An open stance has the golfer facing the target more, and the hips do not need to turn so drastically to the left in the impact zone, thereby taking stress off a left knee replacement.

7. Some orthopedists recommend that their total joint recipients play only if they ride in a cart. There is no scientific evidence one way or the other to support this advice. Based on the European studies quoted earlier, it seems that walking would not be detrimental to the prosthesis and may actually be beneficial to the lifespan of the total joint replacement. Therefore, if the patient/golfer wishes to walk while playing golf, and it causes no discomfort, I do not think a total joint replacement is a contraindication to this. I would recommend that they use either a pull-cart or a caddy, however. Carrying a golf bag would be quite stressful to the artificial joint.

SUMMARY

The final word on total joint replacements in golfers has yet to be written. It appears from the opinions of orthopedists who specialize in joint replacement and from the results of a study of patients with total hip and knee replacement that it is possible for patients to remain active golfers with no significant increase in symptoms or rates of revision of the implants.

In addition, from the standpoint of helping patients who desire to continue to play golf as they get older, the following quote from Borden[6] seems most appropriate:

From a philosophical standpoint, I am a firm believer in helping individuals with arthritis to enjoy a good quality of life. I know how important golf is to individuals of all ages from both a social and competitive point of view. My experience has been gratifying with these individuals. It can be quite depressing for an individual facing retirement to know that he will have to give up a sport which he can finally play when he wishes and which he loves. Total joint arthroplasty had allowed the vast majority of these individuals to continue the sport during their retirement years and has clearly improved their quality of living. Isn't that what it is all about?

ACKNOWLEDGMENTS

I would like to thank John J. Callaghan, MD (Department of Orthopedics, University of Iowa Medical Center), and Donald E. McCollum, MD (Division of Orthopedics, Duke University Medical Center), for their assistance in preparing the survey on which this chapter was based.

REFERENCES

1. Aldinger, G and Gekeler, J: Aseptic loosening of cement-anchored total hip replacements. Arch Orthop Traumat Surg 100:19–25, 1982.
2. Amstutz, HC: Personal communication, July 18, 1988.
3. Arborelius, MM, Carlsson, AS, and Nilsson, BE: Oxygen intake and walking speed before and after total hip replacement. Clin Orthop 121:113–115, 1976.
4. Beckenbaugh, RD: Total joint arthroplasty — the wrist. Mayo Clin Proc 54:513–515, 1979.
5. Black, DM, et al: Computerized tomographic determination of vertebral density after total hip arthroplasty. Clin Orthop 198:259–263, 1985.
6. Borden, LS: Personal communication, July 22, 1988.
7. Callaghan, JJ: Personal communication, July 7, 1988.
8. Chandler, HP, et al: Total hip replacements in patients younger than thirty years old. J Bone Joint Surg 63A:1426–1434, 1981.
9. Cofield, RH: Personal communication, Aug 19, 1988.
10. Coonrad, RW: Personal communication, Aug 22, 1988.
11. Crowninshield, RD, et al: The effect of femoral stem cross-sectional geometry on cement stresses in total hip reconstruction. Clin Orthop 146:71–77, 1980.

12. Dubs, L, Gschwend, N, and Munzinger, U: Sport after total hip arthroplasty. Arch Orthop Traumat Surg 101:161–169, 1983.
13. Hungerford, DS: Personal communication, July 19, 1988.
14. Insall, JN: Personal communication, July 25, 1988.
15. MacNicol, MF, McHardy, R, and Chalmers, J: Exercise testing before and after hip arthroplasty. J Bone Joint Surg 62B(3):326–331, 1980.
16. Mallon, WJ: "Ask the doctor." Semimonthly column, Golf Digest, Trumbull, CT.
17. Monahan, T: Exercise after total hip replacement. Your Patient & Fitness 1(2):5–10, 1988.
18. Morrey, BF: Personal communication, Aug 17, 1988.
19. Morrey, BF, Bryan, RS, and Dobyns, JH: Total elbow arthroplasty. A five-year experience at the Mayo Clinic. J Bone Joint Surg [Am] 63A:1050, 1981.
20. Neer, CS, Watson, KC, and Stanton, FJ: Recent experience in total shoulder replacement. J Bone Joint Surg [Am] 64A(3):319–337, 1982.
21. Post, M: Personal communication, Aug 24, 1988.
22. Pugh, LGCE: The oxygen intake and energy cost of walking before and after unilateral hip replacement, with some observations on the use of crutches. J Bone Joint Surg 55B(4):742–745, 1973.
23. Ritter, MA and Meding, JB: Total hip arthroplasty: Can the patient play sports again? Orthopaedics 10(10):1447–1452, 1987.
24. Rütten, M: Rudern mit einer Hüfttotalprothese. Z Orthop 117(5):830–832, 1979.
25. Sledge, CB: Personal communication, July 1988.
26. Stauffer, RN and Segal, NM: Total ankle arthroplasty: Four years' experience. Clin Orthop 160:217, 1981.
27. Steinbrück, K and Gärtner, BM: Totalendoprothese und Sport. Münch Med Wochenschr 121 (39):1247–1250, 1979.
28. Stover, CN, Wiren, G, and Topaz, SR: The modern golf swing and stress syndromes. Phys Sportsmed 4:42–47, Sept 1976.
29. Thornhill, TS: Personal communication, July 26, 1988.
30. Visuri, T and Honkanen, R: Total hip replacement: Its influence on spontaneous recreation exercise habits. Arch Phys Med Rehab 61:325–328, 1980.
31. Volz, RG: Total wrist arthroplasty. A new approach to wrist disability. Clin Orthop 128:180–189, 1977.

PART

4

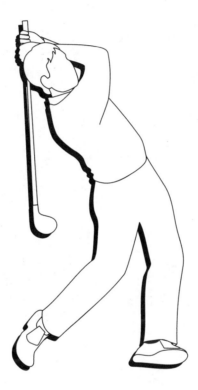

Injuries and Illness

11

Biomechanical Analysis of the Golfer's Back

Timothy M. Hosea, MD
Charles J. Gatt, MD
Eric Gertner, MD

P articipation in golf is increasingly being cited as a cause of lower back injuries. Although golf is not considered a strenuous sport, reports have implicated the golf swing in subjecting many parts of the body, especially the lower back, to large stress loads.[7,9,11,16] Among professional golfers, low back pain has become a well-documented injury, identified as the most common complaint among touring professionals of both the PGA and LPGA tours.[9] It has been estimated that 10 to 33% of touring professionals are playing injured at any one time, and it is also likely that half the group will develop chronic problems.[9] The growing concern over injuries has led to the presence since 1984 of a complete fitness center staffed with athletic trainers and physical therapists at every tour stop. In 1988, for example, close to 90 professionals used the PGA-Centinela Hospital Fitness Center.[13]

Except for freak accidents, golf injuries tend to result from overuse and develop over extended periods. The professional, who spends 8 to 10 hours per day on either the practice range or golf course, may develop serious problems due to improper swing mechanics, practice patterns, or both.

Low back pain has also been cited by amateur golfers as their most common golf-related injury.[7,10] More than 21 million recreational golfers now fill the public and private courses across the United States, and although most play less than do professionals, many are susceptible to injury. Drawn from a wide range of ages and fitness levels, recreational golfers often play sporadically and without a proper warm-up, and they may have relatively poor swing mechanics. Their poor mechanics may make overpracticing especially hazardous. By compensating with even more inappropriate adjustments, amateurs may temporarily improve their score but impose further strain on their bodies. An additional problem in treating back injuries among amateur golfers is that their swing mechanics tend to vary. The professional uses the same basic, well-grooved swing for nearly every shot, but the amateur often has a poorly defined swing with an array of unorthodoxies that lead to deviations in muscle control. These inconsistencies may increase loading of the lower back and leave the amateur more susceptible to injury.

MECHANICS OF THE GOLF SWING

The golf swing imposes stresses on the musculoskeletal system that leave many golfers with chronic ailments. In the 1960s, the advent of improved equipment and more challenging golf courses led professionals to adjust their swings to produce greater distance and improved accuracy. The success enjoyed by this new generation of professionals encouraged imitation, and soon the older, "classic" swing popularized by Bobby Jones and Walter Hagen was replaced by the new, "modern" swing. Since this change, golfers have become painfully aware that these new swing mechanics are physically more demanding.

The classic swing originated in Scotland and was refined in the United States to best use a hickory shaft. It differs from a modern swing in a few respects that are especially important when comparing the effects of both swings on the lower back. The classic style (Fig. 11–1) begins with a backswing using a flatter swing plane and a large hip and shoulder turn, with the hips turning almost as much as the shoulders. On the follow-through, the golfer ends in a relaxed, straight-up-and-down "I" position. The modern swing, on the other hand, relies on a tightly coiled body to store power for maximum club head acceleration at impact. It also uses a large shoulder turn, but unlike its predecessor, the modern swing restricts the hip turn to build torque in the muscles of the back and shoulders (Fig. 11–2). This pro-

vides greater angular displacements and proportionally leads to greater angular velocities on the downswing. The follow-through is characterized by the arched back (the "reverse C" position), with the right shoulder lower than the left for the right-handed golfer and the hands held high over the head. Thus, in contrast to the rhythmic, flowing, classic swing, the modern swing uses all parts of the body to generate a more powerful but stressful swing.

The modern swing is suspected of being a major source of injury suffered by both professional and amateur golfers.[11,16] As discussed in Chapters 13 to 16, these injuries involve all the major upper- and lower-extremity joints, but the most common problem in all groups of golfers is the development of low back pain.[7,9–11] This pain most likely is due to the twisting of the lumbar spine at the top of the backswing, with subsequent derotation and hyperextension through the downswing and follow-through. To understand how lower back injuries occur in golfers, and to be able to develop a program for their treatment and prevention, one must be familiar with spinal anatomy and with the complex forces, kinetic and muscular, that affect the lumbar spine during the golf swing.

ANATOMY OF THE SPINE

The spine is an articulation of bony segments called vertebral bodies (Fig. 11–3). These vertebral bodies protect the spinal cord, located in the vertebral foramen, from injury. The transverse and spinous processes provide sites for ligament and muscle attachments. To allow motion, the vertebral bodies are connected by an interposed intervertebral disc, as well as by the intervertebral ligaments and muscles. The two synovial joints in the posterior aspect of the vertebral body are referred to as the facet joints, and are composed of the superior and inferior articular processes (Fig. 11–4).

The spine is composed of a total of 33 vertebral bodies, which are divided into five sections. The cervical spine comprises the neck area. The thoracic spine articulates with the ribs. The lumbar spine is the lower part of the back and is of most interest to the

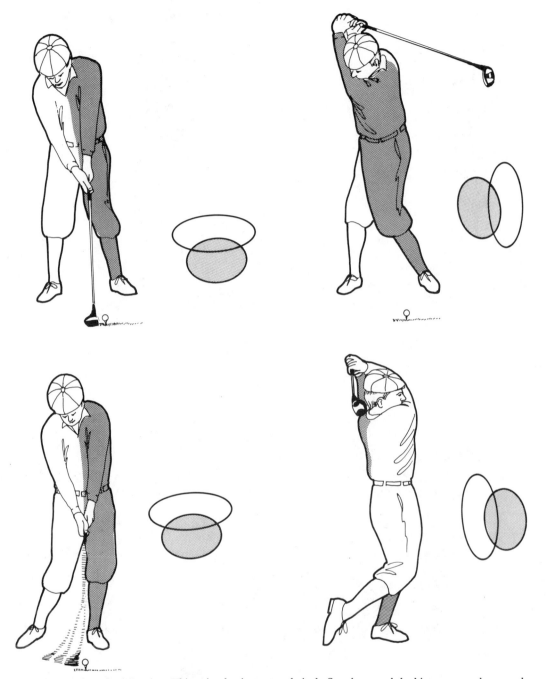

Figure 11–1. The "classic" swing. This swing begins on a relatively flat plane, and the hips turn nearly as much as the shoulders. The follow-through ends with a straight-up-and-down "I" position. (The shaded oval represents the position of the hips; the unshaded oval, the shoulders.)

golfing population. It also is the lowest area that allows movement between the vertebral motion segments or between one vertebral body and another. The vertebral bodies of the sacral and the coccygeal spine are fused.

The ligaments and intervertebral discs allow motion in the cervical, thoracic, and lumbar regions of the spine. The intervertebral disc acts as a thick-walled, deformable shock absorber, which contains fluid under

Figure 11–2. The "modern" swing. This swing emphasizes a large shoulder turn with a restricted hip turn. By increasing the torque of the back and shoulders, this technique leads to greater velocities on the downswing. The finish is characterized by a "reverse C" position. (Ovals as in Fig. 11–1.)

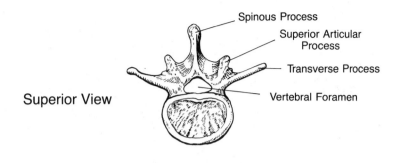

Superior View

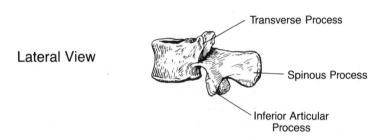

Lateral View

Figure 11-3. Vertebral body anatomy.

pressure. When it is subjected to stress, the disc responds by developing a corresponding increase in intradiscal pressure or remodeling.[1] The other load-sharing structures of the lumbar motion segment are the facet joints. Facet joints help in the distribution of stress applied to the lower back by working in tandem with the intervertebral disc. Studies have shown that the facets carry up to 20% of the spinal compression load in the upright, standing position, and more than 50% of the anterior shear load affecting the lumbar spine in the forward flex position.[12]

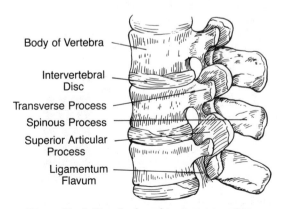

Figure 11-4. Vertebral motion-segment anatomy.

FORCES ON THE LOWER BACK

Four types of forces are imposed on the lower back during a golf swing; three are axially directed, and the fourth is rotational (Fig. 11-5). The lateral-bending force is developed in the lateral-lateral direction, the shear force in an anterior and posterior direction, and the compression force in the cranial-caudal direction. The torsional or rotational force is developed as a result of twisting of the vertebral motion segments about the long axis of the spine. Each force vector develops a unique stress within the lumbar motion segment, the clinical significance of which is related to both the magnitude and type of loading involved as well as to the interaction of the forces. Earlier studies used mathematical models to analyze these forces during performance of static tasks and simple motions such as walking, running, and rowing.[2,6,15] In addition, good correlation has been found between the predicted forces and intradiscal pressure and the myoelectric activity about the lumbar spine with selected positions and activities.[15]

We evaluated the complex motion of the golf swing to identify the lateral-bending, shear, compression, and torsional forces affecting the L3-4 motion segment while

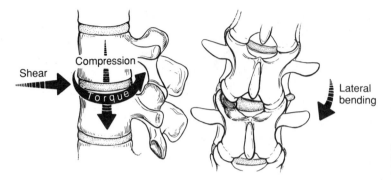

Figure 11–5. Forces affecting the lumbar spine. Shear force occurs in the anterior or posterior direction, compression loading in the cranio-caudal direction, torsion around the long axis of the spine, and lateral bending to the right or left.

swinging a five iron.[5] The myoelectric activity surrounding this motion segment was simultaneously obtained using surface electrodes and was compared with the maximal isometric activity of each particular muscle group. Our study involved four male professional and four male amateur golfers (with an average USGA handicap of 16), in order to detect the differences between these two groups. Each subject was filmed hitting a golf ball off a practice mat by four synchronized video cameras placed around the subject to allow stereoscopic visualization of the location of the reflective markers placed along the spine and extremities during the swing. Simultaneously, myoelectric signals were obtained with each swing. These data were then digitized and transformed into three-dimensional stick figures for use in the mathematical model. This model summed the gravitational, inertial, and muscle forces to determine the total loads at the L3-4 motion segment, whereas the total torque about the long axis of the L3-4 motion segment

was calculated by totaling the associated moments and couples. Large lateral-bending, shear, compression, and torsional forces were found to affect the lumbar spine during a golf swing. Interestingly, the forces were greater in the amateur population and also were associated with larger standard deviations, possibly owing to greater variations in the amateur swing patterns. Findings in the professional group indicated a similar basic swing pattern, with smaller standard deviations.

The amateur golfers generated approximately 80% greater peak lateral-bending and shear loads than did professionals (Fig. 11–6). During a golf swing, the amateurs averaged a peak shear load of 560 N, and the professionals peaked at 329 N. For comparison, peak shear loads in men while rowing averaged 848 N, and weight-lifting activities such as isometric torso lift and squat lift averaged 867 and 690 N, respectively.[4,6] Lateral-bending forces for other activities have not been determined.

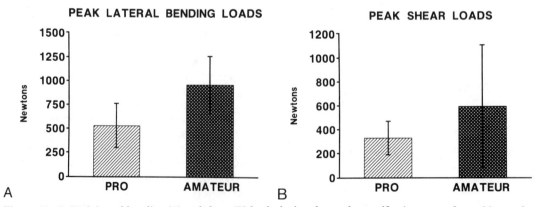

Figure 11–6. Peak lateral-bending (*A*) and shear (*B*) loads during the modern golf swing, as performed by professional and amateur golfers.

Compression of the lumbar spine encompasses a wide range, from nearly 0 while lying quietly, to 400 N while standing, and greater than 4000 N with vigorous activities. Running produces a peak compressive load of three times body weight and rowing, seven times body weight. The golf swing, by comparison, develops a peak compression load of more than eight times body weight in both amateur and professional subjects.

The twisting motion of the lumbar spine during a golf swing produces an average torque of 85.2 Nm in the amateur population, versus 56.83 Nm for professionals. This peak occurred during the transition and downswing phases of the golf swing, as the trunk uncoils. Although quantitated torsional loads have yet to be determined in work or other sporting activities, studies have long associated twisting with the development of low back pain.[3]

Myoelectric Analysis

The overall myoelectric activity of the amateurs while swinging a golf club reached nearly 90% of their peak muscle activity compared with 80% for the professionals. These activity levels parallel the large loads affecting the lumbar spine while golfing. In general, the professionals demonstrated a discrete on-and-off muscle-firing pattern consistent with a grooved swing, whereas the amateurs lacked the same precision.

In general, the left external oblique and, to a lesser degree, the left rectus abdominis and left L3 paraspinal muscles are responsible for the initial twisting of the trunk during the take-away of the club from the address position (Fig. 11 – 7). This firing of the left external oblique, as the shoulder turns to the right producing a lumbar axial torque to the right, is consistent with published

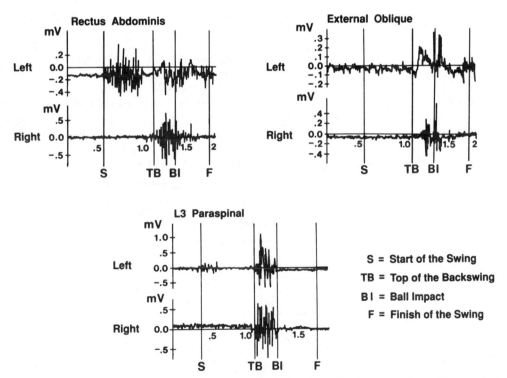

Figure 11-7. The myoelectric activity of the trunk muscles during the golf swing, as performed by a professional golfer. The left-sided muscles initiate the backswing as the torso turns to the right. From the top of the backswing to impact, the paraspinals fire maximally, as do the right-sided muscles, as the torso uncoils to the left. Near the finish, the paraspinals are essentially off, while the anterior (rectus abdominis) and lateral (external oblique) muscles act as stabilizers. (Adapted from Hosea et al,[5] p 47.)

work, which has found external oblique myoelectric activity proportional to the axial torque and shoulder turn to the opposite side.[14]

From the top of the backswing through impact, the muscles on the right side of the trunk lead the swing. In particular, the right external oblique muscle fires maximally, reflecting the torsional force to the left. During this phase of the swing, peak muscle forces occur, corresponding to the peak spinal loading of the shear, lateral-bending, and torsional forces. The right and left paraspinals fire nearly symmetrically during this phase, reflecting their spine-stabilizing action. The right-sided muscles (i.e., the rectus abdominis and external oblique) develop a higher myoelectric peak than their counterparts on the left side.

Swing Analysis

Amateur and professional golfers thus have differences in the magnitude of their spinal loading and muscle activity during the swing. The amateurs' poorer swing mechanics result in larger loads with correspondingly higher myoelectric activity. Ironically, these loads are produced as the amateur swings harder, attempting to achieve an acceptable result.

Although it is important to recognize the peak loads generated during a golf swing, one must also understand how deviations in the basic swing pattern may lead to increased or abnormal loading patterns.

Shear Forces

The shear loading pattern in professional golfers reflects the rapid uncoiling of the trunk associated with rotation of the hip and pelvis. In this example (Fig. 11–8), the professional begins the downswing with an anterior shear direction, which rapidly changes to a posterior loading pattern as the hip and trunk uncoil and the golfer assumes the reverse "C" position through impact and follow-through. On the other hand, the amateur (Fig. 11–9) does not exhibit this smooth uncoiling, but rather presents a jerky move straight from the top, with an increasing posterior shear-load-to-ball impact, while attempting to compensate for a poor turn.

Lateral-Bending Forces

Our example of lateral bending in the amateur golfer (Fig. 11–10) illustrates a classic problem with swinging over the top with a reverse weight shift. From the top of the backswing, the amateur throws his arms and shoulder outside the plane of the swing and thus must compensate by bending the torso to the left to bring the upper extremities and club head back to the ball. In addition, weight is not transferred to the right side during the take-away but rather is kept on the left. Thus this lateral-bending loading pattern begins with the right side loading from the top of the backswing and quickly changes direction so that at impact, the golfer is actually leaning away from the ball.

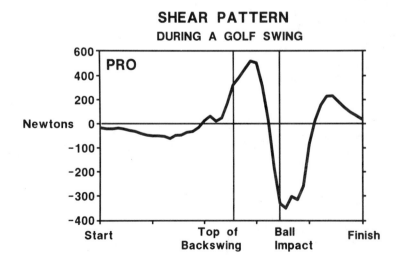

SHEAR PATTERN
DURING A GOLF SWING

Figure 11–8. Shear pattern during the golf swing of a professional golfer. The transition begins with anterior shear loading (positive values), which rapidly changes to posterior loading prior to ball impact. (From Hosea et al,[5] p 45, with permission.)

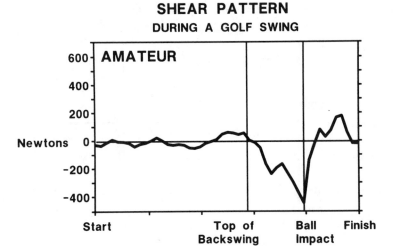

SHEAR PATTERN
DURING A GOLF SWING

Figure 11–9. Shear pattern during the golf swing of an amateur golfer. Unlike the professional, the amateur exhibits a poor turn, and by swinging "from the top" subjects the lower back to an increasing posterior shear load, up to the time of ball impact. (From Hosea et al,[5] p 45, with permission.)

The professional (Fig. 11–11), on the other hand, stays within the swing plane and achieves the desired impact position of leaning to the right. After impact, momentum carries the trunk around to the "reverse C" position, with right spinal lateral bending.

Compression Forces

Compression loading patterns of the lumbar spine are similar for both groups, with a two-peak pattern (Fig. 11–12). The first peak occurs following the top of the backswing, as the club head, hands, and arms start down toward the ball. As the hands pass the waist and proceed overhead on the follow-through, there is a second peak.

Torsional Forces

The torsional pattern of the golf swing (Fig. 11–13) most closely reflects the coiling and uncoiling of the trunk. The peak torque occurs as the upper torso turns to the right and reaches the top of the backswing. During the transition and downswing, there is a sudden, rapid change in the direction of the torsional force that peaks at impact, thus maximizing the coiling action.

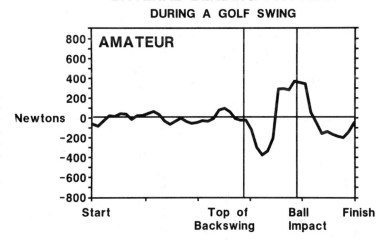

LATERAL BENDING PATTERN
DURING A GOLF SWING

Figure 11–10. The pattern of lateral-bending forces during an amateur's golf swing. Early in the downswing, the amateur leans to the right (negative values); to compensate for faulty swing mechanics, the amateur changes the lateral-bending direction so that he or she is actually leaning to the left, away from the ball, at impact. (From Hosea et al,[5] p 46, with permission.)

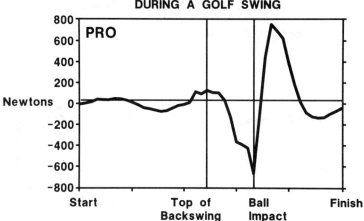

LATERAL BENDING PATTERN
DURING A GOLF SWING

Figure 11–11. The pattern of lateral-bending forces during a professional's golf swing. The professional assumes the "reverse C" position as he or she begins the downswing and leans toward the ball (to the right) at impact. The professional changes direction during the follow-through. (From Hosea et al,[5] p 46, with permission.)

CLINICAL IMPLICATIONS

The loads on the lumbar spine during a golf swing and the muscle forces generated may predispose the golfing population to muscular strains, herniated discs, spondylolysis, and degenerative facet changes with associated spinal stenosis.[1,8,17] The most common cause of low back pain in the golfing population is low back strain or lower back muscle spasms. In our study, the lumbar paraspinal muscle activity averaged 92.4% of maximum voluntary isometric effort. This muscle activity maximally initiates with the beginning of the forward swing and continues to impact with a sudden off-on pattern. Thus the importance of proper warm-up and an off-course strengthening and stretching program prior to commencing play cannot be overemphasized (see Chapters 4 and 12).

The spinal loads developed by swinging a golf club are similar in magnitude to loads that produce disc disruption in cadaver specimens. Our golfers' compression loads ranged from 6000 to 7500 N. In their studies, Adams and Hutton[1] showed that an average compression load of 5448 N produced a prolapsed disc. Fortunately, the speed at which the spine is loaded during the swing actually serves as a protective mechanism for the disc.

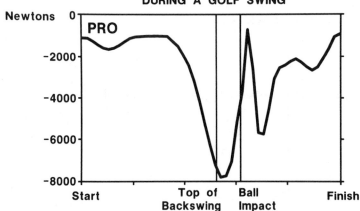

COMPRESSION PATTERN
DURING A GOLF SWING

Figure 11–12. Compression loading pattern during a professional's golf swing. The pattern of two downward peaks was similar for all the golfers, with the first peak occurring around transition and the second when the hands are moving overhead at the finish. (From Hosea et al,[5] p 46, with permission.)

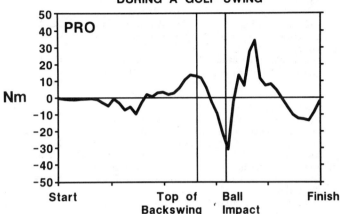

TORSIONAL PATTERN
DURING A GOLF SWING

Figure 11–13. The pattern of torsional forces during a professional golfer's swing. The forces peak at the top of the backswing, as the trunk is coiled to the right (positive values). During the transition and downswing, the trunk uncoils to the left, with the forces peaking at impact. (From Hosea et al,[5] p 47, with permission.)

Although the normal disc is well suited to withstand these compression loads, with aging the disc degenerates and loses its viscoelastic properties, increasing its susceptibility to injury and increasing the amount of load resisted by the facet joints and posterior vertebral structures. This increased loading of the facet joints may also lead to development of lower back pain and disability. Although the lumbar facet joints are well oriented to resist shear loading, when combined with compression forces the facets resist approximately ½ to ⅓ of the shear force, while the intervertebral disc lying between the vertebral bodies resists the remaining force. Thus the shear component of the total force exerted on the lower back during a golf swing puts considerable pressure on the pars interarticularis of the posterior vertebrae of the lumbar spine. Shear forces have been postulated as a mechanical cause of spondylolysis. Our peak shear loads, ranging from approximately 300 to 600 N, are similar to the shear load of 570 ± 190 N, which produced fractures of the pars interarticularis in cadaver specimens tested.[1] Thus the golf swing generates a spinal loading pattern that, over time, may result in a stress-related bony injury of the lumbar spine.

SUMMARY

The golf swing subjects the lower back to rapid, complex, and intense loading patterns. Both amateur and professional golfers demonstrate similar loading patterns, but the amateurs, as a result of poor swing mechanics, develop higher loads compared with their professional counterparts. By using proper mechanics, professionals generate relatively lower loads and better results secondary to greater efficiency.

Nevertheless, the loads on the back predispose the entire golfing population to muscle strains, discogenic lower back pain, spondylolysis, and facet-joint arthritis. Thus it is imperative for all golfers to warm up properly prior to play, to consider practice patterns carefully, and to strive to improve their mechanics through work with a PGA professional. Finally, a general lower back conditioning program should be a mainstay off the golf course.

REFERENCES

1. Adams, MA and Hutton, WC: Mechanics of the intervertebral disc. In Ghosh, P (ed): The Biology of the Intervertebral Disc, Vol II. CRC Press, Boca Raton, FL, 1988.
2. Cappozzo, A: The forces and couples of the human trunk during level walking. J Biomech 16:265, 1983.
3. Farfan, HF, et al: The effects of torsion on the lumbar intervertebral joints: The role of torsion in the production of disc degeneration. J Bone Joint Surg 52A:468, 1970.
4. Hansson, TH, et al: The load on the lumbar spine

during isometric strength testing. Spine 9:710, 1984.

5. Hosea, TM, et al: Biomechanical analysis of the golfer's back. In Cochran, AJ (ed): Science and Golf: Proceedings of the First World Scientific Congress of Golf. E & FN Spon, London, pp 43–48, 1990.

6. Hosea, TM and Boland, AL: Rowing injuries. Postgraduate Advances in Sports Medicine III(XI):1–17, 1989.

7. Jobe, F and Yocum, L: The dark side of practice. Golf 30(3):22, 1988.

8. Kirkaldy-Willis, WH: Pathology and pathogenesis of lumbar spinal stenosis. In Brown, FW (ed): Symposiums on the Lumbar Spine. CV Mosby, St Louis, 1981.

9. McCarroll, JR and Gioe, TJ: Professional golfers and the price they pay. Phys Sportsmed 10(7):64–70, 1982.

10. McCarroll, JR, Rettig, AC, and Shelbourne, KD: Injuries in the amateur golfer. Phys Sportsmed 18(3):122–126, 1990.

11. McCleery, P: "Bad back"—how to avoid an old hang-up. Golf Digest 35(3):58, 1984.

12. Miller, JAA, Haderspeck, KA, and Schultz, A: Posterior element loads in lumbar motion segments. Spine 8:331–337, 1983.

13. Mitchelle, T: Tough enough. Golf 31(1):133, 1989.

14. Pope, MH, et al: Electromyographic studies of the lumbar trunk musculature during the development of axial torques. J Orthop Res 4:288, 1986.

15. Schultz, A, et al: Loads on the lumbar spine. J Bone Joint Surg 64A:713, 1982.

16. Stover, CN, Wiren, G, and Topaz, SR: The modern golf swing and stress syndromes. Phys Sportsmed 4(9):43, 1976.

17. Wiesel, SW, Bernini, P, and Rothman, RH: The Aging Lumbar Spine. WB Saunders, Philadelphia, 1982, pp 23–29.

Back Pain:
Diagnosis and Treatment

· ·

Ned Brooks Armstrong, MD

We golfers are a funny lot. The lure of the game seduces us into spending the afternoon violently twisting our spines while trying to make par. It should come as no surprise, then, that even though golf is touted as a leisure sport, back ailments afflict amateurs and professionals alike. Just think about the likes of Tom Kite, Jack Nicklaus, and Fuzzy Zoeller. They all have suffered some form of back ailment; Fuzzy Zoeller eventually required surgical removal of a lumbar disc.

Studies[9,10] have shown the back to be the most common site of injury in both amateur and professional male golfers, and have put it only slightly behind the elbow and left wrist in female golfers (see Tables 2–1 and 2–2). Faulty swing mechanics are the primary reason for injuries to amateurs, but overuse appears to be the most frequent cause among the professionals. Commonly, injuries are reported to occur at the top of the backswing, after impact, and during the follow-through.[9]

As discussed in Chapter 11, the design of the thoracolumbar spine (middle and lower back) permits flexion forward, extension backward, and lateral bending from side to side. Rotation occurs primarily within the thoracic spine (middle back). As the shoulders and thoracic spine rotate against the lumbar vertebrae during the backswing and follow-through, compression, shear, and torsional stresses increase, especially near the junction of the middle and lower back. These forces have been found to be signifi-

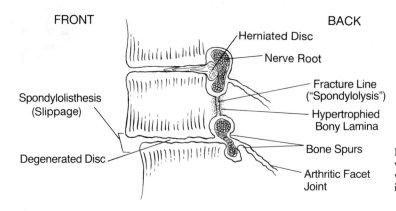

FRONT   **BACK**

Herniated Disc

Nerve Root

Spondylolisthesis
(Slippage)

Fracture Line
("Spondylolysis")

Hypertrophied
Bony Lamina

Degenerated Disc

Bone Spurs

Arthritic Facet
Joint

Figure 12–1. Degeneration of vertebral structures (shown in side view) may cause pain by compressing nerve roots.

cantly greater in amateur golfers than in professionals.[5]

Repetitively stressing the spine eventually can lead to tears of the supporting ligaments and discs and strain of the adjacent abdominal and back musculature. Local fatigue fractures of the pars interarticularis (spondylolysis), possibly with displacement of the spinal column (spondylolisthesis), may occur (Fig. 12–1). Ruptured discs or constant impingement by a narrowed spinal canal may squeeze nerve roots as they exit to the lower extremities, usually causing a lancinating type of back, buttock, and leg pain. A narrowed spinal canal or spinal stenosis occurs more frequently in people more than 50 years of age. Occasionally, repetitive contraction of the serratus anterior muscles (located on the chest wall), which pull the scapula foward, can lead to multiple rib stress fractures that mimic thoracic back pain (Fig. 12–2).[7]

ANATOMY

The vertebrae of the lumbar spine are linked on both sides by joints at adjacent neural arches and are separated in the front by jelly-filled intervertebral discs (see Fig. 11–4). A thick fibrous band, the annulus, surrounds the disc's gelatinous center, the nucleus pulposus. This architecture displaces the vertical forces transmitted along the spine in a radial direction. The annulus restricts the disruption of the nucleus pulposus, while its springlike action compresses it.[8]

When the annulus tears, the disc ruptures. Because it is naturally weaker near the nerve

root, it pins the exposed nerve against the vertebral body–ligamentous arc (see Fig. 12–1). Prior to exiting its foramina, a nerve generally passes adjacent to two disc levels and can be compressed at either site, depending on the site of the rupture. This can lead to a symptomatic picture of two ruptured discs when in reality only one involved level is affecting two nerve roots.[8]

DESCRIPTIVE CAUSES OF LOW BACK PAIN

The causes of low back pain include developmental and structural anomalies (scoliosis, kyphosis, spinal stenosis); neurogenic disorders (arising in the central nervous system, not including nerve roots); trauma to the vertebrae and their associated ligamentous structures, muscles, and soft tissue (spondylogenic); and trauma to the discs, with or without nerve root involvement (discogenic). Generalized muscle strain and ligament sprains are quite common and are included under the heading of spondylogenic. Low back pain may also arise from intra-abdominal (viscerogenic) and blood-vessel (vascular) problems, and from emotional derangements (psychogenic).[8]

The most common causes of golf-related back pain are spondylogenic or discogenic. Although the sport can drive you crazy, an emotional cause for back pain in golfers has not been confirmed in the medical literature. Likewise, no conclusive evidence exists for golf-related intra-abdominal injuries. Table 12–1 summarizes the clinical earmarks of spondylogenic and discogenic low

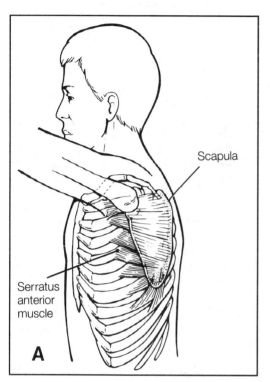

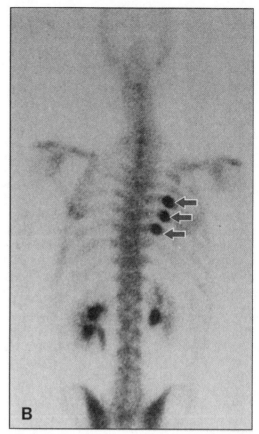

Figure 12–2. (*A*) The digitations of the serratus anterior muscle pass from the external surfaces of the ribs to the anterior surface of the medial scapula. (*B*) A bone scan of a 36-year-old male golfer's thorax reveals increased linear uptake (*arrows*) along the posterolateral aspect of the left sixth, seventh, and eighth ribs, suggesting the presence of three stress fractures. (From Lord and Carson,[7] pp 85 and 82, with permission.)

TABLE 12–1. Common Causes of Low Back Pain in Golfers

Type	Description	Subdivisions
Spondylogenic	Back pain derived from disorders of the spinal column and its associated structures	1. *Osseous.* Pain derived from pathologic changes in the bony components of vertebral columns and sacroiliac joints: traumatic, inflammatory, infective, neoplastic, metabolic, and structural (e.g., scoliosis, spondylolisthesis, spinal stenosis) 2. *Soft tissue.* Pain derived from traumatic and degenerative changes in muscles, ligaments, and fascia
Discogenic	Back pain resulting from structural changes in the intervertebral discs (with or without sciatica)	1. *Disc degeneration.* Gives rise to back pain with or without referred pain to legs, without evidence of nerve root compromise 2. *Disc rupture.* Gives rise to radicular pain with or without back pain, always associated with signs of nerve root tension and occasionally with evidence of impairment of root conduction

Source: Adapted from MacNab,[8] p 230.

back pain. One should keep in mind that subtle variations exist.

DIAGNOSIS OF LOW BACK PAIN

Appropriate x-rays and diagnostic imaging (CT, MRI, and bone scans) are important supplemental ingredients in an examination. However, listening carefully to a golfer's description of his or her symptoms and performing a thorough physical remain traditionally fundamental to the accurate diagnosis of low back pain.

For example, a deep, achy pain that is exacerbated by a change in position (mechanical pain) is more often caused by spondylotic problems and is known as somatic pain. On the other hand, a lancinating pain, especially with numbness or tingling down the legs, most frequently suggests a discogenic cause with nerve root impingement, known as radicular pain. A thorough medical work-up by an internist may prove beneficial, but for most golf injuries, the source of the pain will be musculoskeletal or related to a nerve or disc problem.

Here is one order of examination:

1. Generally evaluate the patient's posture and back topography. Subtle increases in lateral curve (scoliosis) or forward curves (kyphosis) while standing that subside while lying down may indicate nerve root impingement. Palpating a "step-off" or "prominence" of the spinous processes may suggest slippage of the vertebrae (spondylolisthesis), which may appear as hyperlordosis of the back. Muscle atrophy of the buttock and lower extremity usually indicates chronic nerve root involvement.
2. Ask the patient to point with one finger to the most painful "trigger point" or "region" of pain and discomfort. Having the patient draw the involved area on a human diagram helps to define it more precisely.
3. Document the range of motion of the spine and localize associated muscle spasms or tilt of the spine during the motion test. For example, restricted motion with paravertebral muscle spasm and a tendency for the player to lean to the left while standing may indicate a herniated disc pushing on the inner border of a nerve root. Leaning toward the side of the lesion will reduce tension on the nerve root if the disc herniation is medial to the root. The patient will lean in the opposite direction if the disc is ruptured lateral to the nerve root (Figure 12-3). The normal range of back motion is depicted in Figure 12-4.
4. Perform a neurologic evaluation, including tests of muscle strength and deep tendon reflexes. Check for pathologic reflexes indicating spinal cord involvement. Testing sensitivity to pinprick in specific areas of skin (dermatomes) will also help to clarify whether a specific nerve root is involved. Figures 12-5, 12-6, and 12-7 depict the evaluation of the more commonly affected nerve root levels, L-4, L-5, and S-1.

To help confirm nerve-root involvement, neurologic electromyographic studies may be helpful. Myelography, in which dye is injected into the spinal sheath and its displacement on radiographs is used to identify possible disc herniations, has largely been replaced by the noninvasive CT and MRI scans. These procedures are typically done, however, only if needed to resolve questions when clinical evidence is equivocal, when definitive pathology has not been resolved, and particularly if their result would change the plan of treatment. The CT scan usually is better for visualizing bony lesions, whereas the MRI scan is more sensitive for areas of soft-tissue pathology. Myelogram-enhanced CT scans may often clarify suspicious lesions affecting the nerve root lateral to its exit through the foramen.

Two important manual tests for sciatic nerve root involvement include straight leg raising (Lasègue's sign) and the popliteal stretch test (bowstring sign), which test specifically for distortion of the emerging nerve roots by extradural lesions of the lumbar spine. They will be positive if "root tension" is abnormal.

The straight leg raising test is performed with the patient supine (Fig. 12-8). The examiner maintains full extension of the knee

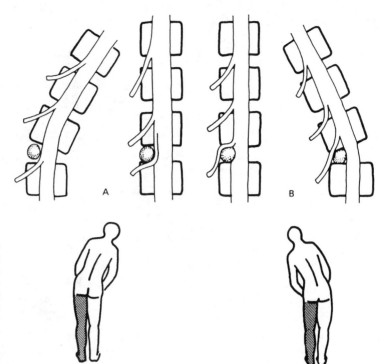

Figure 12-3. (A) When a disc protrusion is lateral to the nerve root, the patient tends to lean away from the side of the lesion to obtain relief of pain. (B) When the disc herniation is in the axilla and lies medial to the root, the patient leans toward the side of the lesion to decrease the radicular pain. (From MacNab,[8] p 173, with permission.)

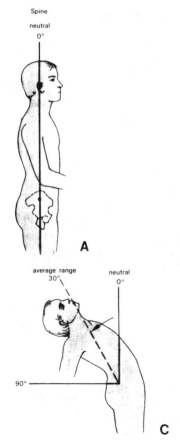

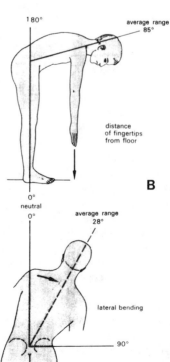

Figure 12-4. (A) Neutral position (0°) of the spine, from the side. (B) The average range of forward flexion of the spine is 85°. One also may measure the distance of the fingertips from the floor. (C) The average range of extension of the lumbar spine is 30°. (D) The average range of lateral flexion is 28°. (From Duthie and Bentley,[4] p 789, with permission.)

113

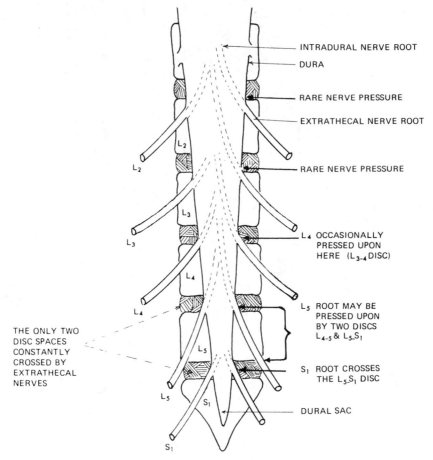

INTRADURAL NERVE ROOT

DURA

RARE NERVE PRESSURE

EXTRATHECAL NERVE ROOT

RARE NERVE PRESSURE

L_4 OCCASIONALLY PRESSED UPON HERE (L_{3-4} DISC)

L_5 ROOT MAY BE PRESSED UPON BY TWO DISCS L_{4-5} & L_5S_1

S_1 ROOT CROSSES THE L_5S_1 DISC

DURAL SAC

THE ONLY TWO DISC SPACES CONSTANTLY CROSSED BY EXTRATHECAL NERVES

Figure 12-5. Relationship of spinal nerve roots to intervertebral discs. The arrows indicate sites of nerve root compression. (Adapted from Cailliet, R: Soft tissue pain and disability, ed 2. FA Davis, Philadelphia, 1988, p 91.)

while raising the leg. If the maneuver produces pain below 70° of hip flexion and, more important, if the pain is aggravated by dorsiflexion of the ankle and relieved by flexion of the knee, then abnormal nerve root tension is strongly suggested. Causing pain in the affected leg by raising the unaffected leg is irrefutable evidence of nerve root compression.

The bowstring sign is the most important indication of nerve root compression. To elicit the bowstring sign, the examiner carries out the straight leg raising test to the point at which the patient experiences some

his or her shoulder (Fig. 12-9). Applying firm pressure to the hamstring will not cause discomfort. Then the knee is allowed to flex and the examiner rests the patient's foot on pain, but applying sudden, firm pressure with the thumbs over the popliteal nerve will produce pain in the leg or in the back if nerve root compression is present. Local pain only in the popliteal space behind the back of the knee is of no significance. The demonstration of root tension is probably the single most important sign in the diagnosis of ruptured intervertebral discs of the lumbar spine.

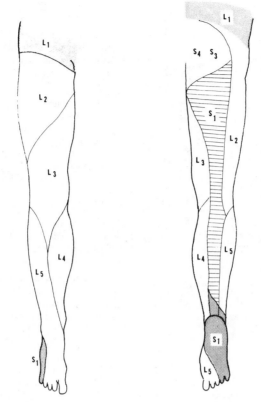

Figure 12–6. Sensory dermatome area map, indicating the distribution of each nerve root. The patient may report "numbness" in this area, and examination will show a diminished sensation to pinprick. Because of patient variation, these areas may overlap. (From Cailliet, R: Soft tissue pain and disability, ed 2. FA Davis, Philadelphia, 1988, p 93, with permission.)

MANAGEMENT OF LOW BACK PAIN IN GOLFERS

Treatment of Acute Injury

Initial Visit

At the initial visit of a golfer with low back pain, the physician should set a positive tone, emphasizing that these problems are not uncommon and generally can be remedied. Studies by Nelson[14] have shown that soft-tissue healing usually is completed by 7 to 8 weeks after a back injury. Nerve tissue, however, which is less resilient than other human tissue, takes longer to heal and is more susceptible to permanent damage.[14]

Treatment Course for Specific Injuries

After the diagnosis has been confirmed, specific treatment protocols begin. For example, any serious bony fracture or an acute disc rupture that leads to sudden loss of bowel and bladder control will require im-

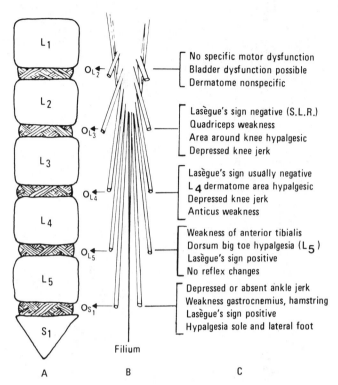

Figure 12–7. Clinical localization of level of disc herniation. At left is a lateral view of the spine showing the relationship of the intervertebral disc to the nerve root (e.g., S-1 nerve root at level of disc between vertebrae L-5 and S-1). At right are listed the clinical manifestations of compression of the various nerve roots as found on neurologic examination. (Adapted from Cailliet, R: Low back pain syndrome, ed 4. FA Davis, Philadelphia, 1988, p 225.)

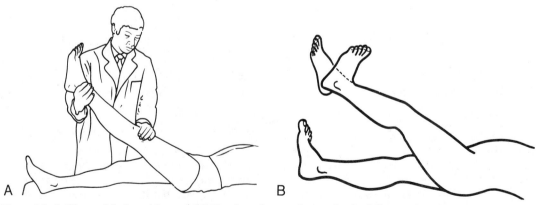

Figure 12–8. The straight leg raising test. (*A*) Note how the examiner maintains full extension of the knee joint while raising the leg. (*B*) At the limit of straight leg raising, if the ankle joint is forcibly dorsiflexed, the golfer may experience increased pain. This maneuver is particularly valuable in those golfers with only minimal limitation of straight leg raising. (From MacNab,[8] pp 174–175, with permission.)

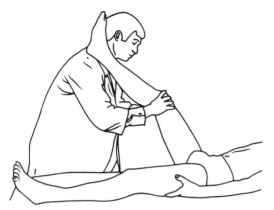

Figure 12-9. Testing for the bowstring sign. (From MacNab,[8] p 175, with permission.)

mediate hospitalization and surgical intervention. For the vast number of overuse syndromes involving soft tissues (muscle strains, ligament sprains, disc and nerve irritations), however, this will not be necessary. Only about 20% of confirmed acute disc herniations (without loss of bowel or bladder control) will ultimately require surgery when monitored over a number of years.[15]

Bedrest

If mild, back pain and related leg pain from nerve root irritation (sciatica) often respond well to a brief period of limitation of activities, along with anti-inflammatory medication, and then gradual return to full activities. For those more severely affected, the Golden Rule is to begin with bedrest and ice applied for 1 to 3 days, emphasizing that less than 2 days of bedrest may not be beneficial.[2,16] It usually helps to have the golfer lie supine with a pillow beneath his or her knees, flexing them 30 to 40°, perhaps with another pillow beneath the most painful part of the back. In this position, vertebral disc pressure, facetal joint forces, and dorsal and abdominal muscle activity all lessen compared with the upright stance.[15]

Medications

Although studies show mixed findings, it may be helpful to use analgesics, nonsteroidal anti-inflammatory medications, and muscle relaxants during this acute period. Injecting trigger points of tenderness with procaine hydrochloride (Novocain) with or without cortisone steroid also may be useful. My experience has shown these modalities to be beneficial 60 to 70% of the time. Medication abuse may become a problem, however, and should be monitored by all parties.

Physical Therapy

Physical therapy should be avoided in the first 1 to 3 days after the onset of pain because it may increase soft-tissue inflammation. After this initial phase has passed, the application of heat and active exercises gradually should begin. Passive exercise such as stretching or manipulation is contraindicated during this early post–acute-injury phase because it increases swelling and scar tissue formation. Manipulation is valuable in chronic cases, however, because it breaks down adhesions resulting from fibrous tissue formation.[4]

Other Treatment Modalities

Transcutaneous electrical nerve stimulation (TENS), ultrasound, and pelvic traction have yielded mixed success. Double-blinded studies have found their benefits to be questionable, but in general none need be totally discredited because they may have positive psychological effects. They should be kept in perspective by both physician and golfer. In particular, it has been found that traction occasionally is helpful in enforcing a prescription of bedrest, which, as emphasized earlier, is the most important facet of conservative management.[15]

Chiropractic Manipulation

In a few reported cases, spinal manipulation (chiropractic care) provided short-term relief for low back pain and sciatica, but careful, controlled studies remain to be done.[2] Manipulative reduction of small disc protrusions has been reported, as well as reductions in the severity of straight-leg-raising tension, but much skepticism remains. Manipulation has been effective in well-defined posterior facet and sacroiliac joint syndromes.[15]

Flexing the spine into the fetal position is often helpful to treat acute episodes of low back pain (with no evidence of nerve root

Figure 12–10. (A) An acute episode of low back pain may be aborted if the golfer pulls his or her knees slowly to the chest and holds the position for 5 minutes. (B) If the pain is severe, it may be easier to assume the same position while lying on one side. (From MacNab,[8] p 136, with permission.)

compression). As shown in Figure 12–10, a player may abort an acute episode of low back pain by lying on his or her back and pulling the knees up to the chest. This position should be maintained for 5 minutes. Again provided there is no evidence of nerve root compression, a flexion manipulation also may be helpful (Fig. 12–11). Occasionally, a physician may manipulate the spinous processes or perform the commonly employed flexion rotation manipulation of the lumbosacral joint to treat acute back pain (Fig. 12–12). To be effective, however, manipulative therapy usually must be performed daily, so that the patient must learn how to perform these maneuvers alone. Figure 12–13 shows one such maneuver.

Back Bracing

After the acute pain and spasm have been relieved, the spinal part must be protected until it heals.[16] Many physicians and therapists oppose the routine use of back braces because they can lead to soft-tissue contracture and muscle atrophy.[15] In some cases, the patient uses the brace as a crutch and becomes psychologically dependent on it.[12] In addition to stabilizing the back, however, lumbar braces compress the abdominal wall, and the support realized with a lumbosacral corset is reflected in an approximately 30% diminution of the intradiscal pressure.[13] More important, often the brace reminds the patient that even though the acute pain and spasm have resolved, the spinal part has not completely healed. As the player improves and the intensity of abdominal and back strengthening exercises increases and the spinal range of motion enlarges, bracing can be discontinued.[16]

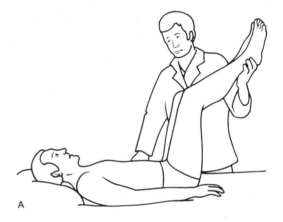

A

B

Figure 12–11. A flexion manipulation. (A) The physician raises the golfer's legs, keeping the knees flexed. (B) By very slowly applying pressure to the heels, the physician pushes the golfer's knees toward the shoulders. The degree of flexion obtained is determined by the golfer's discomfort. This movement is then repeated slowly and rhythmically over 5 minutes. In most, the range of movement achieved by this passive manipulation gradually increases. At the conclusion of the manipulation, the golfer is instructed to flex his or her knees fully and allow them to come down to the bed soles first. (From MacNab,[8] p 137, with permission.)

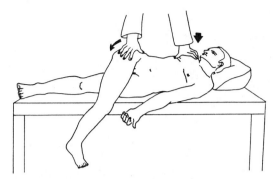

Figure 12–12. Rotation manipulation. (From MacNab,[8] p 138, with permission.)

Figure 12–14 shows a back brace and its application.[8] It may be possible to wear a brace while playing golf, depending on its dimensions. The smaller lumbosacral braces (as opposed to the large polypropylene braces) may be used if comfortable, but the player must realize that chronic use is inadvisable because of the possibility of dependence and of atrophy and weakness of the abdominal and spinal musculature.

Exercise Routines

Exercise routines may include abdominal and pelvic strengthening exercises, antilordotic exercises, pelvic tilts, and crunches (partial sit-ups for the upper abdominal muscles). Patients with discogenic pain are encouraged to perform exercises that improve flexibility of the lower extremities, especially the hamstrings (Fig. 12–15; see also Figs. 18–2 and 18–3).[12]

To transfer power and strength from the legs through the body and out through the club in the golf swing, the golfer needs rigid control of the trunk muscles, which protect

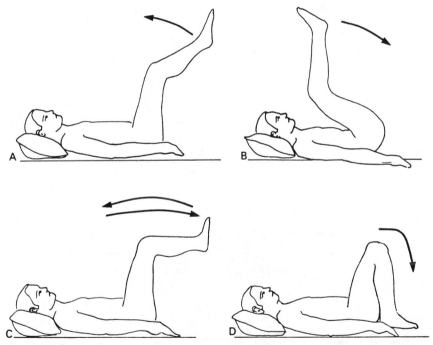

Figure 12–13. A flexion manipulation of the lumbar spine. (*A*) The golfer (in a supine position) should first flex the hips and knees to a right angle, then raise the legs toward the ceiling, keeping the knees slightly bent. Next the golfer attempts to move the feet over his or her head. This maneuver must not be done as a sudden kick; rather, the buttocks are raised slowly and smoothly off the bed by contraction of the trunk flexors, followed by (*B*) lowering the legs just as slowly. (*C*) This movement is repeated several times, each time lowering the legs just to the starting position, with the hips flexed at 90°. The legs must not be lowered to the bed. (*D*) After five "kick-ups," the golfer rests by lowering the legs, putting the feet onto the bed soles first, with the knees fully flexed. Only 10 kick-ups should be performed at a time, repeated three times daily. This maneuver is appropriate for treatment of acute back pain and is not designed to be an exercise program. (From MacNab,[8] p 139, with permission.)

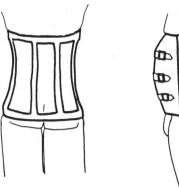

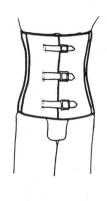

Figure 12-14. A rigid spinal brace with posterior and side steels and a firm abdominal binder. (From MacNab,[8] p 156, with permission.)

the back.[3] This control is accomplished with an isometric trunk strengthening exercise called the "Dead Bug" (Fig. 12-16). The next phase of the program includes exercises to improve strength and balance. Sit-ups (Fig. 12-17) and extension exercises (Fig. 12-18) are done with a large rubber ball, about the size of a beach ball. Other exer-

cises help the golfer to develop flexibility and control. Because the golf swing involves flexion, extension, and rotation, it is important to exercise in every direction (Fig. 12-19).

Aerobic conditioning will make golfers better athletes and thus less likely to sustain back injuries. Stationary cycling, swimming, water exercises, walking, or stationary cross-country skiing all may be used for this purpose. For swimming, the backstroke, side-stroke, and the crawl or freestyle may be recommended, but not the breaststroke, which may cause the back to sway.[12] Micheli and Couzens[12] suggest that the ideal swim stroke for back conditioning is the crawl while using a snorkel and mask. This allows the patient to keep the spine in a neutral position without twisting or turning.

Golfers who experience pain mostly while

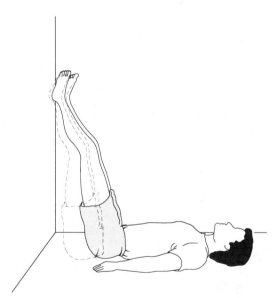

Figure 12-15. Static hamstring stretch. Golfers lie on their backs facing a wall or door. They position their buttocks close to the wall, so that when they raise and extend their legs, their knees do not bend. If their legs bend at the knee, they are too close to the wall and need to move back. Golfers with tight hamstrings may have to start 2 to 3 ft from the wall. They should hold this stretch for 15 minutes and repeat it each day. As the stretch becomes comfortable, they can move their buttocks slightly closer to the wall to increase the stretch. Eventually, they will be able to get right next to the wall. (From Micheli and Couzens,[12] p 193, with permission.)

Figure 12-16. The "dead bug" is begun by lying on the back with the knees flexed and the feet on the ground. A small, folded towel is placed under the lower back. The abdominal muscles are contracted, and the golfer pushes against the towel gently with the lower back. Once this position is comfortable and easy to maintain, the golfer tries to lift one leg without changing the position of the back. The leg is flexed and then straightened. Next, the golfer should lift and straighten the other leg. Other exercises such as arm raises and foot raises can also be done while maintaining the spine in a neutral position. (Redrawn from Duda,[3] p 110, with permission.)

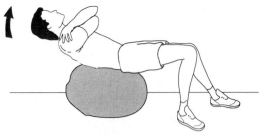

Figure 12–17. Sit-ups performed with a rubber ball help strengthen the abdominal muscles and improve balance. The ball should be placed under the lower back. Fold the arms across the chest, bend the knees, and keep the feet on the ground. Lift the shoulders and upper back off the ball, using the abdominal muscles to do the lifting. Hold this position for 4 to 8 seconds. (Redrawn from Duda,[3] p 110, with permission.)

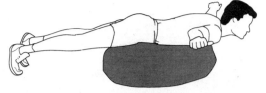

Figure 12–18. The golfer lies with the abdomen on the ball, feet wide apart, and arms extended at the shoulder and touching the floor. Keeping the back in the neutral position, the golfer raises the arms parallel to the shoulders and holds this position for 4 to 8 seconds. Hand-held weights will increase the resistance of this exercise. (Redrawn from Duda,[3] p 110, with permission.)

walking and standing should perform flexion exercises, whereas those who experience pain mostly while sitting or standing that is relieved by walking should perform extension exercises. Meaningful strengthening of the lumbar extensor muscles is only possible when the lumbar spine is moving against resistance. It does not occur when the pelvis moves along with the lumbar spine. Figure 12–20 shows the two types of motion.[14] Lumbar extension exercises with the pelvis stabilized may achieve an average 120% increase in back strength in the fully extended position.[14]

Surgery

Surgical intervention should be considered only if the following three conditions are met:[14]

1. The golfer has failed to achieve maximal functional restoration and has intractable pain that significantly affects activities of daily living.
2. The golfer has made a good-faith effort to get well and does not demonstrate undue signs of symptom exaggeration.
3. A specific lesion can be identified as the cause of pain.

Typical procedures available include:

1. Decompressing and/or extracting a specific lesion by removing surrounding bone (laminectomy).
2. Dissolving an impinging disc using an amplified light source (laser) or enzyme (chymopapain).
3. Stabilizing two or more vertebrae.

Treatment of Chronic Back Pain

Chronic lumbosacral strain presents a more complex problem, and dramatic results should not be expected. Exercises designed to flatten the lumbar curve, increase muscle tone, and improve posture form the central, local treatment. The fitting of a back brace is rarely necessary or desirable, but patients with a pendulous abdomen frequently benefit from the support of a lumbosacral belt or strong corset.[4]

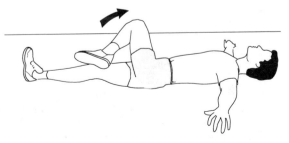

Figure 12–19. The trunk stretch increases the flexibility of the back. The golfer lies on the floor with the arms extended at shoulder height, then rolls over onto the right hip without lifting the arms. Then the left knee is bent, crossed over the extended right leg, and brought to the chest. This position is held for 10 to 15 seconds. The exercise is repeated three or four times, before switching to the other leg. (Redrawn from Duda,[3] p 112, with permission.)

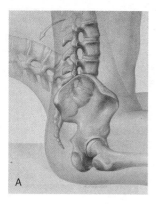 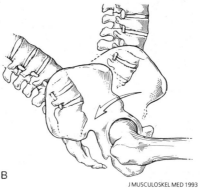

A   B

J MUSCULOSKEL MED 1993

Figure 12–20. (*A*) With the pelvis stabilized, the lumbar vertebrae rotate to the rear in relation to the sacrum. Extension exercises performed in this manner can strengthen lumbar extensor muscles. (*B*) If the pelvis is allowed to move along with the lumbar spine, strength may be maintained but will not improve. (From Nelson,[14] p 78, with permission.)

The RICE approach (rest, ice, compression, and elevation) may be modified to apply to chronic recurrence of acute low back pain related to muscle strains and ligament sprains. The player may rest for 15 to 30 minutes in a comfortable supine position, with ice applied to the affected area. This could be done immediately after onset. Depending on the response, initiation of further treatment can then be considered.

Manipulation as an isolated measure can produce only transient improvement of strain syndromes. However, in long-standing cases, especially if there is evidence of initial trauma, it is valuable for mobilizing joints and breaking down adhesions resulting from excessive fibrous tissue formation.[4]

Prevention of Reinjury

A vital ingredient in the treatment of chronic back pain is prevention of reinjury by education of the player. Recurrent back injuries may be prevented or reduced by teaching the golfer about proper swing mechanics, controlled practice routines, and the maintenance of good physical condition.

The technique of the golf swing has changed over time to gain greater distance with more accuracy. The "classic" swing of Bobby Jones and Walter Hagen was characterized by a long, flowing backswing and large hip turn (see Fig. 11–1). Today's "modern" swing is more tightly coiled, stressing maximum upper-body wind-up with minimal lower-body rotation (see Fig. 11–2). In this type of swing, angular body motions are greatly increased, causing greater stresses on the lumbar spine and hip joints. This type of swing is embodied by a recent article in *Golf* magazine,[11] in which McLean described an "X Factor" determined by calculating the angle between a line through the plane of the shoulders at the top of the backswing and one drawn through the plane of the hips. The factor said to be responsible for the longest drives on the PGA tour is the ratio between the rotation of the shoulders and the rotation of the hips (which creates "rotary tension" and a slingshot effect). Trying to increase this ratio by either increasing shoulder rotation or restricting hip rotation, however, can lead to repetitive damage to the lower back. It should be both effective and anatomically permissible for the shoulders to rotate approximately 90° and the pelvis, 45°. Golfers eager for powerful drives but concerned about back injury also could be reminded that the ratio need not be established at the top of the backswing. The intensity and duration of the compression load on the spine will be reduced if club head lag is developed and sustained as the downswing approaches impact.

The physician also might point out some bad habits that predispose golfers to back problems. For instance, bending over with straight legs to tee up the ball or pick up clubs can increase the pressure within the lower intervertebral discs.[3] Golfers should bend their knees and squat to perform such tasks.

Golfers can adopt some other specific habits to reduce load forces on the spine and allow them to return to their game:

1. They should remember always to play within their own capabilities, body strength, and limits of flexibility.

Trunk control is much easier with a more compact swing, cutting down on the backswing and follow-through.[3]

2. They should develop trunk (spinal), buttock (gluteal), and thigh (quadriceps/hamstring) strength so that address position can be sustained without excessive stress to the lower back. Routine flexibility exercises are also helpful. Some strengthening and flexibility exercises that may be helpful are discussed in Chapter 4.

3. While addressing the ball, apply the "30° Rule": the golfer's knees should be flexed approximately 30°, with a similar degree of forward flexion at the hips from the vertical plane (primary axis tilt). Now the muscles of the torso (spine) and legs are in a dynamically balanced position and the body's center of gravity is as close to its position while standing as upright as possible. Coordinate this with dynamically balanced wrist and shoulder hinging during the swing. Optimal alignment of the club shaft, club head, and face with the target line will occur with reduced stress to the lumbar spine.[1]

4. In the follow-through, they should substitute a more upright posture for the stressful "reverse C" usually recommended as part of the "modern" golf swing (see Figs. 11–1 and 11–2). Lateral bending can be avoided by keeping the shoulders "over" the hips throughout the swing. However, approaching impact lateral bending (secondary axis tilt) should reach but not exceed 30°. This helps keep the clubshaft on the target line without unnecessary stress to the spine.

5. They should establish a warm-up routine prior to playing. The regimens listed in Table 12–2 show how the routine may be adapted to the amount of time available before tee-off.

6. They should make greater use of the arms and wrists during the downswing and follow-through (being careful to sustain clubhead lag). This will lessen shear stress to the lower back.

7. Working with their golf instructor, each player should determine whether he or she is a "swinger" or a "hitter." Although both should focus on controlling the shaft, club head, and club face alignment, a swinger relies on a strong pivot whereas a hitter uses more arm strength.[6] Under-

---

TABLE 12–2. Warm-up Routines for Golfers

Latecomer Warm-up (Total time: 10 min)

STRETCHING (1 MIN)

Stretching before a round increases the flexibility and mobility of your muscles, to promote a bigger body turn and produce more powerful shots. Stretching also reduces the chances of straining a muscle. Try these 20-second exercises: *Neck Rotations:* Tilt your head to the right side and hold; repeat for the left. *Trunk Side Bends:* With hands on hips, bend to each side and hold. *Toe Touches:* Standing erect, bend at the waist and touch your toes; rise slowly. For those suffering from low back problems, this should be performed by sitting on a bench and leaning forward to touch the toes.

DRIVING RANGE PRACTICE (3 MIN)

Hit three shots with the sand wedge, 5-iron, and driver. Spend 1 min hitting each club, from a half-swing with the sand wedge, to a three-quarter swing with the 5-iron, to a full swing with the driver. As you work through the clubs, get a feel for swinging on a flatter plane and increasing the tempo.

If you're hitting a fade rather than your normal draw (or vice versa), play that shot on the course.

PUTTING (4 MIN)

Spend 2 min putting back and forth across the length of the practice green. Each time, try to stop the ball just short of the fringe, to get a feel for the speed of the greens and long lag putts.

For the next 2 min, practice dead-straight 3-footers and short breaking putts.

During this exercise, putt with only one ball. This intensifies your concentration and prepares you for the pressure you'll face on the course throughout the round.

WAITING TO TEE OFF (2 MIN)

Spend 30 seconds making practice swings with the club you plan to hit off the first tee. Concentrate on a low take-away, a full backswing turn, clearing the hips, and reaching a full finish. From swing to swing, increase your tempo slightly while maintaining good rhythm. Take care not to pivot so abruptly during the transition that the hip-to-shoulder turn ratio exceeds 45°.

Spend the remaining 1½ min in relaxed thought.

Early Riser Warm-up (Total time: 45 min)

BODY/FINGER STRETCHES (2 MIN)

Do the same 1 min of stretching exercises recommended for the latecomer. Then stand with your arms extended in front of you at shoulder height, slowly opening and closing your fingers for 1 min.

Stretching your fingers enhances your feel for the club head; that means a better swing and crisper touch shots around the greens.

Continued

TABLE 12–2. *Warm-up Routines for Golfers (Continued)*

ON THE RANGE (10 MIN)

Work through the irons, short to long, hitting three balls with either all the even- or odd-numbered clubs. Go through your complete preshot routine on every third shot, and always hit to specific targets. Then move onto your woods, always hitting fairway wood shots before practicing with the driver. Determine your most effective swing for the day. Focus on minimizing stress to the spine by using good address posture and trying to avoid shoulder rotation beyond 90°.

CHIPPING (5 MIN)

Practice chips of various lengths, three balls at a time. Analyze each chip shot, paying attention to the texture of the grass you're hitting from and the speed of the green. Note whether your chips check up quickly or release. Try to improve distance and accuracy with each subsequent shot to the same hole.

BUNKER PLAY (5 MIN)

Wriggle your feet into the sand to feel the texture. Setting your hips open with an open stance places them in a "cleared" position, reducing stress to the back while executing the shorter bunker shots. For longer shots, identifying the consistency of the sand will enable better body and club control, both helpful in reducing potential stress to the back. Hit shots from varying lies and distances so you're prepared for any sand situation.

PUTTING (20 MIN)

Putt two balls to nine holes set on the practice green. On the longer holes, try to sink the first putt; lag the second as close as you can to the cup. On the shorter holes, take extra time to set your body and blade square to the hole and try to knock both putts in. In each circumstance, work with your address position and stroke so that putting can be done comfortably, with minimal stress to the low back.

FINAL REHEARSAL (3 MIN)

Sit on a bench and take slow, deep breaths to relax. Mentally rehearse a perfectly played first hole, from an opening drive hit down the center of the fairway to the holed birdie putt. This will put you "in the zone" and supply the boost of confidence needed to get off to a good start.

Source: Adapted from McGetrick, M: Be prepared. Golf 1992, pp 64–65.

standing and adhering to the biomechanical principles of each type and avoiding an unorthodox mixture of them will lessen the likelihood of back injury.

8. They should use correct footwear and clubs with appropriate flexibility and weight. Use of higher compression balls is another way that equipment changes may help reduce the stress to the spine.

9. After an injury, they should resume golfing by using a more lofted iron (such as a 7 iron), first chipping, pitching, and punching before working up to full swings, and they should advance to other clubs only as tolerated.

10. While putting, they should maintain as upright a posture as possible, to lessen stress to the lower back. Use of a putter with a longer shaft may help.

SUMMARY

The golf swing is physically demanding and contributes to various types of injuries. The forces generated commonly produce spondylogenic back pain (from disorders of the spinal column or its associated structures) or discogenic back pain (from structural changes in the intervertebral discs).

Steps in diagnosis of low back pain in a golfer begin most importantly with a careful and complete history of the pain and its effects. Diagnostic imaging may be helpful if doubt remains after the examination and if the plan of treatment would be likely to be altered by the findings. The physical examination should include a general evaluation of the posture and the topography of the spine, a careful determination of the area of the pain, evaluation of the range of motion of the spine and of any tilting or leaning, and a neurologic examination including tests of muscle strength and deep tendon reflexes. Tests for Lasègue's sign and the bowstring sign are important to look for sciatic nerve-root involvement.

The harm of deconditioning may be greater than the danger of too much activity during the period of recovery from an injury. After a brief rest and the use of analgesics, anti-inflammatory agents, or other modalities as required, the patient should begin exercises to strengthen the structures supporting the spine. Specific exercises should be selected to suit the type of injury and the structures affected. Improvement of general physical fitness will also help to prevent future injury. The use of back bracing may allow strengthening and conditioning to continue while the back is rested. Surgery should be considered only when other treatments have been tried and have failed, in patients in whom a clearly defined lesion appears to be causing the pain. It should be emphasized that the most common causes of recurrent low back problems in both athletes and nonathletes are (1) not allowing sufficient time for the injured part to heal and (2) lack of appropriate rehabilitation before returning to the pretrauma level of physical activities.[16]

Golfers can help to avoid reinjuring their backs by avoiding extreme shoulder rotation and/or restricted hip rotation during the backswing by replacing the "reverse C" position in the follow-through with a more upright posture and applying the "30° Rule" for primary (hip) and secondary (spine) axis tilt and knee flexion. With careful attention to technique and equipment, golfers can perform effectively without excessive stresses on the spine. A warm-up routine will also be helpful. In the long run, education of golf instructors about the basics of spinal anatomy and the susceptibility of the back to stress injury will contribute many "ounces of prevention" so that fewer "pounds of cure" will be needed.

REFERENCES

1. Armstrong, NB: The natural golf swing. Golf Illustrated, Fall 1991, pp 64–71.
2. Davis, AA and Carragee, ET: Sciatica: Treating a painful symptom. Phys Sportsmed 20(1):135, 1992.
3. Duda, M: Golfers use exercise to get back in the swing. Phys Sportsmed 17(8):110–113, 1989.
4. Duthie, RB and Bentley, G: Mercer's Orthopedic Surgery, ed 8. University Park, Baltimore, 1983.
5. Hosea, TM, et al: Biomechanical analysis of the golfer's back. In Cochran, AJ (ed): Science and Golf: Proceedings of the First World Scientific Congress of Golf. E & FN Spon, London, 1990, pp 43–48.
6. Kelly, H: The Golfing Machine (Geometric Golf). Star System Press, Seattle, 1982, p 9.
7. Lord, MJ and Carson, WG Jr: Multiple rib stress fractures—A golfer overdoes it. Phys Sportsmed 21(5):80–91, 1993.
8. MacNab, I: Backache. Williams & Wilkins, Baltimore, 1978.
9. McCarroll, JR and Gioe, TJ: Professional golfers and the price they pay. Phys Sportsmed 10(7):64–70, 1982.
10. McCarroll, JR, Rettig, AC, and Shelbourne, KD: Injuries in the amateur golfer. Phys Sportsmed 18(3):122–126, 1990.
11. McLean, J: Widen the gap. Golf, Dec 1992, pp 49–53.
12. Micheli, LJ and Couzens, CS: How I manage low-back pain in athletes. Phys Sportsmed 21(3):183–194, 1993.
13. Nachemson, A and Morris, JM: In vivo measurement of intradiscal measurements. J Bone Joint Surg 46A:1077, 1964.
14. Nelson, BW: A rational approach to the treatment of low back pain. Journal of Musculoskeletal Medicine, May 1993, pp 67–82.
15. Rothman, RH and Simeone, FA: The Spine. WB Saunders, Philadelphia, 1982.
16. Rovere, GD: Low back pain in athletes. Phys Sportsmed 15(1):105, 1987.

The Shoulder

James R. Andrews, MD
James A. Whiteside, MD

Today's golfers seem to have more musculoskeletal shoulder problems than their predecessors. Perhaps this can be charged to the use of graphite shafts or explained by society's emphasis on tenacity, determination, and hard practices to ensure success for both the gifted and the not-so-gifted golfer. Television coverage of prestigious golf tournaments not only stimulates spectator interest in the game but also attracts participation, regardless of physical condition and preparation. Those who would not take a power boat out without a Coast Guard course accept the advice of a store clerk as to suitable clubs, purchase the best-looking bag and the most popular brand of shoes, and head for the nearest golf course.

Successful golf is not a game in which muscular strength predominates.[8] Rather, swing technique, fluidity, and finesse are needed for optimal proficiency. Inasmuch as golf can be played by all ages, and for some it may even be addictive, golf cannot be considered an innocuous activity. It is well documented that golf produces musculoskeletal injuries such as tendinitis, sprains, and strains, which tend to be related to repetitive use.[17] Even though McCarroll and Gioe[6] reported that the left wrist, low back, and left hand were more frequently injured than either shoulder in professional golfers, shoulder problems do constitute a major segment of disability in all caliber of golfers. In the game of golf, which primarily is an upper-extremity sport, uniquely, neither shoulder is dominant. Each has a very specific and special function in order to develop proper mechanics. The general practitioner, as well as the referral orthopedic center surgeon and sports medicine specialist, must comprehend this pathology to diagnose correctly, treat expeditiously, and rehabilitate effectively both the recreational and elite athlete.

PREDISPOSING FACTORS

Predisposing factors may make the shoulder more vulnerable to injury from the repetitive stresses of golf and ultimately may limit participation.

Constitutional Factors

Frequently, men and women participate in golf without adequate cardiopulmonary conditioning, and they also neglect the strength and flexibility of arm, back, and leg muscles. Inadequate warm-up, along with improper stroke technique and golf equipment, compound the situation. For optimal participation and enjoyment, the golfer needs to be prepared mentally and physically. Otherwise, constitutional factors may directly or indirectly hamper proper shoulder motion.

Insidious Trauma

Overuse or abuse of the shoulder caused by excessive play in a short period or moderate play over many years in golf, volleyball, racquet sports, swimming, gymnastics, and in throwing in baseball and football, which results in an inflammatory response to microtrauma, remains the major factor in the production of shoulder stress pathology. Weight training with free weights or so-phisticated machines also can contribute unrecognized trauma, just as the normal aging process enhances degenerative joint changes.

Acute Trauma

Questioning about previous shoulder injuries in sports, falls, or vehicular accidents often yields pertinent information about time-loss injuries. Sprains, subluxations, dislocations, and fractures about the shoulder, especially of the clavicle, even when now asymptomatic, may have resulted in unrecognized decreased shoulder/arm motion. Soft-tissue trauma can produce space-occupying heterotrophic bone formation as well as nerve damage.

Postinflammatory Changes

Bursitis, synovitis, rotator cuff and bicipital tendinitis, radiculopathies, and the arthritides of collagen diseases, gout, and psoriasis are clinical entities that frequently involve the shoulder girdle and result in limited disability.

Postinfection Sequelae

Although a relatively rare diagnosis today, septic arthritis and osteomyelitis in earlier years manifested considerable consequences. Acute viral encephalitis, poliomyelitis, and febrile polyneuritis, which yield muscle atrophy and weakness, also have decreased in incidence.

Tumors

Bone cysts, enchondromas, osteochondromas, and malignant growths such as Ewing's sarcoma of the clavicle can involve almost any segment of the shoulder girdle.

Congenital Defects

Absence of the clavicle, dysplasia of the glenoid or humeral head, hyperelastic joints, glenohumeral instability, and perinatal cervical nerve damage are situations that may impart negative shoulder sequelae and decreased function.

Other Factors

Other common predisposing factors that augment shoulder girdle overuse pathology are impingement, labral and rotator cuff tears, previous shoulder surgery, symptomatic previously placed staples and screws, and reflex sympathetic dystrophy.

THE EFFECTS OF GOLF ON THE SHOULDER GIRDLE

Included in the shoulder girdle are the clavicle and the scapula bones, and four articulations—the sternoclavicular, acromioclavicular, scapulothoracic, and glenohumeral. Each relationship reacts to repetitive athletic trauma in a characteristic manner. Predisposing factors also cause typical pathology in these areas. Omitting the significance of any underlying pathology and assuming the shoulder girdle to be in a pristine state prior to the overuse stress of golf usually leads to an unfortunate misdiagnosis.

For the shoulder to function optimally and proficiently in sports and in daily activity requires a harmonious and synchronous balance of muscle activity, working through unimpeded and healthy articulations in a sound, well-conditioned body that is devoid of significant congenital or acquired abnormalities. Previous musculoskeletal injuries must have been ameliorated, muscular strength and flexibility returned to its prior levels, and educated, rational plans instituted with proper supervision. Such a utopian situation is difficult to achieve and even more difficult to maintain.

The practice necessary for proficiency in a sport requires countless repetitions of the same motion to perfect technique and to make the motion second nature. With such use, positively, the dominant limb can increase in strength and size because of muscle hypertrophy and bone enlargement. Negatively, articular cartilage can wear irregularly, and ligamentous and tendinous structures can undergo microtrauma, leading to granulation tissue, scarring, or calcification. Adjacent surfaces that previously moved on each other as smoothly as two thin pieces of silk now, with microscopic scarring, become as rough as two pieces of thick corduroy. When actively moved, this area produces roughness and an irregular excursion of opposing surfaces that is appreciated as noisy crepitation. If the same activity continues, the healed tissue assumes different, less suitable, mechanical properties.[3] Further insults may result in pain, edema, hemorrhage, and fibrosis that can lead to soft-tissue failure at load levels that previously were well tolerated.

The Sternoclavicular Joint

The medial end of the clavicle articulates with and is firmly attached to the manubrium and the cartilage of the first rib.[11,14] While joint integrity depends on its strong ligamentous support, three planes of frequent motion are allowed at the sternoclavicular joint: posterior/anterior, cephalad/caudal, and rotation. Violent lateral forces to the shoulder directed medially or direct trauma to the clavicle are necessary for acute dislocations in the normal joint.

In the modern golf swing, the ligamentous support of the sternoclavicular joint is subject to medially directed forces on the left at the top of the backswing and on the right at the end of the follow-through. In addition, when the right arm is abducted and fully coiled at the end of the backswing and at the beginning of the downswing, there is posterior retraction of the shoulder, which results in anterior sternoclavicular joint stress. Because less force is involved, similar but milder stress is noted on the left sternoclavicular joint at the end of the follow-through. Ordinarily such sternoclavicular joint stress or sprains produce minimal symptoms and findings, but when the ligamentous supports are sufficiently irritated by the repeated microtrauma of stretching, the sternoclavicular joint becomes swollen and tender and may limit full motion. Simple daily motions of reaching and lifting may be affected as well.

The sternoclavicular articulation may develop decreased range of motion from degenerative changes with age and weight training, but it also may develop increased motion as a compensatory mechanism for decreased glenohumeral and acromioclavicular joint mobility.

The Acromioclavicular Joint

The acromioclavicular joint is a diarthrodial articulation between the lateral end of the clavicle and the medial margin of the acromion of the scapula, which usually contains a meniscus or a disc.[11] Its ligamentous support is relatively lax and weak to allow for gliding or sliding anterior/posterior and superior/inferior between the acromion and the clavicle, and rotational motion of the clavicle. Acute ligamentous injuries occur with falls on the point of the shoulder, top of the shoulder, the flexed elbow, and the outstretched hand, predominantly in sports. Such joint injuries, or sprains, are graded I, II, or III with respect to the separation of the clavicle from the acromion or the distance of the coracoid process from the clavicle. Although some controversy remains, nonoperative treatment of grades I and II, and even grade III, can yield favorable results with essentially normal shoulder motion, strength, and stability.

The acromioclavicular joint occasionally is the target of septic and rheumatoid arthritis, gout, and hyperparathyroidism. More often, the acromioclavicular joint reveals degenerative changes or resorption after acromioclavicular separation and mild repeated localized trauma. Osteolytic lesions of the lateral end of the clavicle, which could be secondary to minute fractures, are now noted frequently in avid male weight lifters without an acute episode of trauma. Symptoms in osteolysis[1,14] of the distal clavicle usually are insidious in onset and mildly painful but can progress to cause significant shoulder disability. Disturbing symptoms of aching after exercises and localized pain in golf or after push-ups, chins and dips, or on throwing, are often reported after healed acromioclavicular joint trauma.

In the powerful golf swing of today, the injured or repetitively stressed acromioclavicular joint can be symptomatic in all segments of shoulder biomechanics because scapular motion is involved in essentially all components. However, in the second or power phase of the downswing, the right acromioclavicular joint ligaments are laterally stretched or sprained when the scapula is externally rotated (downward) and the clavicle remains relatively fixed with little rotation on the sternum. A somewhat lesser amount of compression force on the acromioclavicular joint occurs on the right when the right arm crosses the chest just above the horizontal on the follow-through swing. Lateral stretching and medial compression forces are not as severe on the left acromioclavicular joint in the right-handed golfer because of a lesser amount of force employed when the left arm crosses the chest on the take-away and on the follow-through when the left scapula is elevated.

With degenerative changes occurring in the acromioclavicular joint, decreased gliding and rotation may occur alone or in concert with sternoclavicular joint pathology. Should glenohumeral motion be restricted primarily, compensatory increased laxity may develop in the acromioclavicular joint to aid in shoulder motion.

The Scapulothoracic Joint

The scapulothoracic articulation, formed by the ventral surface of the scapula and the posterior chest wall, is capable of moving superiorly by action of the superior fibers of the trapezius, levator scapula, and rhomboid muscles; inferiorly by the inferior trapezius fibers and pectoralis minor; ventrally (anteriorly) by the serratus anterior, pectoralis minor, and, when fixed, the pectoralis major; dorsally (posteriorly) by the rhomboids and middle and inferior trapezius fibers; and rotationally, by a combination of these movements.

Often neglected as a site of shoulder pathology is the anterior or ventral surface of the scapula in relationship to the underlying musculature over the posterior rib cage.[16] In a 2:1 ratio of glenohumeral to scapulothoracic movement, the scapula is intimately related to arm flexion and extension and abduction and adduction motion. With repetitive stress as in repeated golf swings, at times impeded by inadvertently striking unrelenting turf surfaces and inappropriate objects, the costal surface of the scapula may develop osteophyte formation at its inferior medial border. In addition, a bursa located at this junction may become inflamed because of chronic irritation and clinically develop into a palpable, tender mass.

The long thoracic nerve supplies the serratus anterior muscle, which functions as a powerful abductor and rotator, and also draws the medial border of the scapula firmly against the posterior rib cage. During the transition phase of the golf swing, into the acceleration phase of the downswing, the medial border of the right scapula is held in firm opposition to the posterior chest wall. Lesser localized force is noted as the swing is accelerated and continued into the follow-through. On the left side, a similar but less vigorous relationship of the medial scapular edge to the posterior chest wall occurs as the follow-through slows to a stop.

The Glenohumeral Joint

Anatomy

The glenohumeral joint is a relatively unstable articulation that is designed to allow a remarkable amount of motion.[11,14] The much larger head of the humerus is held against a variable and shallow concavity on the glenoid of the scapula. This anatomic relationship is somewhat analogous to a golf ball resting on a tee. If the tee is held horizontally, the golf ball falls away from the tee. Such would be the case with the head of the humerus if it were not for the tendinous, ligamentous, and muscular supports that surround this articulation. The articular capsule of the glenohumeral joint is notably loose and lax to allow for its varied motions, and, except at extremes of motion, it does not function to approximate the bones of this ball-and-socket joint.

The articular capsule is reinforced superiorly by the tendons of the supraspinatus, anteriorly by the subscapularis, posteriorly by the infraspinatus and teres minor, and inferiorly by the long head of the triceps. The coracohumeral ligament provides support to the upper part of the capsule as it blends with the supraspinatus tendon. Although at times difficult to individualize, there are three thickenings of the joint capsule — the superior, middle, and inferior glenohumeral ligaments — that provide additional anterior support. Overlying musculature helps to sustain the integrity of the humeral articulation.

The concavity of the glenoid is deepened by the densely fibrous, triangle-shaped labrum that is attached circumferentially to the margin of the glenoid, which it serves to protect. Peculiarly, the tendon of the long head of the biceps attaches directly to and is contiguous with the superior rim of the labrum (Fig. 13–1).

The shoulder joint is capable of essentially every definable motion. The humerus is flexed by the pectoralis major, anterior deltoid, coracobrachialis, and, when the forearm is flexed, by the biceps; extended by the

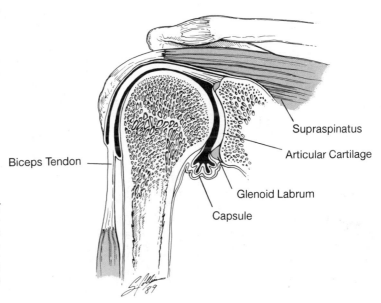

Supraspinatus

Articular Cartilage

Biceps Tendon

Glenoid Labrum

Capsule

Figure 13–1. Coronal section of glenohumeral joint illustrating insertions of supraspinatus and the long head of the biceps tendons. The relationship of the glenoid labrum to the glenoid and to the head of the humerus also is apparent.

latissimus dorsi, teres major, posterior deltoid, and, when the forearm is extended, by the triceps; abducted by the deltoid and the supraspinatus; adducted by the subscapularis, pectoralis major, latissimus dorsi, teres major; externally rotated by the infraspinatus and teres minor; and internally rotated by the subscapularis, latissimus dorsi, teres major, pectoralis major, and anterior deltoid. The humerus is circumducted by a specific combination of these muscles (Fig. 13–2).

Additionally, in abduction shoulder motion, the subscapularis acts to stabilize and roll the humeral head posteriorly in the glenoid to counteract the tendency of anterior subluxation. The supraspinatus, which is in action with the deltoid throughout its entire range of motion, helps to maintain proper glenohumeral relationships. The in-

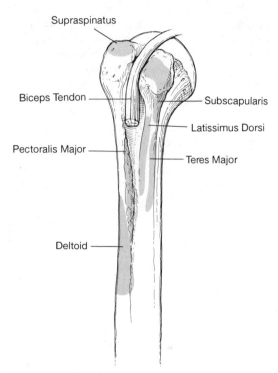

Figure 13–3. Anterior view of right humerus revealing insertions of supraspinatus and subscapularis muscles on greater and lesser tubercles, respectively. Also shown are insertions of pectoralis major on the crest of the greater tubercle and latissimus dorsi on the intertubercular groove of the humerus.

fraspinatus and teres minor, in abduction, give a firm and steady counterforce to help prevent anterior displacement and help pull the humeral head down. In relation to the shoulder, the latissimus dorsi holds the humeral head back, extends the humerus, and depresses the shoulder. The lower fibers of the pectoralis major also depress the shoulder girdle (Fig. 13–3).

Effects of Repetitive Overuse

Repetitive overuse of the shoulder in athletics yields definitive rotator cuff pathology related to the sport technique. Disregarding pathology in the sternoclavicular, scapulothoracic, and acromioclavicular joints (which must be considered in the clinical setting), and focusing only on the glenohumeral joint, the overuse injury scenario begins with microtrauma of the rotator cuff tendons, especially of the supraspinatus, infraspinatus,

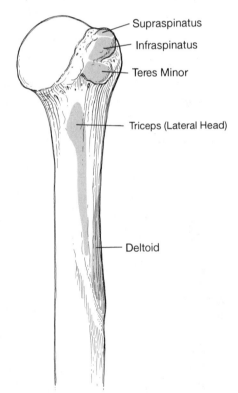

Figure 13–2. Posterior view of a right humerus revealing insertion of the supraspinatus, infraspinatus, and teres minor muscles on the superior middle and inferior facets of the greater tubercle, respectively. Also shown are insertions of the deltoid muscle on the deltoid prominence and origin of the lateral head of the triceps muscle.

and, less commonly, the tendon of the long head of the biceps. Soft-tissue inflammation and thickening occur locally, along with pain on exertion, which is followed by muscle weakness, especially in abduction and external rotation. If not rested and rehabilitated, the injured tissue tears, microscopically at first and then macroscopically. As noted arthroscopically, initially the undersurface of the injured rotator cuff becomes friable and fibrillated before exhibiting further deterioration into a split-thickness or full-thickness tear. The bicipital tendon may also reveal similar erosion and a decrease in substance. At the same viewing, the glenoid labrum is usually found to be a secondary participant in the development of this repetitive injury. As the normal glenohumeral relationship and motion are impeded by a change in soft-tissue restraints, dynamic stabilizers, and muscular activators, the head of the humerus is allowed more anterior-posterior gliding on the rims of the glenoid labrum. The labrum initially reacts by exhibiting fibrillated wearing away, followed by substance cleavage tears, and then possibly avulsion from its glenoid attachment (Fig. 13 – 4). Roughness and erosion of the articular cartilage over the adjacent portion of the head of the humerus also may be obvious arthroscopically (Fig. 13 – 5).

Subacromial Space. The subacromial space above the glenohumeral capsule, at times referred to as the acromiohumeral articulation, is not immune to this repetitive overuse activity. Concurrent pathology is noted in the subacromial lining of the bursal sac as it becomes irritated and swollen while normal bursal fluid is thickened and production increased. The superior surface of the rotator cuff, as seen when the arthroscope is passed into the subacromial bursa, may also reveal a fibrillated response of irritation. The acromion, when viewed from underneath at arthroscopy, may exhibit periosteal thickening and injection. The inferior ligament of the acromioclavicular joint may be noted to be more abundant and intensely white. Spurring may be seen on the distal clavicle. The coracoacromial ligament is often broadened and more dense. These findings are the result of impingement of the head of the humerus on the acromion and adjacent tissues in abduction and flexion and represent a continuum of the primary rotator cuff overuse pathology.

Pain. As more soft-tissue and osseous pathology develops, proportionately more pain is appreciated. Pain results in less active shoulder motion, muscle weakness, and then atrophy of the rotator cuff muscles and inelastic changes in the tendons. Clinically, in some, the entity of adhesive capsulitis or fibrosis of the articular capsule develops from this progression of a pain-weakness-atrophy-pain sequence in the ongoing syndrome of rotator cuff tendinitis. Obviously, the rotator cuff as well as the glenoid labrum degenerates with the cumulative activity of age, but in an athlete, the primary cause is over-

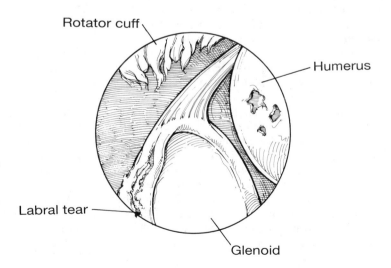

Figure 13 – 4. The production of shoulder pathology in the persistent golfer. Overuse results in rotator cuff tendinitis, from which a sequence of conditions ensues that in turn produces interrelated, altered clinical states. (ROM = range of motion.)

Rotator cuff

Humerus

Labral tear

Glenoid

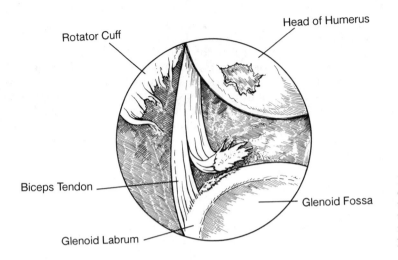

Figure 13-5. Artist's conception of an undersurface rotator cuff tear, partial biceps tendon rupture, and cortical defect of the humeral head as viewed through the posterior portal via arthroscopy.

use in a short period of time. Playing with pain can be carried to the extreme of abuse by an individual who is under pressure from a society that regards only winners as heroes.

Shoulder Instability

The most significant predisposing factor to complicate athletic glenohumeral dysfunction is instability. Whatever its cause, instability added to an already very mobile joint is paramount to disappointment for the athlete in reaching full sport potential. Unrecognized overstretching of the rotator cuff in normal child's play, recreational activities, organized sports, and competitive endeavors, even without time-loss episodes, may occur insidiously. If the mechanism of activity included abduction, external rotation, and posterior flexion (extension), stretching of the anterior capsule may have occurred during which, when the shoulder was subjected to an episode of similar acute trauma, the humeral head may have subluxated or dislocated anteriorly. Repeated anterior subluxations tend to produce anterior labral lesions; anterior dislocations may also produce posterolateral compression fractures of the humeral head (Hill-Sachs lesions) and fractures of the greater tuberosity or of the anterior glenoid rim (Bankart lesion[8]). The axillary nerve is frequently stretched or impinged in anterior dislocations, which may result in transitory deltoid and teres minor weakness.

More related to genetic laxity and less a result of athletic activity is posterior subluxation and dislocation of the humeral head. An injury from falling forward on the outstretched hand that produces adduction, internal rotation, flexion (the opposite of anterior instability of the humerus), laxity of the posterior capsule, and weakened infraspinatus tendinous support is necessary to create posterior instability of the glenohumeral joint. The glenohumeral joint is more liable for posterior subluxation or dislocation if the normal posterior tilt of the glenoid (2 to 12°) is congenitally increased, or if the humeral head is misshapen. Repeated posterior dislocations produce characteristic osseous lesions in the anteromedial humeral head and, at times, fractures of the posterior glenoid rim of the scapula and the lesser tubercle of the humeral head. Traction injuries to the suprascapular nerve may be noted clinically, with weakness in supraspinatus and infraspinatus muscle action and poorly localized pain.

Multidirectional instability of the glenohumeral joint, though less frequent, is potentially more disheartening for an aspiring athlete who requires maximal, coordinated upper-limb activity, such as is needed in golf.

The glenohumeral joint and other areas of the unstable shoulder girdle can be the focus of related pathology, especially calcific tendinitis and degenerative changes, which enhance pain production and limit productivity.

Impingement

The clinical finding of impingement in the shoulder, as expounded by Neer[13] in 1972, ultimately refers to the absolute importance of maintaining the humeral head dynamically centered against the glenoid. If rotator cuff musculature becomes ineffective because of weakness, atrophy, adhesions, or lack of flexibility, muscle imbalance and abnormal motion ensue. If contraction of the deltoid were unopposed, the humeral head would be displaced up against the coracoacromial ligament and acromion. If the infraspinatus and teres minor were deficient in externally rotating the head of the humerus in abduction, the greater tubercle would impinge on the subacromial bursa and acromion-acromioclavicular joint–coracoacromial arch complex. The centering and active stabilization of the humeral head depends on normal rotator cuff activity and interaction, together with the actions of the latissimus dorsi and the long head of the biceps tendon. Any compromise of the biomechanics in the glenohumeral joint due to asynchronous rotator cuff action leads to further deterioration of supporting soft and osseous tissues and the production of shoulder motion dysfunction and discomfort.

Reversibility of Pathology

If only mild to moderate rotator cuff tendinitis is present, essentially complete reversibility of pathology centered around the rotator cuff is expected by reduction of the amount of repetitive shoulder motion, followed by rehabilitation. Once repeated episodes of rotator cuff tendinitis have occurred, however, resulting in scarring and muscle imbalance that produces impingement, complete reversal of symptoms by these conservative means (although they should be attempted) is problematic. Should actual osseous lesions and soft-tissue tearing be evident, conservative measures and specific surgical intervention may restore only 85 to 90% of the previous shoulder function. Obviously, the best results in restoring function are obtained when medical intervention is employed early in order to prevent progression of pathology to an unforgiving and very painful state.

Effects of the Golf Drive

The long game in golf is power-dependent. On today's longer courses, the golfer is well aware of the length of the carry and roll of the drive. However, the typical golfer gives little thought to the determinants of the total length of a shot. Disregarding environmental factors and the elasticity and weight of the ball, the club head mass and its speed at impact primarily determine the length of the drive.[7] Distance then is a measure of the efficient recruitment and timely application of muscle action about the shoulder, which propels the club from a momentary standstill to maximum velocity near impact.

Figures 13–6 through 13–12 are drawn from photographs taken from above and slightly behind a former professional golfer hitting tee shots in a biomechanical laboratory setting, to show shoulder/arm positioning.

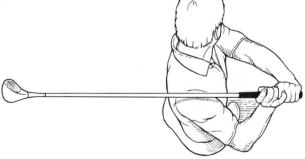

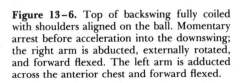

Figure 13–6. Top of backswing fully coiled with shoulders aligned on the ball. Momentary arrest before acceleration into the downswing; the right arm is abducted, externally rotated, and forward flexed. The left arm is adducted across the anterior chest and forward flexed.

Setup. After club selection, the golfer grips the club, addresses the ball, aligns the feet, hips, and shoulders for the desired direction, and sights the target. A waggle may be used to relax muscle tension. The force and direction needed, along with environmental factors, are computed. Failure to follow a prescribed physical and mental routine of shot preparation may lead to poor mechanics and erratic shot-making.

Backswing. In the backswing, the right supraspinatus abducts the humerus while the left subscapularis is active as the arm is internally rotated and adducted across the anterior chest.[2] Other musculature is dynamic but relatively quiet and acts as joint stabilizers. When fully coiled at the top of the backswing, the anterior segment of the right articular capsule is wound proportionately taut (Fig. 13–6). If the right supraspinatus is weak, the right deltoid overacts, abnormally, raising the humeral head. If the left subscapularis is weak, it is less able to help prevent anterior subluxation. On both the right and the left, restraints must be poised to prevent stretching of the soft tissues and abnormal humeral-head movement when the forceful downswing begins.

Downswing. In the acceleration phase of the downswing, more total force is expended on the right than on the left, with the moderate firing of the right pectoralis major, latissimus dorsi, and subscapularis.[5] These muscles adduct and internally rotate the arm and need to be counterbalanced by increased infraspinatus and teres minor activity. Should these external rotators be weak, unwanted posterior gliding of the humeral head and posterior capsule and infraspinatus

stretching are possible. On the left, in the first phase of the downswing, the subscapularis is moderately active as the latissimus dorsi aids in adduction and internal rotation. Also on the left, there must be increased activity of the cuff muscles to check the primary activators and maintain a proper glenohumeral relationship.

In the power phase of the downswing, near-maximal force is generated on the right by the latissimus dorsi and pectoralis major, and somewhat less by the subscapularis (Fig. 13–7). Correspondingly, more activity is also seen in the stabilizers. The long head of the biceps at the elbow counterbalances the full extension activity of the triceps and proximally holds the humeral head up against the glenoid.

On the left in the power phase, near-maximal electromyographic (EMG) activity is noted in the subscapularis and slightly less in the pectoralis major and latissimus dorsi.[4] Maintenance activity of the supporting muscles is again necessary to maintain normal functional glenohumeral activity. Should such support be diminished or overwhelmed by the power activators, soft-tissue stretching and subluxation can follow.

In the power segment of the downswing, on both the right and the left, the greatest amount of activity is exerted by the subscapularis, pectoralis major, and latissimus dorsi muscles (Fig. 13–8). The supraspinatus, infraspinatus, teres minor, and deltoid muscles play a lesser role. Additional force is developed by a large moment of rotation transmitted from the counterclockwise uncoiling of the hips and trunk to the origins of the pectoralis major and latissimus dorsi on the

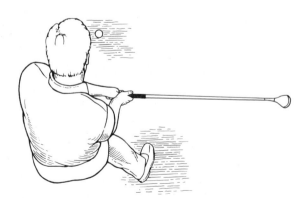

Figure 13–7. Beginning of the power phase of the downswing. The right arm is adducted to 0° and still is externally rotated. The left arm is adducted and internally rotated. The shoulders are aligned about 45° off the ball.

Figure 13-8. Mid-power phase. Near-maximal internal rotator muscle activity in the right shoulder and early forceful abductor activity in the left shoulder. Hands and arms are close to the trunk and are obscured by forward rotation and depression of both shoulders.

Figure 13-9. At impact; maximum clubhead velocity. Both arms are essentially fully extended (forward flexed). The right shoulder is further depressed, and the left is elevated as significant abduction ensues. Both shoulders are aligned parallel to ball placement.

chest wall.[18] This portion of the downswing is potentially injurious to the glenohumeral joint and surrounding tissues if there is not a balance in total motion, right shoulder to left shoulder and intrinsically on each side, because of the considerable magnitude of power generated.[15]

Impact. Just at impact or at the conclusion of the downswing, the club head should be traveling at its maximum velocity.[10] Both arms are resisting the centrifugal force of the club on the hands. At this point, the anterior capsular structures and restraints are fully operational, comparable to throwing a softball underhand on the right side and simultaneously hitting a low backhand with a racquet on the left (Fig. 13-9). Should the club head strike an immovable object, momentarily the arms would continue their motions before the weaker external rotators and the abductors could decelerate bilateral glenohumeral motion. This

would allow each humeral head acutely to ride forward upon and damage the anterior labral rim. A milder, more gradual, but cumulative deleterious effect on anterior capsular and supportive muscular structures would be expected from years of practice and from the frequent production of divots.

The relationship between the intrinsic rotator cuff musculotendinous units and the glenohumeral joint will affect the success of the swing. If muscle imbalance, tendinitis, or improper humeral head seating is present, there will be a disturbance in the critical orientation of the club face to the ball and in the smooth application of the correct speed.

Follow-through. As in other sports, the follow-through or deceleration phase of the golf swing permits gradual slowing of the club and body movements after impact (Fig. 13-10). On the right, the pectoralis major and latissimus dorsi slow to a moderate level

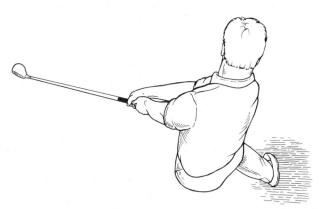

Figure 13-10. Early deceleration phase of follow-through with left arm abducted and right arm adducted. The right shoulder is hidden under the chin as the head maintains previous ball alignment.

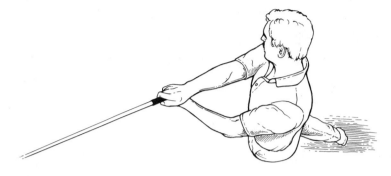

Figure 13–11. Midway through the follow-through phase. The left shoulder is forward flexed, and the right shoulder is adducted across the chest. The ball trajectory is followed by rotation of the trunk and head.

of activity along with a slightly greater subscapularis contraction, while the supraspinatus, infraspinatus, teres minor, and deltoid firing remains at a low level.[5-12] Should the long head of the bicipital tendon be weakened by inflammation and erosion, the function proximally of holding the humeral head down is diminished when the right elbow is flexed. As the right arm assumes a cross-chest position, further irritation of the anterior labrum can take place, especially if the external rotators are inefficient (Fig. 13–11).

Proper follow-through on the left at the glenohumeral joint is dependent on continued near-maximal subscapularis activity and moderate firing of the pectoralis major, latissimus dorsi, infraspinatus, teres minor, and supraspinatus muscles. If intermuscular synchronism is negated by joint erosion or soft-tissue pathology, existing glenohumeral joint and rotator cuff lesions are augmented. As left-sided recoiling proceeds to a stop, abduction above 90° is produced by increased deltoid activity (Fig. 13–12). Impingement can ensue at this point, especially if superimposed on tendinitis, wear, and inflexibility due to healed scarring and aging.

Research on the Golf Drive

The foregoing discussion relies extensively on the research of Dr. Frank A. Jobe and coworkers[5,12] in EMG studies of the rotator cuff during the golf swing.

PREVENTION OF INJURIES

Prevention of injury in any sport is difficult and this is particularly true in golf. Golf, unfortunately, maintains an image of ease,

relaxation, and comfort. No nasty collisions are seen by viewers on television. Players' physical incapabilities are not popular topics in sports columns, and the game itself appears so effortless. High-level golf, however, depends on proper physical and mental preparation. Not only should the purchase of equipment be individualized, but it should be used, initially at least, under professional tutelage. General conditioning must be evaluated and brought up to optimal status because proficient golf requires both considerable muscle power and refined motor skills. Flexibility is especially important for proper shoulder action and the prevention of back problems because of the rotation and extension so necessary in the modern drive swing. Leg strength cannot be neglected because fatigue is reflected in improper shifting of weight and uncoiling on the downswing. Good anaerobic conditioning enhances the explosive energy expenditure needed for

Figure 13–12. Completion of the follow-through, fully uncoiled. In this golfer, the left shoulder is abducted and externally rotated, while the right shoulder is adducted horizontally and forward flexed. However, the position at this stage of the swing may vary widely even among professionals.

power. Aerobic conditioning allows the golfer endurance to perform optimally for 18 or more holes. Once golfers appreciate their need for strength and endurance, in-season and off-season conditioning programs can be instituted and maintained.

Prevention of time-loss injuries requires the recognition of the warning signs of the overuse injuries of sprains, strains, and in-flammation of soft tissues. Pain, weakness, and loss of mobility are the hallmarks of problems that need to be medically investigated, not ignored through continued play. In addition, once injured, a golfer should not play unrestricted golf until the area is pain-free, flexible, and fully rehabilitated. Early use of anti-inflammatory medication and the trainer's techniques of application of ice under a compression wrap, elevation (if possible) of the involved area, and restricted activity are the first line of care in golf, just as in a collision sport. Prevention also extends to deploring the use of alcohol and drugs when playing golf.

TREATMENT RECOMMENDATIONS

Once a definitive anatomic diagnosis has been established (by careful clinical assessment and appropriate imaging studies) as to the cause of pain, weakness, or decreased flexibility in the golfer's shoulders, medical treatment, which relies heavily on rehabilitation, is instituted (Table 13–1). The goal is to return to optimal preinjury status.[9] Initially, the familiar acronym of RICE is implemented. The "R" indicates restricted activity, not rest; the "I" stands for ice, not immobilization; the "C" denotes compression, not comfort; and the "E" here means elimination of the trauma, not elevation; all of which is the application of proven, good, common medical sense. Immediately after this practical phase of treatment is fulfilled, the second phase, which concerns reestablishing full flexibility, is begun. Range-of-motion exercises are encouraged within the tolerance of pain. The golfer is encouraged to persevere, even with discomfort, under the supervision of a trainer/physical therapist, using just the weight of the extremity at first and then using a pulley system or plastic T-bar to push with the asymptomatic arm to increase the arc of motion. As tolerance

TABLE 13–1. Treatment Recommendations After Clinical Assessment of Shoulder Pathology

Phase	Treatment	Extent
Phase I	R Restricted activity	Continue daily routines
	I Ice	15 min 4 × day
	C Compression	Elastic wrap to shoulder
	E Elimination of trauma	Stop offending motions
Phase II	Reestablish flexibility and range of motion	Exercise within pain tolerance
Phase III	Begin strengthening with elastic bands and weight	Exercise through full range of motion
Phase IV	Restart selected stroke production	Evaluation of stroke mechanics
Phase V	Progress to multiple club use	Isokinetic shoulder evaluation
Phase VI	Return to match/tournament play	Continue maintenance rehabilitation exercises
Phase VII	Failure of conservative management	Anesthetic/steroid injection
	Repeat phases I–VI If unsuccessful, proceed to	
Phase VIII	Arthroscopic shoulder evaluation and treatment	Open surgical procedures, especially for instability
	Repeat modified phases I–VI	

increases, light wrist or hand weights are added, and repetitions are increased.

Once flexibility is demonstrated, phase III strengthening exercises are begun for the shoulder in general and then specifically for certain muscle groups. In order to stabilize the scapulothoracic articulation, which must act as a platform on which the upper extremity performs, the rhomboid, trapezius, serratus anterior, and levator scapular muscles need to be functionally exercised. The external rotators—infraspinatus, teres minor, and, to a lesser extent, supraspinatus; the internal rotators—subscapularis, pectoralis major, and latissimus dorsi, and, to some degree, teres major; and the deltoid, biceps, and triceps muscles are by necessity strengthened both eccentrically and concentrically by planned and individualized techniques (see Chapter 4). The goal should be to reestablish proper strength and balance through the functional range of motion in both the anterior and posterior shoulder.

Phase IV allows for the return of partial stroke production. At this juncture, swing mechanics should be evaluated by a qualified professional, using both simple methods and sophisticated, digitized photographic techniques. Because functional biomechanical deficits or inefficiencies may have been learned or secondarily produced when early symptoms were present and "played through," it is now necessary to substantiate the adage that practice does not make perfect, but perfect practice makes perfect.

In phase V, a progressive program of multiple club use as well as increasing distance and number of swings is instituted before return to actual practice on the course is recommended. At this point, the level of total body preparation, including trunk, back, and lower extremities, must be returned to preinjury status. Positive mental adjustments need to be made before return to active competition (see Chapter 5). In this phase, an isokinetic evaluation of both shoulders is most useful in ascertaining any persistent muscular or torque deficiencies that can be modified by specific training techniques. It is wise to recall that, in general, female golfers are more flexible than male golfers and have essentially the same endurance, but they do lack comparable strength and power. Consequently, each treatment plan must be prescribed on an individual basis.

Phase VI encompasses the return to match or tournament play, completely recovered physically and mentally, rested, and using proper swing techniques while continuing rehabilitative exercises. By far, most of the early shoulder problems in golfers do resolve with appropriate treatment and rehabilitation and allow the athlete to return to action.

Failure of this diligently used treatment/rehabilitation protocol to reestablish the golf game quite often is a sign of underlying structural conditions that roughly can be grouped under three headings: overuse, abuse, and loose. "Overuse" indicates repetitive overload with structural failure and microscopic tearing of the musculotendinous rotator cuff, articular cartilage damage, and glenoid labral and bicipital tendon wearing. "Abuse" refers to playing through painful symptoms that indicate inflamed, damaged tissue, muscular imbalance, and structural abnormalities. Such strenuous action leads to traction injuries, such as pectoralis major avulsion and lateral acromion apophysitis. Continuation of golf when some part of the swing is painful also produces abnormal mechanics that are structurally counterproductive and merely compound the problem. "Loose" denotes elements of joint laxity observed as anterior, posterior, or combined soft-tissue instability of the glenohumeral joint, either congenital or acquired by repetitive use. In this condition, the humeral head is functionally unstable in the glenoid fossa during the forceful golf swing. Anterior, posterior, or multidirectional subluxation then occurs, which further damages the anterior and posterior capsular support structures, the glenoid labrum, and the articular surface of the humeral head, and stretches the axillary nerve anteriorly and the suprascapular nerve posteriorly. This symptom complex progresses with unrestrained activity to allow for impingement of the humeral head up against the subdeltoid bursa, the acromion, and the coracoacromial ligament. As weakness of the glenohumeral joint stabilizers increases, the deltoids' pull upward is relatively unopposed, and with further imbalance, allows the humeral head more effectively to encroach and impact up against the "roof" of the glenohumeral joint.

When conservative management (phase VII), which may include an anesthetic/steroid injection, has been carefully monitored and diligently performed, but pain, crepitation, instability, or decreased range of motion and strength persists, operative intervention should be considered (phase VIII). Arthroscopic evaluation of the shoulder by a skilled orthopedic surgeon is now a definitively helpful surgical procedure. Small arthroscopic instruments are introduced through multiple portals, first into the glenohumeral joint, and a preliminary assessment is made of the integrity and laxity of the joint. The prominent articular surface of the humeral head is scanned for erosion

(Hill-Sachs lesion). If found, the area is burred down to bleeding cancellous bone. Looking down on the glenoid, the labrum is evaluated for wearing, which is shaved, or an avulsion, which is sutured, if possible. The glenoid itself is explored for possible fractures at its margin (Bankart lesion). The bicipital tendon/superior labrum junction is inspected and probed for stability. The bicipital tendon itself is shaved if it is roughened. Just adjacent is the undersurface of the rotator cuff. Often, it is damaged, as noted by fibrillation, and this area is smoothed down to bleeding tissue with a rotating instrument. If a frank tear in the rotator cuff is identified, it can be débrided to allow for healing.

In the second part of the arthroscopic shoulder procedure, the instruments are introduced into the subdeltoid space and the superior surface of the cuff is evaluated for inflammation, fibrillation, and tearing. This surface of the cuff is also smoothed by proper motorized instrumentation. Attention is then directed to the acromioclavicular/coracoacromial arch complex. Should signs of impingement be obvious, acromioplasty is performed by burring away the undersurface of the acromion, the adjacent clavicle, and any osteophytic formation, and by cauterization of local soft tissue. When completed, this procedure allows additional room for the excursion of the head of the humerus in the golf swing without violent encroachment of surfaces.

No matter how well the arthroscopic surgery was performed, all phases of rehabilitation, similar to those employed in the nonoperative treatment, must be undertaken daily, progressed in a step-wise fashion, and completed in order to ensure maximum clinical results. Once back to active participation, the golfer needs to perform maintenance exercises faithfully at least three times a week to help prevent recurrent shoulder symptoms.

Should anterior or posterior capsular shifts be required to inhibit anterior or posterior shoulder subluxations, or if suturing of more significant rotator cuff and labral tears is needed, open procedures are performed after arthroscopic identification of the problem. Return to the previous level of competitive golf, even with excellent adherence to treatment/rehabilitative regimens, is difficult. Often, the ultimate performance level is a measure of innate mental toughness.

SUMMARY

Briefly stated, to play golf well, two good shoulders are required. The shoulder girdle, its joints, soft tissue, and muscle coverings play a vital part in the total body effort to strike a golf ball. It may be argued that the shoulder is not the most vital link in swing mechanics, but there is little question that shoulder pathology very often hinders effective golf.

Failure to have and restore bilaterally normal shoulder musculature, to develop and maintain proper swing mechanics, and to recognize the early physical signs of overuse are the cardinal sins of the avid golfer. Such obdurateness is not unusual for either men or women and reflects both the lack of notoriety that injury prevention and treatment receives in the golfing community and the dearth of medical education and counseling available for golfers. The lack of physicians knowledgeable in prevention, treatment, and rehabilitation compounds the situation. Most golfers do not want to hear and will not accept the dreaded advice, "Stop playing," unless there is a reasonable and usually successful plan to treat and rehabilitate the injured area.

Although repetitive overuse injuries are the most common cause of shoulder pathology in golfers, previous insults, incomplete recovery, and deterioration of general body strength and conditioning play a less recognized causative role. Inflammation of the rotator cuff musculotendinous units initiates a clinical pattern that, at first, is reversible. With continued repetitive insults, soft-tissue structures microscopically tear, articular cartilage degenerates, osseous tissue produces osteophytes, and the labral rim erodes. At this stage, spontaneous reversibility is doubtful. When scarring, decreased range of motion (or the opposite, instability), and impingement occur, surgical intervention and rehabilitation usually are necessary for recovery.

Total body conditioning before embarking into golf participation is optimal. However, special attention should be given to the rotator cuff relationship to the glenohumeral joint. Just as in throwing and racquet sports, the supraspinatus, infraspinatus, teres minor, and subscapularis muscles must work competently, synchronously, and smoothly. There can be no muscle imbalance in the internal-external rotators if a fluid swing is desired. Prevention also should include bilateral strengthening of the pectoralis major and latissimus dorsi muscles that are so necessary for propulsion. In essence, to play golf proficiently, normal bilateral shoulder function and proper mechanics are required.

REFERENCES

1. Cahill, BR: Osteolysis of the distal part of the clavicle in male athletes. J Bone Joint Surg 64A(7):1053–1058, 1982.
2. Carlsoo, S: A kinetic analysis of the golf swing. J Sports Med Phys Fitness 7:76–82, 1967.
3. Cofield, RH and Simonet, WT: The shoulder in sports. In Symposium on Sports Medicine, Part II. Mayo Clin Proc 59:157–164, 1984.
4. Fleisig, GS: Analysis of a mechanical model of the golf swing. Unpublished B.S. thesis, Massachusetts Institute of Technology, 1984.
5. Jobe, FW, Moynes, DR, and Antonelli, DJ: Rotator cuff function during a golf swing. Am J Sports Med 14(5):388–392, 1986.
6. McCarroll, JR and Gioe, TJ: Professional golfers and the price they pay. Phys Sportsmed 10(7): 64–68, 70, 1982.
7. McCarroll, JR: Golf. In Schneider, RC, et al (eds): Analysis of Sports Techniques. Williams & Wilkins, Baltimore, 1985, pp 270–287.
8. McCarroll, JR: Golf. In Schneider, RC, et al (eds): Sports Injuries: Mechanisms, Prevention, and Treatment. Williams & Wilkins, Baltimore, 1985, pp 290–294.
9. Middleton, K: Prevention and rehabilitation of shoulder injuries in throwing athletes. In Nicholas, JA and Hershman, EB (eds): The Upper Extremity in Sports Medicine. CV Mosby, St Louis, 1990, pp 767–780.
10. Milburn, PD: Summation of segmental velocities in the golf swing. Med Sci Sports Exerc 14(1):60–64, 1982.
11. Moseley, HF: Athletic injuries to the shoulder region. Am J Surg 98:401–422, 1959.
12. Moynes, DR, et al: Electromyography and motion analysis of the upper extremity in sports. Phys Ther 66(12):1905–1911, 1986.
13. Neer, CS: Anterior acromioplasty for the chronic impingement syndrome in the shoulder. J Bone Joint Surg 54A:41–50, 1972.
14. Resnick, D: Shoulder pain. Orthop Clin North Am 14(1): 81–97, 1983.
15. Schulenburg, CAR: Medical aspects and curiosities of golfing. The Practitioner 217:625–628, 1976.
16. Sisto, DJ and Jobe, FW: The operative treatment of scapulothoracic bursitis in professional pitchers. Am J Sports Med 14(3):192–194, 1986.
17. Stover, CN, Wiren, G, and Topaz, SR: The modern golf swing and stress syndromes. Phys Sportsmed 5(9):43–47, 1976.
18. Williams, KR and Cavanaugh, P: The mechanics of foot action during the golf swing and implications for shoe design. Med Sci Sports Exerc 15(3):247–255, 1983.

The Elbow

William D. Stanish, MD, FRCS(C), FACS
Mark I. Loebenberg, MD
John W. Kozey, MSc

he elbow is the most common site of tendinitis in golfers. Both the medial and lateral epicondyles are regularly affected. The chronic nature of these injuries has puzzled physicians for decades and frustrated countless avid golfers who lead vigorous and active lives, yet suffer from severe pain every time they swing a club.

Recent advances in the understanding of the biochemical processes in tendons and their rehabilitative capabilities have led to the development of new and successful treatments for tendinitis. By treating the muscle-tendon unit as one physiologic entity, physicians and therapists have been able to speed up the rehabilitative period and have had great success in eliminating the chronic nature of tendinitis. This is especially encouraging for golfers because tendinitis in the elbow accounts for close to 10% of all golf-related injuries.[3]

DEFINITIONS

Tendons are fibrous tissue, ropelike in structure, that connect muscle to bone. Muscles produce the forces that precipitate all movement, and tendons transmit the force generated by the muscle to the limb being moved. Tendons are continually subjected to tremendous strains in all sports, including golf. The forces produced by the large muscles of the arms, legs, and trunk must be transmitted through the tendons to the bones in order to generate the movements that are essential (or in some cases not essential) to the golf swing.

Perhaps nowhere in the body is this strain on the tendon more evident than in the elbow. All the major muscles of the forearm narrow into two tendons that insert into the medial and lateral epicondyles at the base of the humerus. The lateral tendon, known as the common extensor tendon, extends into those muscles that control extension in the wrist. On the medial side, the common flexor tendon applies forces from the flexor muscles of the forearm. Because both of these tendons narrow into small origins, the muscle forces create very high stresses (force per unit area).

The precarious position of these tendons, situated between the strong force-producing muscles of the forearm and the relatively rigid humerus, makes them particularly prone to injury. Whether tendon injuries result from direct blows, excessive tensile force, or low-magnitude, highly repetitive forces, the body's response to injury is always "inflammatory" in nature. "Tendinitis" is simply the generic name given to describe the inflammatory response in tendons.

Most incidents of tendinitis are classified as overuse injuries. The tendon is loaded repeatedly until it is unable to withstand further loading, at which point damage occurs, and the body activates its "biologic splint," the inflammatory response. Overuse injuries can result from any activity with repetitive motions, and they are common in sport and industry. In fact, tendinitis in the elbow is so often associated with sports that the syndrome has entered the vernacular as "tennis elbow." Tennis elbow (lateral epicondylitis) is quite simply a tendinitis that affects the lateral epicondyle, or outer aspect, of the elbow. The medial epicondyle is similarly affected by a tendinitis known as "golfer's elbow" (medial epicondylitis). Physiologically, the two syndromes are identical. They differ only in their anatomic position. Tennis elbow and golfer's elbow are far from exclusively associated with their respective sports, however. In fact, it is very common for a right-handed golfer to suffer from tennis elbow in the leading left elbow and golfer's elbow in the following right elbow.

TENDINITIS AND THE GOLF SWING

Tennis elbow and golfer's elbow develop primarily because of the continual loading of the elbow tendons while the wrist is either in forced flexion or extension. The tremendous torques created by the long moment arm of the golf club and the high stresses placed on the wrists at the beginning of the downswing and at the moment of impact with the golf ball combine to make elbow tendinitis a very common ailment. A proper golf swing and sound training often can alleviate tendinitis in the elbows by reducing hyperextension and hyperflexion of the wrists while under strain.

The golf swing has been analyzed[1,4,5,7] and adjusted countless times in the past 60 years. There is no doubt that the modern golf swing is considerably more aggressive than the leisurely swings of years past. The modern golfer swings with greater speed and around a much more controlled arc, creating both greater joint moments and more repetitive stresses. This change naturally places a much greater load on the tendons of the elbow.

To determine when and where the elbow undergoes strain during the golf swing, we will examine five stages: the backswing, transition, downswing, impact, and follow-through. It is thought that each of these stages has an ideal physical position and common positional faults. Injuries probably result from abnormal stress on the muscles and tendons, caused by a less-than-perfect swing. Although the exact point or action that causes particular injuries is not precisely known, this section highlights the various actions most likely to account for injuries to the elbow in golf.

Backswing

Very little physical stress is put on the elbows or forearms during the take-away. Because the wrists should move only slightly as part of the one-piece take-away, a negligible strain is placed on the tendons of the elbow. It is important to bring the club back slowly and smoothly, however, to minimize the eccentric load on the muscles of the forearm and wrists at the moment of transition to the downswing, thus minimizing tendon strain.

Transition

It is critical that the golfer achieve the correct position at the top of the backswing and that the transition to the downswing be made with a fluid motion. On reaching the transition stage, the shoulders are coiled, the hands are swung high, and the arms are extended, thus stretching the forearm muscle. The peak negative moment of force at the wrist exists during the transition from backswing to downswing. During this time, the club head is still moving in the direction of the backswing, and the wrists must exert a force on the club to arrest this motion and initiate the downswing. This force must be exerted while the right wrist is dorsiflexed and the right elbow flexor mass is stretched. This extends the common flexor tendon and places it under a great deal of strain; medial epicondylitis may result.

A slower, smoother backswing, allowing the wrists to cock naturally, causes less force on these muscles and tendons. At the transition to the downswing, stress is reduced if motion is begun by the hips, with forward arm motion then initiated by the shoulders, not the wrists. The common swing fault of "casting" the club into the swing (similar to the action of casting a fishing rod) or "hitting from the top" not only is bad for the golf game but also may be a major contributor to the development of medial epicondylitis.

Downswing

The peak positive moment of force of the entire golf swing exists milliseconds before impact.[5] At this point, the club is moving at close to its maximum velocity, and the golfer squares the club face by rotating the forearms. The right wrist remains dorsiflexed, which maintains the stretch of the right elbow flexor muscles. This extended position of the right wrist is difficult to maintain, however, because the forward momentum of the long club exerts a force on the wrist to move into flexion. Many golfers attempt to "decelerate" their swing prior to impact because they feel "out of control" when they are about to strike the ball. By attempting to hold their wrists back, they place tremendous strain on the right common flexor tendon. The golfer can avoid some of this strain by swinging freely and allowing the club's velocity to "uncock" the wrists naturally.

Impact

At impact, the back of the left hand should face the target, as the forearms continue to rotate. In physical terms, the golf ball, although stationary, must be viewed as a force acting against the movement of the club and the arms of the golfer. Just after impact, the club and the hands of necessity decelerate somewhat because of the force exerted by the ball (and even more, by the divot) against the club. This deceleration, especially when taking a divot, requires significant counteracting forearm muscle force to maintain control of the club face and places a further strain on either the lateral or medial epicondyle; consequently, the overwhelming majority of elbow injuries probably take place during the impact phase of the swing.

The left wrist is now beginning to extend, and the right wrist to flex.[4,5] Extending the left wrist involves the contraction of the lateral extensor muscle mass, stretching the lateral tendon so that it must absorb the force of the ball while in an activated state. Similarly, the reaction force of the impact would attempt to extend the right wrist, adding to the forces on the wrist flexors. Actively "uncocking" the wrists, rather than allowing them to break naturally, increases the stresses of impact at the elbow.

Follow-through

Although the follow-through may produce other injuries, epicondylitis would be a rare result because the stress of the downswing and impact on the wrists and elbows has lessened considerably by this stage. It is often helpful for the golfer to concentrate on certain aspects of the follow-through in order to reveal symptoms of mechanical faults in the previous stages of the swing, but nothing inherent in the follow-through directly promotes either tennis elbow or golfer's elbow.

SYMPTOMS AND DIAGNOSIS

The onset of either tennis elbow or golfer's elbow cannot be prevented entirely with swing corrections. Avid golfers place huge strains on their elbows thousands of times each season, and tendinitis is sometimes an unavoidable consequence. Although the onset of these syndromes is often gradual, the earlier patients and their doctors recognize its appearance, the earlier rehabilitation and tendon strengthening can begin.

Both syndromes develop similarly, with essentially the same symptoms, treatment, and prognosis. The principal symptom associated with either medial or lateral epicondylitis is pain over the respective epicondyle. This pain may also radiate upward along the upper arm and downward along the inside or outside of the forearm, depending on whether the tendinitis is medial or lateral. A very distinct tender point can be elicited by pressure on the inflamed epicondyle. In severe cases, marked bruising over the epicondyle may also occur.

Depending on its severity, epicondylitis causes varying degrees of disability. In mild cases, some pain is felt only when the golfer swings a club. In more severe cases, sufferers may find themselves unable to perform even simple, everyday functions, such as lifting a coffee cup, opening a car door, or shaking hands. All of these problems result from a weakness in the wrist that inhibits the hand's ability to grasp objects with strength.

Usually a diagnosis of epicondylitis can be determined through a series of simple tests. If pain is induced at the lateral epicondyle when the hand is dorsiflexed against resistance, the complaint can be diagnosed as tennis elbow. If pain is experienced at the medial epicondyle from volar (palmar) flexion, an accompanying diagnosis of golfer's elbow can be made. Tendinitis is by far the most common of all elbow injuries, and if the evidence points to tears of the common extensor or flexor tendons, it is safe to assume so and pursue treatment accordingly.

If the patient does not respond to treatment, various differential diagnoses can be made. Primary among these syndromes are entrapments of either the radial nerve (for lateral epicondylitis) or ulnar nerve (for medial epicondylitis), degenerative arthritis or rheumatic disorders, or radiating pain caused by degenerative changes in the cervical spine in the region of the fifth and sixth cervical vertebrae.

Radial nerve entrapments are exceedingly rare, but ulnar nerve entrapments are quite common and occur almost as frequently as golfer's elbow. Some sensory loss in the fourth and fifth fingers may develop. Palpation of the nerve may cause pain. The principal differential technique is to volarflex and dorsiflex the wrist against resistance, depending on the site of injury. If pain is elicited over the appropriate epicondyle, the inflammation is tendon-related.

The most common degenerative change that can occur as a result of chronic epicondylitis is the development of heterotopic calcification.[2] A roentgenogram will confirm this diagnosis. Conservative treatment will usually not be very successful, but a local steroid injection can be used to great benefit.

TREATMENT

The list of treatment techniques for epicondylitis includes almost every option available to the modern physician and physiotherapist. Rest, local steroid injections, systemic nonsteroidal anti-inflammatories, ice, ultrasound, heat, deep friction massage, manipulation, bracing, and surgery all have been used. The very existence of such a variety of techniques, however, and the number of patients who have experienced many, or all, of them, should serve as convincing evidence that none alone is entirely successful.

The rehabilitation of the golfer to full recovery can be subdivided into four stages:

1. **Relief of Acute and Chronic Inflammation.** A symptomatic approach is necessary to relieve the patient's pain. This is best accomplished through the liberal use of ice and sometimes oral nonsteroidal anti-inflammatory drugs to control the inflammation. Brief periods of rest may be necessary in acute stages. Immobilization should be avoided, because the accompanying muscle atrophy retards the return to full activity.

2. **Increased Forearm Muscle Strength, Flexibility, and Endurance.** A major philosophical change has taken place recently in the treatment of medial and lateral epicondylitis.[6] A greater emphasis is now placed on exercise rehabilitation, in order to restore muscle strength and therefore place less strain

on the tendon unit (see also Chapter 18). This emphasis stems from the knowledge that decreased flexibility causes the muscles to be overstretched during eccentric contraction, and overloading of either the flexor or extensor muscles is the most widely recognized factor in the cause of epicondylitis. Maximum strengthening of the muscle must necessarily include eccentric exercise because this is the nature of the force producing the injury and because eccentric exercise produces the greatest tensile force on the tendon.

During physiotherapy, control of loading on the muscle is carried out by altering the speed of movement or the amount of resistance. A starting weight of 2 lb (1 lb for smaller individuals) in acute cases is sufficient. Weights of up to 5 lb could be used in less severe cases. Warm-up may be effectively provided by local heat application for a few minutes or by general body exercise.

Physiotherapies for tennis elbow and golfer's elbow are the same from a procedural standpoint but are essentially mirror images of each other. The treatment for tennis elbow works the extensor muscles, and the treatment for golfer's elbow works the flexor muscles. The patient with lateral epicondylitis stretches the wrist extensors by pronating the forearm with the elbow extended and then passively volarflexing the wrist. This flexing may be done with the opposite hand or by placing the flexed hand on a support of a suitable level (Figs. 14–1 and 14–2).

The patient suffering from medial epicondylitis stretches the wrist flexors by supinating the forearm with the elbow extended and then passively dorsiflexing the wrist. This is accomplished in the same manner as earlier.

Following three 30-second stretches, the patient sits with the forearm supported so that the hand and weight are beyond the support (Fig. 14–3). Then the weight is lowered and raised freely. The emphasis is on the change in the muscle action from eccentric on the way down to concentric on the upward motion. The weight is lowered slowly and then raised quickly (Fig. 14–4).

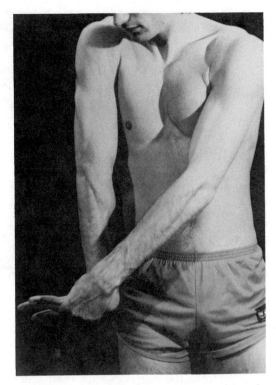

Figure 14–1. Stretching the wrist extensors: active assisted.

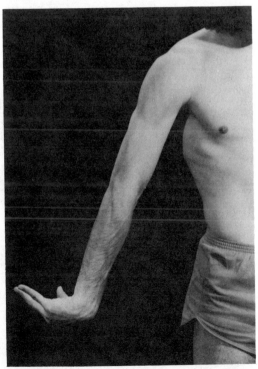

Figure 14–2. Stretching the wrist extensors: active.

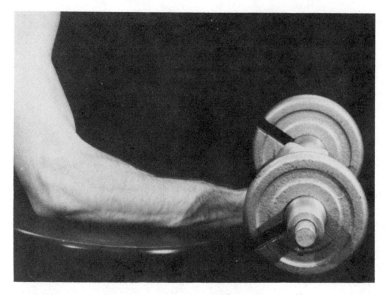

Figure 14–3. Strengthening for tennis elbow: extension before dropping weight "to catch."

The exercise is repeated 30 times, in three sets of 10. The exercises differ only slightly for tennis elbow and golfer's elbow. Tennis elbow sufferers perform the exercises with their palm facing down; those with golfer's elbow leave their palm facing upwards.

The stretching exercises are then repeated, and ice is applied to the inflamed epicondyle. One very convenient method of doing this is to freeze a paper cup full of water and use this to rub gently over the area for 5 minutes. It may be placed back in the freezer and reused. Alternatively, an ice cube with a stick frozen inside it or crushed ice in a damp towel may be used.

The entire session should take about 20 minutes and be performed daily. It may be 2 or 3 weeks before symptoms begin to abate. During this interval, the patient should be checked regularly to ensure that the program is done regularly and correctly and progresses

Figure 14–4. Strengthening for tennis elbow: dropping weight "to catch" before moving back to extension.

when indicated. The yardstick of discomfort (or absence of it) near the end of 30 repetitions determines when the speed or resistance should be changed.

3. **Decreasing the Moment of Force at the Wrist.**

   a. *Altered swing technique.* These alterations were discussed previously. It is wise to consult a golf professional to discuss swing changes. The pro will be best qualified to point out the deficiencies in the golfer's swing that might lead to tendinitis.

   b. *Equipment changes.* Very few equipment changes are available to the golfer to alleviate the symptoms of tendinitis in the elbow. Because pain is most often experienced when gripping the club, a larger grip will make grasping somewhat less demanding. Grip size is limited by the physics of the golf swing, however, which demands a free and easy swing with fluid and uninhibited movement of the wrists.

   c. *Elbow support.* The use of a forearm brace (as shown in Fig. 18–15) is suggested to relieve symptoms during the treatment period. The exact mechanism of action of this brace is unclear, but it appears to function by providing a reactive force against the contracting muscles, and either spreads the force over a wider area or decreases the contractile pull on the epicondyles. The brace is applied snugly to the relaxed forearm just prior to activity and is removed immediately afterward.

4. **Surgery if Conservative Treatment Fails.** After all conservative treatments have been thoroughly explored, surgery may be considered. A small incision is made over the affected epicondyle and a tenotomy is performed. The tendon is lengthened to reduce the force per unit area.

SUMMARY

A proper understanding of both the biomechanics and pathophysiology of epicondylitis allows great insight into the rehabilitation of these syndromes. A coordinated effort involving the patient, physician, therapist, and golf professional can, in most cases, eliminate both the acute and chronic aspects of tendinitis. Increased concern with the muscle strength and not just with the alleviation of symptoms will unquestionably diminish the number of chronic cases of epicondylitis among golfers and return thousands to the fairways in a more expedient fashion, much less susceptible to recurrent injury.

REFERENCES

1. Budney, D and Bellow, DG: Kinetic analysis of a golf swing. Research Quarterly 50(2):171–179, 1979.
2. Matthews, P and Leyshon, R: Acute calcification in tennis and golfers elbow. Rheumatology and Rehabilitation 19:151–153, 1980.
3. McCarroll, JR and Gioe, TJ: Professional golfers and the price they pay. Phys Sportsmed 10(7):64–70, 1982.
4. Nagao, N and Sawada, Y: A kinematic analysis in golf swing concerning driver shot and No. 9 iron shot. J Sports Med Phys Fitness 13(1):4–16, 1973.
5. Neal, RJ and Wilson, BD: 3-D kinematics and kinetics of the golf swing. International Journal of Sports Biomechanics 1(3):221–232, 1985.
6. Stanish, WD and Curwin, S: Tendinitis: Its etiology and treatment. DC Health and Co, Lexington, MA, 1984.
7. Stover, CN, Wiren, G, and Topaz, S: The modern golf swing and stress syndromes. Phys Sportsmed 4(9):42–47, 1976.

The Wrist and Hand

· ·

Arthur C. Rettig, MD

I njuries to the wrist and hand are common problems in the golfer. In a questionnaire by McCarroll[20] sent to 226 professional golfers, there were 106 injuries to the wrist and 28 injuries to the hand. Injuries to the left wrist ranked first in the total number of injuries compared with other body parts. Hand and wrist injuries accounted for 37% of the total injuries in this series. The left wrist was injured in 94 golfers (23.9% of all injuries) and the right in 12 (13.7%). The left hand was injured in 28 (7.2%), the right in none.

ACTIONS OF THE WRIST AND HAND DURING THE GOLF SWING

The golf swing may be broken down into five phases: (1) set-up; (2) backswing; (3) transition; (4) downswing; and (5) follow-through. Following the set-up, the backswing starts with the take-away phase, consisting of rotation of the shoulders, hips, knees, and lumbar and cervical spine to the top of the backswing. This is accompanied by radial deviation of the left wrist at the top of the backswing, with dorsiflexion and radial deviation of the right wrist.

Tendinitis of the wrist may be associated with this phase of the swing. In the third and fourth phases of the swing (transition and downswing), as the player begins to hit the ball, the right wrist is at maximum dorsiflexion and the left ulnar nerve, right elbow, and forearm muscles are under tension. During the downswing phase, the left wrist, hand, and elbow are more often injured by compression. Such injuries include carpal fractures and carpal tunnel syndrome. The greatest number of injuries occur during this phase of the swing, with 73 of the wrist injuries and 16 of the hand injuries occurring in this phase.[20]

The final phase is the follow-through. After the golfer strikes the ball, the left forearm supinates and the right forearm pronates, with accompanying lumbar and cervical spine rotations. The follow-through phase accounts for the least number of wrist and hand injuries, with only nine wrist injuries and four hand injuries occurring in this phase.

In the elite golfer in mid-downswing, the left wrist is radially deviated and in neutral flexion or a very slight volar flexion. The right wrist is radially deviated and maximally dorsiflexed. The left forearm is pronated, and the right forearm is supinated. During impact, the position of flexions of the wrist does not change appreciably; both wrists ulnarly deviate to neutral and slightly beyond. In addition, and of primary importance, the forearms rotate; the left forearm supinates and the right forearm pronates. This rotation begins at mid-downswing and continues through impact to mid–follow-through. The so-called uncocking of the wrists is in actuality the result of forearm rotation, which creates an illusion of uncocking.

DIAGNOSIS AND TREATMENT OF INJURIES

Injuries to the wrist and hand can be subdivided into overuse and acute traumatic injuries. The vast majority of injuries in the golfer are overuse-type injuries due to repetitive motions and to the forces acting about the wrist and hand during the golf swing. Acute traumatic injuries may be seen with sudden impact loading, such as when the golf club strikes the ground, a rock, or another object, causing sudden deceleration in the swing.

Wrist and hand injuries may be divided into categories of tendinitis, impaction or impingement syndromes, ganglia, sprains, stress fractures, compression loading syndromes, distal radio-ulnar joint syndromes, nerve compression syndromes, and vascular problems.

Tendinitis

Tendinitis is the most common problem seen in the wrist and forearm of the golfer. It is due to the repetitive dorsiflexion and palmar flexion motions of the right wrist and the radial deviation, ulnar deviation motion of the left wrist, and extremes of pronation and supination. Ulnar deviation of the left wrist occurs only minimally, just prior to impact, but it occurs at a high rate of speed while the wrist is under high degrees of stress. Tendinitis is seen in both wrists and may involve the extensor carpi ulnaris, extensor carpi radialis longus and brevis, flexor carpi ulnaris, and flexor carpi radialis.

The golfer will have aching and sometimes burning pain in the affected tendon (or tendons) and along the course of the muscle belly. Physical examination will reveal tenderness in the specific tendon or tendons involved, as well as pain when the patient is asked to resist dorsiflexion or palmar flexion of the wrist corresponding to the tendon and muscle involved. Intersection syndrome (crossover syndrome)[15] occasionally occurs because of repetitive dorsiflexion and palmar flexion. This is a frictional tendinitis caused by intersection of the extensor carpi radialis brevis and longus and the extensor pollicis longus with resulting inflammation. In this specific case, crepitus may be felt dorsally over the area of the tendinitis in addition to tenderness in this area.[12]

Treatment of tendinitis of the wrist extensors and flexors consists of immobilization, rest, and anti-inflammatory medications. Rest is provided through immobilization in a volar cock-up splint (Fig. 15–1) for 10 to 14 days, followed by modification of daily activities and sports. The wearing time of the splint depends on the severity and duration of pain, that is, the golfer complaining of constant, throbbing pain during activities is instructed to wear the splint continuously. Pain is closely monitored (pain scale, disability index, and pain evaluation) and dictates the advancement of the golfer through three phases of treatment. Pain monitoring must be an integral aspect of any success-oriented program.

Phase I consists of icing (two to three times a day) followed by transverse massage to release the microscopic and macroscopic adhesions constricting the underlying anatomy[7]

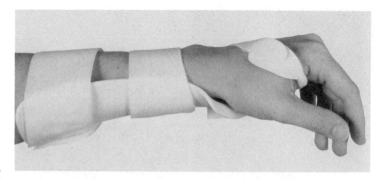

Figure 15–1. Volar cock-up splint.

(Fig. 15–2). Icing decreases inflammation (because of its vasconstricting effects) and assists with pain management because it decreases nerve conduction velocity.[16] Stretching is also advocated, pre-exercise and post-exercise, to increase the resting length of the musculotendinous unit.[1,6]

Physical therapy treatments are recommended during phase I if symptoms have been present for more than 1 month (prior to seeking medical attention) and pain is constant. Phonophoresis with 10% hydrocortisone cream is advocated by some authors for reduction of inflammation.[13] In addition, this author suggests use of low-volt electrical stimulation, which promotes healing and manages pain through a biofeedback mechanism. Even though minimal information is available on using this type of low-intensity stimulation, successful results have been reported with athletes when conventional methods have failed.[13]

Phase II is introduced when pain has decreased to a tolerable level. It includes an eccentric exercise program, as described by Stanish, Rubinovich, and Curwin.[29] These exercises subject the tendon to additional load while minimizing the stress on the tendon insertion.[6] Three sets of 10 repetitions are performed twice a day. If pain has persisted over several months and muscle atrophy has developed, exercises for increasing grip and pinch strengths are indicated. Grip and pinch strengths are tested serially with a dynamometer and pinchmeter respectively (Fig. 15–3).

Phase III includes a functional progression golf program, which can be simulated in the clinic (Fig. 15–4), as well as exercises for improving coordination and strength. The

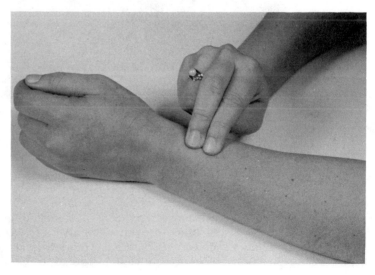

Figure 15–2. Transverse (cross-friction) massage.

Figure 15–3. (*A*) Grip strength is tested with a dynamometer. (Courtesy of Jamar, Asimow Engineering Co.) (*B* and *C*) Pinch strength is tested with a pinchmeter, using the positions shown. Strength is reported by taking an average of three trials.

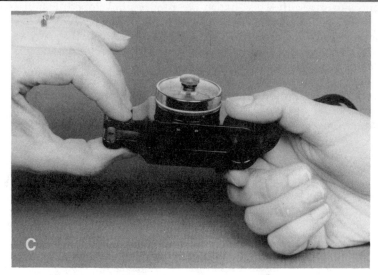

Nirschl R-U wrist brace (Fig. 15–5) is recommended for wrist sprains and tendinitis because it limits only the extreme ranges of movement. (The R-C wrist brace provides full wrist support and is therefore used after minor fractures.) These braces prevent rein-

jury for the golfer preparing to return to the course.

Return to golf is permitted when grip and pinch strengths are symmetric, little or no tenderness is present, and adequate functional training has been completed. (See

Figure 15-4. The golf swing can be simulated as part of a functional progression golf program in the clinic, using the Impulse. (Courtesy of Totem, Inc.)

Chapter 18 for a further discussion of rehabilitation.)

De Quervain's Tenosynovitis

De Quervain's syndrome (tenosynovitis of the first dorsal compartment) is a specific tendinitis that deserves special attention. This is common in the left wrist of right-

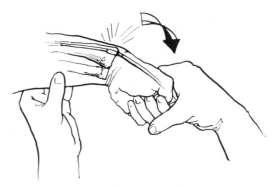

Figure 15-6. Finkelstein's test.

handed golfers because of the radial deviation of the wrist during the backswing and ulnar deviation of the wrist at high speed near impact.[20] Physical examination reveals tenderness over the first dorsal compartment tendons, over the radial styloid, and just proximal and distal to the styloid. The pathognomonic physical sign is Finkelstein's test[9] (Fig. 15-6), in which the thumb is grasped by the fingers, flexing it under a clenched fist, while passive ulnar deviation of the wrist is performed. This elicits significant discomfort over the first dorsal compartment. Radiographic films are usually negative, although occasionally calcification in the first dorsal compartment area is noted.

Treatment of de Quervain's syndrome involves rest, usually in a thumb spica splint with the thumb in functional position (Fig. 15-7), and use of nonsteroidal anti-inflammatory medications. We also recommend a series of two or three steroid injections

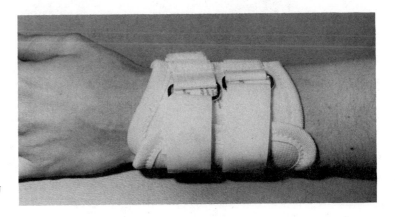

Figure 15-5. The Nirschl R-U wrist brace.

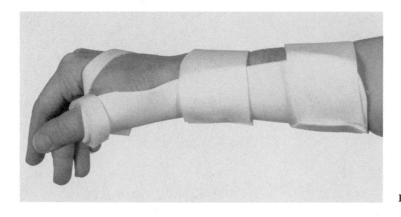

Figure 15–7. Thumb spica splint.

within the tendon sheath, approximately 2 weeks apart. Symptoms will usually resolve in 6 weeks with this treatment. Rehabilitation is then initiated and consists of a stretching program, eccentric exercises (Fig. 15–8), and strengthening. Icing and transverse massage to the extensor pollicis brevis and abductor pollicis longus are prescribed. The golfer may return to competition when there is no tenderness, strength has returned to normal, and he or she has completed the functional progression.

Impaction or Impingement Syndromes

Impaction or impingement syndromes are also the cause of wrist pain in many golfers.

Dorsal and radial impingement occur in the left wrist during the backswing, particularly at the top. Dorsal impingement also may occur in the right wrist of the right-handed golfer.

During repetitive dorsiflexion and palmar flexion of the wrist, as well as on radial and ulnar deviation, impingement occurs between carpal bones and between the carpus and distal radius or ulnar styloid. Pain results from these repetitive impactions or impingements.

The radioscaphoid impaction syndrome is the most common impingement syndrome due to forceful dorsiflexion.[8] In this syndrome (which may result from a single forceful injury, although it is usually the result of

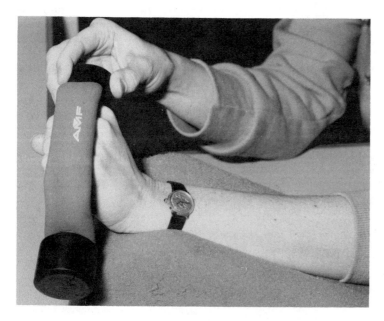

Figure 15–8. Eccentric exercise for wrist extensors. Start in extension. Extensor muscles are contracted as the wrist moves in flexion. Use a maximum of 2 lb, 20 repetitions.

repetitive hyperextension stress), symptoms of pain, weakness, and tenderness in the dorsal radial aspect of the wrist are present. Such tenderness is usually aggravated by dorsiflexion. Point tenderness over the scaphoid rim may be elicited with the wrist in dorsiflexion and ulnar deviation.[17] Radiographic films occasionally show a small ossicle continuous with the scaphoid rim on the lateral views. Pain from this syndrome is often felt in the right hand of golfers near impact. Treatment of this condition includes rest, splinting, and an occasional steroid injection. In protracted cases that do not respond to nonoperative treatment, surgical exploration may be performed, with débridement of the dorsal aspect of the scaphoid and dorsal rim of the radius.

The radial styloid impingement syndrome is similar to the scaphoid impaction syndrome except that symptoms are usually noted over the anatomic snuffbox and are produced by radial deviation, with pressure exerted on the scaphoid tuberosity from the radial styloid.[17] Tenderness is present on the palmar aspect of the radial styloid and may be elicited by forced radial deviation. This occurs in the left wrist of golfers due to extreme radial deviation during deceleration of the club head near the transition from backswing to downswing. Treatment of this condition, as above, includes rest and splinting. Simple technical points such as slowing down the backswing may be helpful in preventing recurrence of this problem. Radial styloidectomy may be necessary in long-standing cases that do not respond to conservative treatment.

Impingement syndromes may also occur in the ulnar aspect of the wrist, the most common of which is a triquetral hamate impingement.[9,17] This is the result of repeated forceful extension and ulnar deviation, which may occur in either wrist of the golfer, usually during impact or follow-through. Tenderness is usually present over the triquetral hamate joint line, and ulnar deviation with dorsiflexion may reproduce the symptoms. Localization may be made more precise by judicious use of lidocaine or bupivacaine as a diagnostic test for relief of symptoms. Treatment involves rest, splinting, and anti-inflammatory medications as needed. Occasionally, exploration and chei-

lectomy of the dorsal articular surface of the hamate or triquetral rim may be necessary.

Occult or Overt Ganglia

Dorsal ganglia, whether overt or occult, are also a common cause of wrist pain in the golfer. These are usually the result of repetitive dorsiflexion of the wrist.[17] Physical findings include tenderness of the dorsal aspect of the scapholunate joint. In an overt ganglion, a semimobile cystic mass may be palpated, most commonly between the extensor carpi radialis brevis and extensor digitorum communis tendons at the scapholunate joint. Treatment of ganglia depends on the degree of symptomatology and ranges from conservative treatment, aspiration and injection, to the definitive treatment, exploration and resection.

Sprains

Sprains may occur in many joints of the wrist and hand. Carpometacarpal sprains occur as a result of carpal extension and flexion, with the flexion mechanism being most frequent.[14] Pain is usually on the dorsum of the distal aspect of the carpus. It is more common at the second metacarpal trapezial joint and least common at the fifth metacarpal hamate joint. Diagnosis is made by point tenderness, and occasionally a click may be produced by holding the distal carpal bone and manipulating the metacarpal. Injection with lidocaine or bupivacaine into the joint may be used to improve diagnostic accuracy. Acute injuries usually respond to splinting for 3 to 6 weeks, with rehabilitation following resolution of symptoms.[19] In chronic, resistant problems, arthrodesis of the appropriate carpometacarpal joint may be necessary.

Chronic sprains of the carpometacarpal joint or basilar joint of the thumb sometimes affect the left hand of the right-handed golfer. Again, diagnosis can be made by means of point tenderness and use of diagnostic injections. In prolonged cases, some degree of instability may exist. Usually it will respond to simple splinting, but if the instability continues to be a problem, an Eaton-type reconstruction of the basilar joint may be indicated.[10]

Injuries to the metacarpophalangeal joint of the thumb may also be seen in the golfer because of stress on the ulnar collateral ligament. The examination reveals tenderness along the ulnar collateral ligament of the metacarpophalangeal joint. Care must be taken to evaluate carefully for chronic instability. If chronic instability and pain are a problem, reconstruction may be indicated.[22,28]

Stress Fractures

The most common stress fracture seen in the golfer is the fracture of the hook of the hamate in the left hand of the right-handed golfer. This has been well described by Stark and associates,[30] Eaton and colleagues,[10] and Torisu.[32] The mechanism is chronic abutment of the end of the club on the ulnar palmar aspect of the left hand (Fig. 15–9). The fracture may occur with no single incident or with a single traumatic incident, such as the club's striking the ground, a rock, or other obstacle. This fracture is also seen in other sports, such as tennis and baseball.

The golfer frequently complains of ulnar wrist pain, which may be somewhat diffuse, and often describes pain over the dorsum of the wrist ulnarly. Physical examination reveals maximum tenderness over the hook of the hamate, which is approximately 1.5 cm distal and radial to the pisiform bone. The hook of the hamate lies on a line between the pisiform bone and the second metacarpal

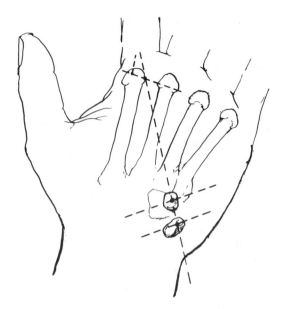

Figure 15–10. Alignment of the pisiform bone and second metacarpal head.

head[3] (Fig. 15–10). Plain radiographs are usually negative for this entity; it is important to obtain carpal tunnel views and a special supination view described by Stark and colleagues.[30] Even with the special views, diagnosis may be in doubt, and a work-up consists of a bone scan and carpal tunnel tomograms or computed tomography (CT) scan to document the lesion.

Attached to the hook of the hamate are the flexor digiti minimi brevis, the opponens digiti minimi, and the transverse retinacular ligament. Secondary to the pull of these structures, the fracture does not readily unite and becomes a chronic painful problem that prevents the golfer from playing. Complications of fractures of the hook of the hamate include ulnar neuropathy and rupture of the flexor profundus tendons to the small finger and occasionally the ring finger.[30] The treatment of this lesion, once diagnosis is made, usually resides in surgical excision of the ununited fragment. Casting for 3 to 6 weeks may be undertaken, but unless this is done in the acute stage, results are poor. Excision is performed through a palmar approach, taking care to protect the motor branch of the ulnar nerve.[3] The wrist is immobilized for 10 days to 3 weeks, followed by a rehabilitation program. The

Figure 15–9. Abutment of the club on the left hand (in a right-handed golfer) can cause fracture of the hook of the hamate.

average return to golf in the 28 cases reported in the literature is 8 to 10 weeks.[3,30] Usually full hand function and symmetric grip strength are achieved following surgery.

Ulnar Compression Syndromes in the Golfer

The left wrist of the golfer is subjected to ulnar compression forces during the downswing and follow-through phases of the swing. During this time, ulnar compression syndromes secondary to repetitive stresses may arise. These syndromes include triangular fibrocartilage tears, triquetral styloid impaction syndrome, chondromalacia of the lunate, and triquetral hamate impaction. Triangular fibrocartilage problems are thought to be secondary to a combination of predisposition of a patient who has an ulnar-plus wrist and repetitive ulnar compression stress loading.[4,23] An "ulnar-plus wrist" refers to a radiographic finding in which the distal ulna is less than 1 mm shorter than the subchondral bone of the distal radius on neutral rotation radiograph view (Fig. 15–11). In patients with this finding, a greater stress is placed on the ulnar aspect of the carpus, frequently causing ulnar-sided wrist pain. A degenerative tearing of the triangular fibrocartilage should be in the differential diagnosis of the golfer complaining of ulnar wrist pain, particularly if he or she has an ulnar-plus wrist.

Physical findings include tenderness over the triangular fibrocartilage area just distal to the ulnar head, pain with resisted ulnar deviation with the forearm pronated, and occasionally palpation of a click or crepitus with ulnar deviation.

Radiographs are important, particularly to look for an ulnar-plus variant, but they usually are unremarkable other than this. In chronic conditions, sclerosis over the subchondral bone of the ulnar head and the ulnar aspect of the lunate may be present.[23] Diagnosis of a full-thickness triangular fibrocartilage tear may be made by wrist arthrogram.[2] We recommend the triple-injection technique because a single injection of the radiocarpal joint may miss a tear that a distal radio-ulnar joint injection may pick up.[33] When a diagnosis remains suspected but has not been confirmed, wrist arthroscopy may

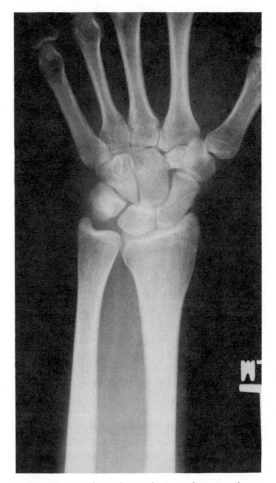

Figure 15–11. Ulnar-plus variant on the neutral rotation view.

be used and is quite helpful for treating flap tears of the triangular fibrocartilage.[27] These may be débrided at the time of arthroscopy, and in some cases the golfer can return to the sport within 3 to 6 weeks.

Conventional treatment includes splinting, anti-inflammatory medications initially, and, occasionally, cast immobilization for a short time. This may be followed by rehabilitation and return to play. In conditions with the ulnar compression syndrome, the use of a Nirschl-type wrist splint, which restricts the full extremes of both dorsiflexion and palmar flexion and radial and ulnar deviation, is recommended. Some golfers may use this on return to their sport. In chronic conditions in which ulnar-plus variance is present, ulnar shortening may be indicated to relieve compressive forces in the triangular fibro-cartilage.[24]

Triquetral lunate ligament injury is another entity in the differential diagnosis of ulnar wrist pain. Its diagnosis is sometimes difficult,[18] although physical findings usually reveal tenderness at the triquetral lunate articulations.[26] Pain with the shuck test, in which the lunate and triquetrum are manipulated against each other during radial and ulnar deviation, is a useful test for this entity. Plain radiographs occasionally show a break in Shenton's line of the wrist or in the proximal triquetral lunate border, particularly in the motion views, but radiographs are usually normal. Initial treatment includes splinting and anti-inflammatory medications. In protracted cases, an arthrogram may be obtained to detect full-thickness tears. Triquetral lunate arthrodesis may be performed in resistant cases, although the results of this are variable.[17,18]

Particularly in the golfer with an ulnar-plus wrist, the ulnar aspect of the triquetrum may impinge on the ulnar styloid.[17] This ulnar styloid triquetral impingement syndrome is analogous to the radial styloid-scaphoid impaction syndrome. Physical findings include pain over the ulnar styloid and ulnar aspect of the triquetrum, and symptoms may be reproduced by means of ulnar deviation, particularly in pronation. Plain radiographics are frequently unremarkable except that they may show an ulnar-plus deformity. In prolonged cases, a bone scan may be useful because it may show increased uptake in the styloid and triquetral area. This syndrome frequently responds to rest, although occasionally ulnar shortening is indicated.

Distal Radio-ulnar Joint Syndromes

The forearm in the golfer is subjected to rapid alternation of pronation and supination during the swing. The right wrist is in near-full supination in mid-downswing and goes through almost a full range of motion to pronation during the follow-through.[20] The left wrist is in pronation in the backswing and goes through a rapid supination with ulnar deviation prior to and during impact and into the follow-through. These motions, performed repetitively, can lead to injury in the area of the distal radio-ulnar joint. Injuries in this area include sprains of the distal radio-ulnar joint ligament, chondromalacia of the ulnar head, and subluxation of the extensor carpi ulnaris.

Sprain of the distal radio-ulnar joint capsule usually occurs with pronation for the dorsal aspect and supination for the volar aspect.[17,33] Injuries to the dorsum are more common. Diagnosis may be made by point tenderness over the ligament capsule involved and pain with resisted pronation for dorsal injuries and with resisted supination for volar lesions. Radiographs are usually not helpful in making a diagnosis. Most often, simple immobilization and anti-inflammatories will suffice, followed by rehabilitation.

Chondromalacia of the ulnar head may be seen in activities involving compression loading of the distal radio-ulnar joint in pronation and supination.[17] Diagnosis may be made by palpation of tenderness over the ulnar head that is quite specific and pain with resisted ulnar deviation with the wrist pronated. A local injection of lidocaine may be quite helpful in confirming the diagnosis. Treatment with splinting and anti-inflammatory medications may result in resolution of the problem; however, if a significant chondral lesion is present, exploration and debridement of the distal radio-ulnar joint may be indicated as a last resort.

Subluxating extensor carpi ulnaris tendon is another entity that may be noted in the golfer, although it is more common in the tennis player. This occurs when the wrist is ulnarly deviated and forcefully supinated.[11] The extensor carpi ulnaris may be palpated radial to the ulnar head in supination, and it is held in place by the sheath and medial wall, which is reinforced by fibers called the linea jugata[31] (Fig. 15–12). In recurrent ulnar deviation and supination activities, the sheath occasionally becomes stretched to the point where the tendon subluxates over the ulnar head when performing this motion. This is quite painful and interferes with function. Occasionally an acute episode of subluxation will occur, but the condition is usually chronic.

Physical examination reveals tenderness along the extensor carpi ulnaris tendon as it passes over the ulnar head.[31] Symptoms may be reproduced by ulnar deviation against resistance in supination. This may produce ei-

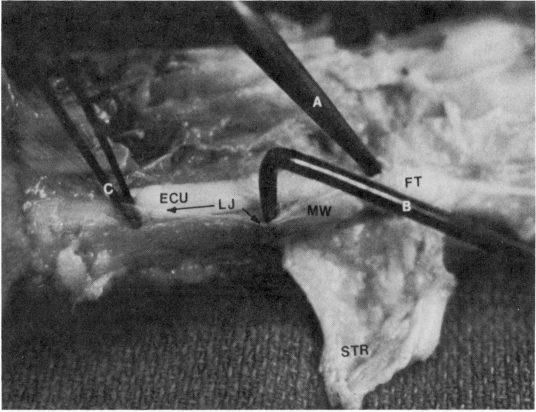

Figure 15–12. The extensor carpi ulnaris tendon (ECU) is normally restricted from ulnar subluxation by the medial wall (MW), the accompanying linea jugata fibers, and the fibrous tunnel. With disruption of the MW, ulnar subluxation of the ECU may occur. Probe A is inserted into the fibrous tunnel (FT) for the ECU; probes B and C elevate the linea jugata (LJ); STR is the supratendinous retinaculum. (From Taleisnik,[31] p 36, with permission.)

ther pain or subluxation. Occasionally, subluxation may actually be observed and palpated. Injection of lidocaine into the tendon sheath may confirm the diagnosis. If the diagnosis is uncertain, arthrography should be performed to rule out underlying pathology in the ulnar aspect of the wrist, such as a triangular fibrocartilage tear. Initial treatment involves immobilization in the neutral position in a modified long-arm splint or cast. This may result in healing of the sheath to the extent that subluxation is prevented.[11] If this is not satisfactory, reconstruction of the sheath may be indicated. This requires immobilization for approximately 6 weeks following the surgery, and the golfer would be out of the sport for approximately 10 to 12 weeks.

Nerve Compression Syndromes

Carpal Tunnel Syndrome

The main nerve compression syndromes seen in the golfer are carpal tunnel syndrome and Guyon's canal syndrome. The carpal tunnel syndrome is the most common nerve compression seen in all sports, and it is due to repetitive dorsiflexion and volar flexion of the wrist with resistance. Carpal tunnel syndrome is usually attributed to the forces across the wrist during the downswing.[20]

Symptoms of this disorder are well known and include paresthesias of any one or all of the thumb, index, long, and ring fingers.[19] The golfer may also complain of volar wrist pain, and the pain may be particularly bothersome at night, often awakening the patient with paresthesias. The patient may also complain of pain when attempting to grip objects or during activities in which the wrist is stressed, such as driving a car.

Characteristic physical findings include a positive Tinel's sign over the carpal tunnel and the most diagnostic test, a positive Phalen's sign.[21] On physical examination, two-point discrimination is usually normal, although in severe cases it may be impaired. Motor function is usually intact, but weakness of the median nerve–innervated thenar musculature may be present.

A diagnostic injection of lidocaine with a short-acting steroid may be carefully placed in the carpal tunnel. This frequently relieves or reduces symptoms nearly completely, although this relief may be transient. Treatment includes splinting, anti-inflammatory medications, and rest. For protracted cases, carpal tunnel release may be indicated.

Guyon's Canal Syndrome

The ulnar nerve may also be compressed at the wrist as it passes through Guyon's canal with the ulnar artery (a canal bordered proximo-ulnarly by the pisiform; disto-radially by the hook of the hamate; superficially [volarly] by the volar carpal ligament; and deeply [dorsally] by the triquetro-hamate joint capsule).[15,25] Any activity involving repetitive wrist dorsiflexion and palmar flexion may result in this syndrome. These patients complain of paresthesia in the small and ring fingers and occasionally in the entire hand. They usually complain of ulnar wrist pain.

Physical findings involve a positive Phalen's sign, tenderness over Guyon's canal, and positive Tinel's sign in this area. Two-point discrimination to the small finger and ulnar half of the ring finger may be impaired. There may be some weakness of ulnar-innervated hand muscles, although this is usually only seen in late cases. Ulnar-innervated intrinsics account for approximately 40% of grip strength. Treatment of Guyon's canal syndrome consists of splinting, rest, and anti-inflammatory medication. In protracted cases, exploration and decompression of the ulnar nerve may be indicated.

Compression of Digital Nerves

Compression of digital nerves may be present in the golfer, although this is quite unusual. Pressure from the grip on the volar radial aspect of the index metacarpal may result in a compression syndrome of the radial digital nerve of the index finger.[9] This may be diagnosed by a positive Tinel's sign over the area of compression and occasionally by impaired two-point discrimination over the radial digital nerve. Usually, padding the golf club handle to relieve pressure on this area or slightly changing the golfer's grip will resolve the problem. Such padding is technically illegal by USGA rules, however. Outside of competition it may be done as a temporary measure. For chronic problems there are specially made, large, extra-padded grips that are legal (Golf Pride, Eaton Corp., Laurinburg, NC).

Vascular Syndromes

The vascular syndromes of the ulnar aspect of the wrist have a clinical picture similar to that of Guyon's canal syndrome and may on occasion be seen in the golfer. These include the hypothenar hammer syndrome, in which abutment of the club head and the ulnar aspect of the wrist may result in thrombosis of the ulnar artery.[5,25] Allen's test is sometimes helpful in differentiating ulnar wrist pain secondary to nerve compression from a vascular problem.

SUMMARY

Injuries to the wrist and hand in the golfer are common. A precise diagnosis is important and may usually be made by a thorough physical examination. Additional studies including radiographs, bone scan or technetium radionuclide imaging, tomograms, and wrist arthrogram are occasionally indicated.

Most injuries are amenable to conservative treatment consisting of rest, splinting, anti-inflammatory medications, and a functional rehabilitation program. Attention to proper mechanics of the golf swing is important when returning to the sport. Following injury, efforts should be made to correct technical errors and to avoid overpractice to prevent reinjury.

A balanced upper-extremity strengthening and stretching program, as well as an adequate warm-up period prior to play, is important in the prevention of injury to the wrist and hand.

REFERENCES

1. Adams, JP, et al: Hand and Wrist Pain. Charlottesville, The Michie Company, 1987, p 107.
2. Bowers, WH: The distal radioulnar joint. In Green, DP (ed): Operative Hand Surgery, Vol 2, ed 2. Churchill Livingstone, New York, 1988, pp 939–989.
3. Carter, PR, Eaton, RG, and Littler, JW: Ununited fracture of the hook of the hamate. J Bone Joint Surg [Am] 59A:583–588, 1977.
4. Coleman, HM: Injuries of the articular disc of the wrist. J Bone Joint Surg 42B:522, 1960.
5. Conn, J Jr, Bergan, JJ, and Bell, JL: Hypothenar hammer syndrome: Post-traumatic digital ischemia. Surgery 68:1122–1128, 1970.
6. Curwin, D and Standish, MD: Tendinitis: Its Etiology and Treatment. DC Heath and Co, Lexington, MA, 1984.
7. Cyriax, J: Textbook of Orthopaedic Medicine, Vol 1. Balliere Tindall, London, 1982.
8. Dauphine, RT and Linscheid, RL: Unrecognized sprain patterns of the wrist (abstract). J Bone Joint Surg 57A:727, 1975.
9. Dobyns, JH, Sim, FH, and Linscheid, RL: Sports stress syndromes of the hand and wrist. Am J Sports Med 6:236–253, 1978.
10. Eaton, RG, et al: Ligament reconstruction for the painful thumb carpometacarpal joint. J Hand Surg [Am] 9:692–699, 1984.
11. Eckhardt, WA and Palmer, AK: Recurrent dislocation of extensor carpi ulnaris tendon. J Bone Joint Surg 6:629–631, 1981.
12. Froimson, AI: Tenosynovitis and tennis elbow. In Green, DP (ed): Operative Hand Surgery, Vol III, Chap 53. Churchill Livingstone, New York, 1988, pp 2117–2134.
13. Gieck, JH and Saliba, EN: Application of Modalities in Overuse Syndromes. Clin Sports Med 6:448–449, 1987.
14. Joseph, RB, et al: Chronic sprains of the carpometacarpal joints. J Bone Joint Surg 6:172, 1981.
15. Kleinert, HE and Hayes, JE: The Ulnar Tunnel Syndrome. Plast Reconst Surg 47:21–24, 1971.
16. Knight, KL: Cryotherapy: Theory, Technique and Physiology. Chattanooga Corp, Chattanooga, TN, 1985, Chapter 2.
17. Linscheid, RL and Dobyns, JH: Athletic injuries of the wrist. Clin Orthop 198:141–151, 1985.
18. Linscheid, RL and Dobyns, JH: Lunotriquetral sprains. Presented at the annual meeting of the American Society for Surgery of the Hand. Baltimore, MD, Sept 1988.
19. Linscheid, RL and Dobyns, JH: Wrist sprains. In Tubiana R (ed): The Hand, Vol 2, Chap 102. WB Saunders, Philadelphia, 1985, pp 970–985.
20. McCarroll, JR: Golf: Common injuries from a supposedly benign activity. J Musculoskel Med 5:9–16, 1986.
21. Milford, L: The Hand. In Crenshaw AH: Campbell's Operative Orthopaedics, Vol 1, 4th ed. Mosby, St Louis, 1963, pp 139–314.
22. Neviaser, RJ, Wilson, JN, and Leivano, A: Rupture of the ulnar collateral ligament of the thumb (gamekeeper's thumb). J Bone Joint Surg 53A:1357–1364, 1971.
23. Palmer, AK and Werner, FW: The triangular fibrocartilage complex of the wrist, anatomy and function. J Hand Surg 6:153–162, 1981.
24. Palmer, AK, et al: Partial excision of the triangular fibrocartilage complex. J Hand Surg 13:391–394, 1988.
25. Parubsky, GL, Brown, SI, and Urbaniak, FR: Ulnar artery thrombosis: a sports-related injury. Am J Sports Med 14:170–175, 1986.
26. Reagan, DS, Linscheid, RL, and Dobyns, JH: Lunotriquetral sprains. J Hand Surg 9A:502, 1984.
27. Roth, JH, Poehling, GG, and Whipple, TL: Arthroscopic Surgery of the Wrist. Instr Course Lect 37:183–194, 1988.
28. Smith, RJ: Post-traumatic instability of the metacarpophalangeal joint of the thumb. J Bone Joint Surg 59A:14–21, 1977.
29. Stanish, WD, Rubinovich, RM, and Curwin, S: Eccentric exercise in chronic tendinitis. Clin Orthop 208:65–68, 1986.
30. Stark, HH, et al: Fracture of the hook of the hamate in athletes. J Bone Joint Surg [Am] 59:575–582, 1977.
31. Taleisnik, J: The Wrist. Churchill Livingstone, New York, 1985, p 36.
32. Torisu, T: Fracture of the hook of the hamate by a golf swing. Clin Orthop 83:91–94, 1972.
33. Vesely, DG: The distal radio-ulnar joint. Clin Orthop 51:75, 1967.

The Lower Extremity

· ·

John R. McCarroll, MD

HIP INJURIES
THIGH INJURIES
KNEE INJURIES
INJURIES OF THE LOWER LEG
PREVENTION OF INJURIES

There is a trend in golf instruction to pay more attention to the upper body. Foot and leg action is not taught much. Certainly, the torso, arms, and hands play important roles in the golf swing. Every golfer should first learn a sound swinging motion using those body parts. Correct foot and leg movement is important, though, to promote good rhythm, balance, and tempo.

In the golf swing at set-up (Fig. 16–1), the knees are spaced comfortably apart with the weight distribution varying from club to club. During the backswing (Fig. 16–2), the left hip is rotated, the left foot rolls inward to the right, and the left knee moves along with it, putting stress on the medial side of the knee so that it is pointing behind the ball when the backswing is completed. During transition and downswing (Fig. 16–3), the gap between the knees widens. The left knee is moving laterally to the left with stress being placed on the lateral side of the knee so it can accept the shift of weight to the left. This left knee action is one of the most important parts of the swing because it encourages coordinated movement of the torso, arms, and hands. Through downswing and into follow-through (Fig. 16–4), the knee gap narrows as the weight drives on to the outside of the left foot. The right knee moves toward the left, placing medial stress on this knee. During this part of the swing, the left hip rotates out of the way, with weight transferred from the right to the left side.

Injuries to the lower extremity, although not as frequent in golf as upper-extremity injuries, can be very bothersome.[1,2] They prevent proper weight shift and rotation during the swing, prevent bending and stooping, and hamper the ability to walk during golf. There are no reports on specific injuries to the lower extremity in our literature, but McCarroll and colleagues[1,2] found in studies on professional and amateur golfers that the knee was injured in 6.6% of professionals and 9.3% of amateurs. The hip was injured in 1% of the professional golfers and 3% of the amateur golfers (Table 16–1).

Figure 16–1. Golfer's stance at set-up. The knees are spaced apart, and weight is distributed equally between the feet.

Figure 16–2. Golfer's stance during backswing. The left foot and knee are rolling inward as the swing reaches its top.

Figure 16–3. Golfer's stance approaching impact. The left knee is moving to the left as weight shifts to that side.

Figure 16–4. Golfer's stance through downswing into follow-through. The right knee moves to the left as the hip rotates in the same direction, transferring weight completely to that side.

TABLE 16-1. Golf Injuries in the Lower Extremity

Injury Site	Professional (n = 393)	Amateur (n = 708)
Knee	6.6%	9.3%
Hip	1.0%	3.1%
Ankle	2.0%	2.5%
Feet	3.3%	1.7%
Thigh (groin)	1.2%	1.1%
Calf	0%	0.6%

Source: Adapted from McCarroll and associates.[1,2]

This chapter discusses injuries to the hip, thigh, knees, and calf areas, as well as their treatment.

HIP INJURIES

Injuries to the hip are extremely uncommon in the golfer. The most common injury seen in our clinic is greater trochanteric bursitis. Inflammation of the bursa overlying the greater trochanter is most often seen in the female golfer. It appears to be caused by rotation of the hip during practice or to be secondary to overuse in the golfer who plays golf frequently and does a lot of walking on uneven terrain. On physical examination, there is pain to palpation directly over the greater trochanteric area of the hip. The pain can also be elicited by external rotation and abduction of the hip. Many times, one finds a very tight tensor fascia lata muscle and iliotibial band on the lateral side of the hip and thigh. the patient must also be examined closely for leg length discrepancy and gait abnormalities. Treatment includes rest, ice, anti-inflammatory medication, and physical therapy, which may include cross-friction massage of the tender area, ultrasound, and stretching of the tight tensor fascia lata or iliotibial band. Very rarely is steroid injection needed. Surgery is considered only as a very last resort.

I have seen five male golfers between 35 and 40 years of age who have osteoarthritic changes of both hips. These golfers complain of loss of hip motion, especially abduction and internal rotation. They also complain of aching following or during a round of golf. None of these golfers had any past history or any medical reasons that would cause this osteo-arthritic condition. Radio-graphs revealed early arthritic changes about the hip, with narrowing of the joint space. On physical examination, there was loss of abduction and internal rotation. There was also reproduction of pain with forced internal rotation of the hip. Four out of five of these golfers responded to anti-inflammatory medications and physical therapy. One, however, continued to progress to the point that he had to undergo a total joint replacement in one hip (see Chapter 10). He is now back to playing golf without difficulty except for some mild problems in the other hip.

THIGH INJURIES

Golfers can also suffer strains of the quadriceps, the hamstring, and the groin muscles. These are most often treated with rest, ice, compression, and physical therapy and usually respond well to this form of treatment.

KNEE INJURIES

Injuries to the knee joint are the most common injuries seen in the lower extremity. They are most commonly either tears of the menisci or patellofemoral problems.

Most of the injuries to the menisci during a round of golf occur during a twisting or bending action. In some cases, an acute injury may cause a meniscus tear and immediate locking of the knee. More commonly, however, injuries to the meniscus occur in the older golfer, in whom posterior horn flap tears are common. These tears are usually due to years of friction from the femur and tibia putting stress on the meniscus with repeated actions of twisting and bending. The posterior horn has trouble securing nutrients, and mucoid degeneration occurs in its depths. With a twisting or stooping action, the underside of the degenerated meniscus tears loose to form a flap. This flap catches in the joint, causing locking, popping, giving way, and pain. The golfer usually complains of pain over the medial joint line. Lateral meniscus tears are very rare in this age group. The pain is increased with bending or twisting motions. Many times, there are episodes of locking or catching of the knee joint. One of the other common complaints occurs at night when the patient is sleeping. If the injured knee makes contact with the opposite knee, pain occurs, which may awaken the patient. Many patients will tell you that they must sleep with a pillow between their knees to prevent this type of pain.

On physical examination, the most common finding is pain to palpation along the medial joint line. One may also see a cystlike swelling over the joint line. Pain can be reproduced by rotation of the lower leg on the femur while extending and flexing the knee with the examiner's fingers at the joint line (the McMurray sign).

Radiographs should include a standing anteroposterior view, lateral view, and patella view (I prefer the Merchant view) of the knee. One may see findings of early arthritic changes that may help in the diagnosis and treatment of these problems. The use of magnetic resonance imaging (MRI) is very helpful in the diagnosis of meniscal injuries in the knee.

After proper diagnosis, arthroscopic surgery is usually recommended, and after a period of rehabilitation, the golfer usually can resume activities without difficulty.

Many golfers present with patellofemoral complaints of pain with walking, climbing, and bending. They may complain of pain in the back of their knee and aching into the calf and thigh after long periods of sitting (movie sign). This pain may represent overuse syndromes, patella subluxation, lateral pressure syndrome, or may be a result of acute trauma due to abnormal or faulty swing mechanics.

Many golfers, especially women, have malalignment problems associated with a wide pelvis, large Q-angles, and pronation of the feet. This places increased stress on the patellofemoral joint during the golf swing, when valgus forces are applied to the knee during different phases of the swing. Other overuse problems can result from tight hamstrings, tight heel cords, and foot pronation. The quadriceps must work harder to overcome tight hamstrings, so that increased force occurs between the patella and the femur. Tight heel cords mean that knee flexion is needed to make up for the lack of shock-absorbing dorsiflexion at the ankle,

thus causing more force across the patella. Foot pronation internally rotates the tibia, causing the patella to translate or shift laterally. Increased shift can cause abnormal stress and pain in the patellofemoral joint, which is enhanced with valgus force applied during the golf swing.

In examining the patellofemoral joint, the physician should look at the patella tracking through a full range of motion of the knee, noting any abnormalities such as lateral riding of the patella. The examiner should next look for abnormal gait patterns. When the patient stands and walks, you can many times observe malalignment problems of the lower extremity, especially pronation of the feet. Following this part of the examination, one must palpate the patella looking for crepitus, popping, and instability.

Both overuse and malalignment problems usually can be treated with physical therapy, which includes quadriceps strengthening, stretching of the hamstrings and heel cords, and anti-inflammatory medication. Orthotics can be used to correct pronation of the foot and are also very helpful in correcting patellofemoral problems. If conservative treatment does not relieve the problems, one must consider patella subluxation, lateral pressure syndrome, or medial synovial plica syndrome in these patients. These conditions may require surgical treatment.

INJURIES OF THE LOWER LEG

Injuries to the calf are very rare in golf, as evidenced by the 0.6% incidence in Table 16–1. The only calf injury that I have seen in a golfer is a strain of the medial head of the gastrocnemius, many times called "tennis leg." The pain may be sharp and acute, and the player may think that he or she was struck in the calf with a golf ball. The area becomes swollen and ecchymotic. The athlete with a mild strain notes a generalized aching in the calf; more calf pain is associated with dorsiflexion of the ankle, and tenderness occurs in the medial belly of the gastrocnemius. In mild strains, the calf should be iced for 20 minutes at a time and stretched. A lift is usually added to the inside of the shoe under the heel to allow calf shortening, which promotes healing. In severe strains, rest is very important and crutches should be used, with the foot held in plantarflexion. After a period of 3 to 4 weeks of healing, strength and stretching exercises are started. The golfer returns slowly to activity, wearing a lift in the shoe for another 4 to 6 weeks. After the injury heals, the golfer should always be on a stretching program before playing.

PREVENTION OF INJURIES

The lower extremity is very important in golf because it is the foundation around which the golf swing takes place. Conditioning for golf is extremely important to strengthen the lower extremities for both power and endurance. The golfer needs endurance strength in the legs because, in some tournaments, 36 holes are played in 1 day. The golfer must be able to climb steep hills and hit a ball at the top. This strength comes from repeated exercises for the legs and lower extremity. It is also important that the golfer gain flexibility to prevent injuries in the lower extremities, such as patellofemoral problems. A program of walking, biking, running, or even swimming to build endurance in the legs and the rest of the body is extremely important in the off-season to maintain fitness for golf season when it arrives. Other exercises for strengthening and conditioning the lower extremity are discussed in Chapter 4.

SUMMARY

Although the incidence of injuries to the lower extremity in golf is low, they do occur, and knowledge of them is important in treating the golfer. Even more important is maintaining strength and flexibility in the lower extremity to ensure proper golf mechanics, to prevent injury, and to increase the longevity of one's ability to play the game.

REFERENCES

1. McCarroll, JR and Gioe, TJ: Professional golfers and the price they pay. Phys Sportsmed 10(7):54–70, 1982.
2. McCarroll, JR, Rettig, AC, and Shelbourne, KD: Injuries in the amateur golfer. Phys Sportsmed 18(3):122–126, 1990.

Medical Control of Illness and Injury

· ·

M. William Voss, MD*
with the assistance of
Edward A. Palank, MD, FACC
and Claude T. Moorman, III, MD

RISK FACTORS

The medical control of injury and illness that may occur during golf play is best established if the physician in charge assumes the role of a team physician in anticipating and planning for possible events. The principles will cover both the management of the everyday golfer on the public or private course and the care of participants in both amateur and professional tournament play—not only the golfers themselves but also those serving in support of them and the spectators.

Four principal factors should be considered in establishing medical control for injury and illness that may occur as a result of

---

*Deceased.

golf participation:[24] (1) personal factors, (2) the nature of the sport, (3) environmental factors, and (4) weather conditions. These factors, alone or in combination, may result in situations ranging from the minor incident to the life-threatening emergency.

Personal Factors

Golfers, those who work in support of them, and tournament spectators may be of any age, and the range of their health status may be equally broad. Because no preparticipation medical examination is required for the recreational golfer, a wide variety of acute and chronic medical conditions may be found among them. As discussed in Chapter 8, because so many recreational golfers are of retirement age and older, the incidence of cardiovascular disease is relatively high, and acute exacerbation or complications of these conditions are not unusual during golf participation.

Even more common may be persons suffering from varying degrees of asthma or other chronic obstructive pulmonary diseases. Their allergic sensitivity may lead to acute anaphylactic events with serious consequences. Also relatively common is type II diabetes mellitus, often poorly controlled. Malignancies, both recognized and unrecognized, also may result in complications associated with golf participation.

Although the risk of injury should not be greater for women than for men, providing that their general level of physical conditioning is equal, the potential for skeletal fracture often is increased in older women because of the relative frequency of osteoporosis. Other factors, such as nutrition and substance abuse, should be comparable between the sexes and will vary according to age and competitive level.

The Nature of the Sport

A number of factors inherent in the nature of the sport may contribute to the occurrence of injury and illness. First are the characteristic time and recurrence of play. Although the measured distance of 18 holes on a golf course may be only 5 miles, the golfer walking it may cover twice that distance over a period of 4 hours or more. Even

using a cart, the golfer will walk several miles over a similar time period. The physical hazards of play involve the swing of the club, which places strain on the musculoskeletal system, the risk of being hit by a club or ball (although rare), and some risk of injury by the cart. Psychological stress induced by the nature of the game may be severe and disabling. Interactions with other persons should be governed by the traditional courtesies long associated with the sport, as well as by local safety rules, but these are sometimes forgotten or ignored.

Environmental Factors

The characteristic setting of golf involves a playing field spread out over 100 or more acres of chiefly grassy terrain that may also include rocks, hollows or crater-like formations, sandy areas, trees, streams, lakes, and roads. Most courses have hilly areas, some with a grade of as much as 20 to 30%, requiring on occasion four times more footpounds of work as walking across level ground. Golfers may be injured when clubs strike rocks or trees, and balls may rebound, striking companions or spectators. Falls into deep bunkers or water hazards are not uncommon.

The grasses and foliage themselves pose a hazard to golfers. Antigens from grasses, weeds, and wildflowers endanger the allergic, and toxic chemicals may be used as fertilizers, herbicides, and insecticides. Dermatitis from exposure to such Toxicodendrons as sumac, poison ivy, and poison oak, which may abound in the rough areas along the fairways, is reasonably common. Stinging and biting insects such as bees, hornets, wasps, and ticks may add to the miseries. Poisonous snakes and even more formidable reptiles, alligators, may be encountered in subtropical climates, and confrontations with rabid animals, though infrequent, are highly dangerous.

Weather Conditions

Weather is a considerable factor for the golfer because although golf is sometimes practiced in an air-conditioned, sheltered environment, it is played outdoors and throughout the year in widely varied geographic locations. The risk factors include solar radiation, heat and humidity stress, high winds, lightning, and airborne antigens and pollutants. Despite the use of spiked soles on golf shoes, inclement weather also increases the risk of falls on slippery surfaces. For the extremely dedicated golfer, hypothermia and frostbite can be added to the list of dangers.

The greatest and most common weather-related risks result from heat and sunlight exposure. High air temperature combined with high relative humidity create heat stress for the golfer that may cause cramps, heat exhaustion, or heat stroke. Exposed areas of skin may be subjected acutely to sunburn, and chronically to accelerated aging, activation of herpes simplex, and malignant growths. The results of these exposures may be modified in the individual golfer according to age, general health, and intake of toxic substances.

Airborne substances are somewhat hazardous to all golfers but most hazardous to those with allergic constitutions or chronic pulmonary disease. Toxic air pollutants are most damaging in conditions of warmth, humidity, and low air circulation, producing smog.

PROVISION OF MEDICAL SERVICES FOR GOLF TOURNAMENTS

Any golf course may have a medical advisor or medical advisory committee, but most golfers depend for medical services on their personal physician or on a consultant. It is certainly helpful, but not essential, to receive advice from a physician who understands golf and its particular problems, perhaps as a player.

A golf tournament, on the other hand, especially one that is part of one of the professional golf tours or an amateur championship, presents a challenge whose extent is measured by the numbers and level not only of the participating golfers but also of the other accompanying persons and spectators. Medical coverage of such a tournament requires careful advance planning and a team approach.[23] It is reasonable to assume in planning such an event that all the medical resources of the community will be available,

and usually they are. Nevertheless, a front line of medical professionals must be directly available at the golf course to meet the special needs of all those involved in and associated with the tournament. These professionals will make diagnoses, initiate necessary treatment, and, when required, provide entry into the health care system of the community. They can be recruited and assigned according to their specialties and disciplines into five categories:

► Sports medicine includes all medical events related to the practice and play of golf by the golfers and their caddies. Individuals providing these services will be chiefly physicians, physical therapists, and athletic trainers.

► Emergency medicine handles all acute medical events involving all persons on the golf course and in its immediate environs. The individuals available for these services will include physicians, athletic trainers, first-aid personnel, and ambulance attendants.

► Primary care medicine provides non-emergency medical and therapeutic services for the golfers' associates and families and for tour and local officials. This service will be provided chiefly by physicians and physical therapists.

► Industrial medicine covers medical events affecting support service personnel, volunteers, employees of the local club, and media representatives. This service will be provided by physicians, first-aid personnel, and physical therapists.

► Crowd medicine is principally first aid but may include some emergency medical service. It is handled primarily by trained and qualified first-aid and paramedical personnel.

For practical purposes, these categories overlap and are not mutually exclusive.

Sports Medicine

The sports medicine of golf is described and discussed in the other chapters of this book. These services are carried out for golfers by the appropriate professionals on a continuing basis. Problems arising during the times of tournaments can be attended to by professionals on the site, and they may also fall under the headings of emergency and primary care medicine.

Emergency Medicine

Emergency medicine can and does include any medical event that requires immediate attention. The critical emergencies are those that involve vital systems and constitute threats to life. The author's experience has identified the six medical emergencies listed in Table 17–1 as the most common and critical in golf.

Cardiac Arrest

The risk factors and incidence of cardiac arrest, the most frequent cause of sudden death on the golf course, are discussed in Chapter 8. In cases of cardiac arrest, prompt initiation of cardiopulmonary resuscitation is necessary to save lives.[9] Usually it must be maintained until advanced cardiac life support can be supplied by a trained emergency team.[15] Every golf tournament should have such a team stationed at the site during the active hours of practice and play. Their equipment should include ventilators; oxygen; a defibrillator; endotracheal tubes; medications such as epinephrine, lidocaine, and atropine; syringes; and intravenous equipment with containers of appropriate intravenous fluids. The standards and guidelines for cardiopulmonary resuscitation and emergency cardiac care were published by the 1985 National Conference on Cardiopulmonary Resuscitation and Emergency Cardiac Care.

Coma

Coma can be described as an abnormal, deep stupor occurring as a result of an illness or injury. The victim cannot be aroused

TABLE 17–1. Critical Medical Emergencies in Golf

Cardiac arrest
Coma
Anaphylaxis
Respiratory arrest
Heat stroke
Lightning strike

TABLE 17–2. Causes of Coma

Alcohol or other toxic drug
Epileptic seizure
Diabetes
Hyperinsulinemia
Uremia
Infection, high fever
Cerebral stroke
Lightning strike
Heat stroke
Cardiac arrest
Brain injury, cervical fracture
Psychosis

from this state by external stimuli. Coma must be distinguished from syncope (fainting), which may be of vasovagal origin, as in longstanding or emotional shock or fear, or may be due to transient cardiac standstill (Stokes–Adams), hyperventilation, or hypoglycemia. Syncope is self-limiting with supportive care.

The common causes of coma are listed in Table 17–2. The first consideration in the emergency management of coma should be to see that the victim has the ability to breathe independently and that the airway is maintained. Second should be that blood circulation continues or can be restarted. External examination and the observations and history from bystanders may help to establish a tentative diagnosis.

The standby emergency ambulance or cardiac resuscitation team can be called directly to the location of the comatose person to provide first aid and transportation to a medical facility. In their absence, a telephone call to 911 or other appropriate emergency number should bring medical and emergency assistance. The medical team at the site should take charge and coordinate emergency treatment and transportation. When a person in a coma is to be moved or transported, it should be assumed that his or her neck may be broken until it can be ascertained with some reliability that it is not.

Anaphylaxis

Anaphylaxis is the most serious IgE-mediated reaction that can occur on a golf course. Immediate recognition and prompt treatment are necessary for survival. The list of agents capable of causing anaphylaxis is growing in length, because it includes a variety of proteins, polysaccharides, haptens (small, incomplete antigens), and synthetics. Of these, the most common encountered in the play of golf is protein hypersensitivity to venom from the suborder Apocrita (stinging species) of the order Hymenoptera. This includes mainly superfamilies of wasps and bees and some stinging ants. About half of the anaphylaxis deaths in the United States annually are due to insect stings.

Although the reaction may be confined to local manifestations such as urticaria and angioedema, the systemic reaction occurs as bronchospasm and shock because of falling blood pressure. The clinical symptoms and signs are itching, faintness, tightness in the chest, wheezing, dyspnea, abdominal cramps, and collapse. Laryngeal edema and bronchospasm cause hypoxia, and falling blood pressure results from reduced venous returns because of extravascular leaking.

The pathophysiology appears to center around IgE produced by an antigen that sensitizes the mast cell. Subsequent exposure to the antigen results in an IgE antigen and antibody complex that causes the sensitized cell to release the mediators of anaphylaxis, histamine, kinins, prostaglandins, slow-reacting substance of anaphylaxis, and heparin chymase.

The treatment of choice[14] is the subcutaneous injection of 0.5 mL of a 1:1000 dilution of epinephrine close to the site of the sting. This may be repeated every 15 minutes until the condition is controlled. In desperate circumstances, epinephrine in a 1:50,000 dilution is administered intravenously. An intravenous line should be established and kept open for the slow infusion of isotonic saline solution, to which may be added (for adults) 50 mg of diphenhydramine, or 4 mg/kg (up to 500 mg) of aminophylline, or 125 mg of methylprednisolone. If volume replacement does not restore organ perfusion adequately, 5 to 20 μg/kg of dopamine may be administered intravenously. The use of a tourniquet to localize the antigen to an extremity may be helpful.

It is essential to maintain an airway and provide oxygen inhalation. In severe angioedema, endotracheal intubation may be necessary, and failing that, tracheostomy. Rapid transport to the nearest hospital or medical care facility should accompany all of these emergency measures.

Those who are at high risk for anaphylaxis are persons with a history of hay fever, eczema, and asthma; individuals with a history of anaphylaxis; or those with a blood relative who has had anaphylaxis. High-risk persons should carry injection kits containing 1:1000 epinephrine in small syringes for emergency use by themselves or others in isolated areas. They also should be advised to consult with an allergist/immunologist for possible desensitization prior to exposure in high-risk areas.

Respiratory Arrest

Acute respiratory failure may occur on the golf course as a result of bronchial asthma (sometimes with the presence of exercise-induced bronchospasm), or from airway obstruction due to aspiration of a foreign body. Both situations are preventable, but when they occur they require immediate management, which may be lifesaving.

The person with asthma may have omitted taking his or her regular medication or may be in a situation in which a higher dose is required. Those who have suffered from exercise-induced bronchospasm in the past should have taken the necessary medication before beginning exercise. Wheezing, coughing, and dyspnea may be followed by cyanosis, confusion, tachycardia, and even by fainting if arterial oxygen tension falls below 50 mm Hg and treatment has not taken place. Treatment involves the administration of epinephrine or other bronchodilator therapy, and in some cases oxygen inhalation. Rapid transport to a medical care facility is advisable.

Probably the foreign body most commonly aspirated on the golf course is liquid or food. Liquid is usually cleared spontaneously by the victim, but even a small particle of food may become wedged under the epiglottis and choke the victim by asphyxiation in a few minutes. It is usually possible to dislodge such an obstruction by inserting a finger into the pharynx of the victim to dig it out. The Heimlich maneuver is successful if the obstruction is located in the upper pharynx, at the entrance to the esophagus.

Heat Stroke

Heat cramps, heat exhaustion, and heat stroke represent advancing stages of the body's reaction to heat stress. They may occur separately, however, and their prevention and management require knowledge both of their causes and mechanisms and of their possible interrelations in the affected individual.

The human body attempts to maintain its internal temperature within the narrow range around 37°C (98.6°F) in which it functions most comfortably and effectively. Its control mechanisms, if properly prepared and supported, can withstand relatively high external air temperatures and substantially increased workloads, which generate internal heat. The body eliminates heat by convection, conduction, radiation, and evaporation. The first three depend primarily on exposure of the skin to air and on air movement around it. Together they account for relatively small amounts of heat loss, however; under high heat stress about 95% of heat loss must occur through evaporation, almost 90% of which occurs in sweating. Thus, relative humidity rather than the absolute air temperature is the critical factor in producing heat exhaustion and heat stroke, which has occurred at air temperatures of 70°F when relative humidity was 80%. People may be able to function normally in dry air at 120°F, although they may be uncomfortable and require large amounts of water.

Because golf is played principally in warm climates and during seasons in which high temperatures and relatively high humidity are common, the average golfer will be subjected periodically to heat stress. Even though the physical activity of the golf swing is insufficient to raise internal body temperature very much and the effort of walking the course and carrying the golf bag may be taken care of by the cart, the golfer who is not properly prepared to cope with heat stress may become its victim. Ken Venturi's profound heat stress at the 1964 US Open, as recounted in Chapter 1, may have been exacerbated by the fact that he had spent the preceding months playing in much cooler temperatures. Porous, lightweight, loose-fitting clothing, such as short-sleeved, open-necked shirts and shorts, will help to prevent heat stress, as will white or light-colored clothes, which will reflect rather than absorb heat.

Heat cramps result from loss of body water, particularly from sweating. They begin in the feet and legs, and without intervention will involve muscles of the trunk and finally the upper extremities. They are entirely preventable by drinking water freely before and during the golf game. As discussed more fully in Chapter 6, other fluids are also satisfactory, except those that are alcoholic, which tend to increase dehydration. Salt tablets are not necessary, and taken in excess they may be harmful.

Heat faintness or syncope also can result from dehydration, especially when the individual is fatigued and perhaps forced to stand in strong, direct sunlight. It can be prevented by maintaining good hydration and taking advantage of shade and places to rest when they are available.

Heat exhaustion is most apt to occur in those who continue activity through or despite cramps and faintness. Extreme dehydration produces profuse sweating, headache and dizziness, mental confusion, and eventually collapse. Prevention involves maintaining water intake, removing sweat-soaked equipment, and seeking rest in a cool environment.

Heat stroke occurs when internal body temperature continues to rise and sweating stops.[13] It can be fatal unless effective treatment is instituted immediately, including removal of clothing, placing the victim at rest, applying external cold packs, and restoring water orally and by vein. The patient should be transported by ambulance to the closest medical facility immediately.

All golf courses should have cool water available around the course at convenient locations near golf tees. Course marshals should be alert to spot those who appear to be showing the effects of heat stress and should be prepared to provide them with assistance. Some courses have carts carrying fluids that circulate during busy times on hot days.

Lightning

In 1991, two spectators were killed by lightning at professional golf tournaments, one at the US Open in Chaska, Minnesota,

TABLE 17-3. USGA Rules Pertaining to Lightning

Protection of Persons Against Lightning

As there have been many deaths and injuries from lightning on golf courses, all clubs and sponsors of golf competitions are urged to take every precaution for the protection of persons against lightning.

Attention is called to Rules 6-8 and 33-2d.

The USGA suggests that players be informed that they have the right to stop play if they think lightning threatens them, even though the Committee may not have specifically authorized it by signal.

The USGA generally uses the following signals and recommends that all Committees do similarly:

Discontinue Play: Three consecutive notes of siren, repeated.

Resume Play: One prolonged note of siren, repeated.

6-8. Discontinuance of Play

    a. WHEN PERMITTED

        The player shall not discontinue play unless:

        1. the Committee has suspended play;

        2. he believes there is danger from lightning; . . .

    b. PROCEDURE WHEN PLAY SUSPENDED BY COMMITTEE

        When play is suspended by the Committee, if the players in a match or group are between the play of two holes, they shall not resume play until the Committee has ordered a resumption of play. If they are in the process of playing a hole, they may continue provided they do so without delay. If they choose to continue, they shall discontinue either before or immediately after completing the hole, and shall not thereafter resume play until the Committee has ordered a resumption of play.

    PENALTY FOR BREACH OF RULE 6-8b: *Disqualification.*

33-2. The Course

    d. COURSE UNPLAYABLE

        If the Committee or its authorized representative considers that for any reason the course is not in a playable condition or that there are circumstances which render the proper playing of the game impossible, it may, in match play or stroke play, order a temporary suspension of play, or, in stroke play, declare play null and void and cancel all scores for the round in question. When play has been temporarily suspended, it shall be resumed from where it was discontinued, even though resumption occurs on a subsequent day. . . .

Source: United States Golf Association and The Royal and Ancient Golf Club of St. Andrews, Scotland,[22] pp 28–29, 81, 105, with permission.

and one at the PGA Championship in Carmel, Indiana. As a result, the PGA Tour has instituted a local rule that is in effect at all their events and slightly contradicts USGA Rules pertaining to the suspension of play, listed in Table 17-3. Whereas the USGA Rules usually in effect allow players to finish the hole they are playing, the new PGA Tour local rule requires all players to discontinue play immediately at the sound of the siren indicating a play stoppage because of lightning. This rule was instituted because it was believed that if players continue to play, spectators may continue to watch them and thus be placed at risk. Stopping play immediately is intended to give spectators a better chance to seek shelter. Unfortunately, suitable shelter often is not available when a storm occurs, and warning may be inadequate. Tournament directors continually monitor approaching electrical storms, using equipment sensitive up to about 200 miles.

Pocket-sized lightning detection devices are available that sense a radio frequency emitted by lightning, with a range of approximately 20 miles. Because lightning strikes often precede the rainfall of a storm, such devices would be especially useful for individual golfers.

The most common cause of death in persons struck by lightning is cardiac arrest with asystole.[3] Respiratory arrest may also occur, the result of electrical current paralyzing the brain's respiratory center. Morbidity and mortality may depend on the degree of apnea because respiratory arrest often persists even after cardiac rhythm has been restored.[20] Neurologic effects are also common; Cooper's study[3] found that after lightning injury 86% of patients were confused or amnesic, 72% lost consciousness, and 69% experienced paralysis. Most of the deficits resolved, but some permanent impairment of the central nervous system has been reported.[1,3] Other injuries may include cutaneous burns, often linear or featherlike in appearance, and hearing loss, generally secondary to rupture of the tympanic membrane.[3] Cataracts can present days to months following injury.[1,20]

The immediate treatment of the lightning victim is aggressive cardiopulmonary resuscitation. Because apnea may persist after cardiac rhythm is restored, it is important to continue with respiratory support. Most lightning victims should be admitted to the hospital for observation of both cardiac and neurologic complications.

Caution is the best way to avoid lightning injuries. Players and spectators should get off the course when lightning nears. Rule 6-8a[22] allows a player to discontinue play if he or she believes there is danger from lightning, even if play has not been suspended. Those unable to obtain shelter in a building or automobile should seek refuge in a dense wooded area, avoiding lone trees, hilltops, and ponds or other water. Elevated greens and open fairways also should be avoided. If no shelter is available, one should lie flat on the ground, preferably in a ditch or bunker. Players should discard clubs, umbrellas, and golf spikes, all of which are excellent conductors of electricity. Although automobiles, with their full enclosure and rubber tires, are generally safe, golf carts are not.

Primary Care Medicine

Primary care medicine may involve the services of a family practitioner, internist, gynecologist, surgeon, dermatologist, ophthalmologist, otolaryngologist, urologist, or dentist. These services may be provided away from the site at private medical offices, clinics, or hospitals. Screening for such services can be performed by one or more primary care physicians on site.

The Effects of Sunlight on the Skin

The recurrent exposure of skin areas to the sun makes dermatology particularly important to the golfer. The chief concern is the ultraviolet (UV) spectrum of sunlight, from 200 to 400 nm, which escapes total atmospheric filtering. The middle portion of this band (UV-B, 290 to 320 nm) is responsible for sunburn, suntan, and chronic changes that include thickening and wrinkling of the skin, actinic keratoses, basal and squamous carcinoma, and possibly malignant melanoma. UV-A (320 to 400 nm) produces phototoxic, allergic, drug, and prophyric reactions. UV exposure is greatest during the summer months and at midday and is increased by reflectance off water or sand and by high altitude (a 4% increase for each 1000 ft above sea level). Clouds influence UV intensity but do not eliminate exposure.

The most frequent medical event due to solar radiation is sunburn. The degree of the burn is related both to the dose of solar radiation and to the genetic nature of the skin, especially pigmentation. Melanin, a polymer contained in the melanosomes of epidermal basal cells, serves as a UV filter. Although black people have a protective advantage in the number of melanosomes, even black skin may be sunburned. A first-degree burn, characterized by redness and pain, is treated by removal from sun exposure, use of an oral analgesic, and local treatment. Topical anesthetic agents should be discouraged because of their sensitizing effect. Corticosteroids in an aerosol spray are widely used. Second-degree burns, characterized by blistering, are best treated in an office or hospital environment, where intense therapy is available, with close follow-up and proper attention to potential complications such as infection. If the burns become third-degree, skin grafts may be necessary.

Long-term damage to chronically exposed skin areas (in golfers, the head, neck, hand, arms, and sometimes the legs) is characterized by premature aging of the skin with patchy areas of diffuse erythema, brown pigmentation, ecchymosis, telangiectasis, atrophy, and wrinkling. Actinic keratoses present either as scaly, flat areas on an erythematous base, or as hypertrophic, thick, white-to-red papules, often with cornified masses of material. These are premalignant lesions. Following biopsy to determine the presence of malignancy, these lesions can be treated by shave excision, cryosurgery, or topical fluorouracil.[25]

Long-term exposure to solar radiation also may damage the lens of the eye, as discussed in Chapter 7.

Prevention of skin damage by exposure to sunlight can be aided by the use of peaked caps or broad-brimmed hats to protect the face, and especially by the use of sunscreens. Sunscreens are available as creams and in alcohol-based solutions that adhere more effectively when exposed to sweat and water. They are rated by a formula that produces a sun protection factor (SPF); SPF-15 theoretically means that exposure for 15 hours would equal 1 hour without a sunscreen. There does not appear to be any advantage to products with an SPF over 15. The principal active ingredient of many sunscreens is para-aminobenzoic acid (PABA), effective against UV-B; broad-spectrum screens contain benzophenones and cinnamates, which also absorb UV-A. Reflectors such as zinc oxide are nearly 100% effective but are difficult to keep in place and less esthetic in appearance. Persons exposed to excessive amounts of sun should also give constant attention to the general health of the skin, by refraining from cigarette smoking, eating a balanced diet, and replacing skin oil lost through routine use of strong soaps.

Contact Dermatitis

Another dermatologic problem affecting golfers and others who frequent golf courses is contact dermatitis from the *Rhus* genus of the cashew family. Poison sumac (*R. vernix*), poison ivy (*R. toxicodendron*), and poison oak (*R. diversiloba*) are found in the rough and around trees on many courses. Plant identification is not difficult; the ivy plant or vine has a triple leaf, as does the oak. Sumac has a characteristic multiribbed, thin leaf with a yellow or red blossom (Fig. 17–1).

The clinical course of the dermatitis is marked by a delayed (1 to 2 days) appearance of erythema and pruritus, progressing rapidly to the formation of weeping vesicles and bullae. Treatment is both systemic and local. Antihistamines such as diphenhydramine hydrochloride (Benadryl) are taken orally to relieve pruritus and weeping of the skin; severe cases may require oral use of prednisone for 10 days to 2 weeks. Topical corticosteroid creams and ointments are applied to the affected areas. Hyposensitization prior to each golf season is helpful to some but must be repeated annually.

Figure 17–1. Poison ivy, poison oak, poison sumac (*top* to *bottom*). (From Thomas, CL [ed]: Taber's Cyclopedic Medical Dictionary, ed 17. FA Davis, Philadelphia, 1993, p 1546, with permission.)

Lyme Disease

Despite their best efforts to stay on the fairway, all golfers sometimes find themselves among the trees and tall grasses of the rough. There they may encounter a small tick, *Ixodes dammini*, the principal vector of Lyme disease. This infection, caused by the spirochete *Borrelia burgdorferi*, is a potentially serious and debilitating disease that may affect the skeletal, cardiovascular, and central nervous systems.[5] The most common vector-borne infection in the United States, it has been identified in 43 states, with the highest incidence in Massachusetts, Connecticut, New York, New Jersey, Pennsylvania, Wisconsin, and Minnesota.[2,21]

The majority of patients (but not all) display a pathognomonic rash, erythema chronicum migrans, within days to weeks of the bite. This appears as a red papule at the site of the bite; a bright red, expanding rash appears outside a blanched area surrounding the papule and lasts for 3 to 4 weeks.[17] Many individuals also experience flulike symptoms during this period, with headache, myalgia, stiff neck, fever, and fatigue.[18] Untreated patients may later develop arthritic syndromes; neurologic abnormalities, including meningitis, peripheral neuritis, and cranial nerve palsy;[17] and cardiac involvement.[19] Serologic studies may confirm the diagnosis in patients with the characteristic clinical syndrome. Early and effective antibiotic treatment will usually prevent the later effects.

Cutting back the rough has been recommended[4] to try to keep the mice that commonly carry the ticks from coming into the playing area. The use of pesticides is impractical to control the tick population because of the difficulty in penetrating vegetation.

Personal protection is the most effective way to avoid Lyme disease, including long pants tucked in at the ankles. If these are a light color, the ticks may be easier to detect. Permethrin (Permanone) has been shown to be effective in repelling and killing ticks, but it should be applied only to clothing, never bare skin. Careful removal of the entire tick (pulling it off slowly with tweezers just behind the head) within the first 24 hours may avoid transmission of the infecting organism,[11] but many patients never notice the bite because the tick is so small.

Rabies

Fortunately, rabies is rarely encountered by golfers in the United States,[6] but it should be suspected when anyone is bitten by a bat, raccoon, skunk, fox, or squirrel. If the animal is identified and captured, it should be held for observation and possible later killing by animal control officers.

Snakebite

Two families of poisonous snakes are indigenous to the United States: the Elapids (coral snake) and the Crotalids (pit vipers, including the rattlesnakes, the copperhead, and the cottonmouth). Approximately 45,000 snakebites occur annually, of which 8000 are inflicted by venomous snakes.[7] About 70% of venomous snakebites occur in the Southeast.[10] In 20% of these bites, however, no venom is injected.

Pit vipers, which are responsible for 98% of venomous snakebites, are characterized by a triangular head, elliptical eyes, and well-developed fangs. Expert identification of the snake, if it can be *safely* captured or killed, is desirable to assist with definitive management at the hospital. Some harmless snakes superficially resemble poisonous ones.

TABLE 17–4. First Aid for Venomous Snakebite

Identification of snake
Constriction band
Suction extractor
Immobilization of extremity (splint)
Evacuation to medical center

Timely application of appropriate first aid (Table 17–4) can minimize risk of mortality and morbidity in the victim. It should be noted, though, that fatalities are rare in healthy adults. A light, preferably elastic, constriction band is applied 2 inches above the bite. It is important that the band be loose enough to slip a finger beneath easily. This will allow for occlusion of the lymphatics (where the venom spreads) without dangerous arterial and venous restriction. The old recommendation to cross-cut the wound and apply mouth suction has been discarded; laymen with no knowledge of anatomy may cut nerves or arteries, and bacteria in the mouth can cause serious infection. Instead, the use of a suction extractor is recommended. This device creates up to 1 atmosphere (760 mm Hg) of negative pressure at the wound site to remove the venom. It is applied directly over the bite, with no incision, and is left in place during transport. If it is applied within 3 minutes, up to one third of the venom can be removed. Next, the bitten extremity should be immobilized, to delay absorption of the venom and diminish local tissue damage.[12] Golf clubs or tree branches can be used as a makeshift splint. The victim should be put at rest to decrease absorption of the venom into the circulation.

The most important step in the care of a snakebite victim is rapid transport to a medical center for definitive treatment. Ambulation is not advised; the victim should be transported in a cart or litter if necessary. Thus the availability of ambulance transport at a tournament is the most important factor in the care of snakebite victims. The use of antivenin is only indicated for people having severe systemic reactions to the bite and is not part of first aid treatment.

Prevention of snakebite on the golf course depends on wearing protective clothing and shoes to protect the feet and legs, walking slowly through thick rough and wooded areas while being alert for snakes, and avoiding putting one's hands in places where a snake could be hiding. Snakes seek to avoid humans.

Exposure to Toxic Chemicals

Chemicals used on a golf course as insecticides, fungicides, pesticides, and herbicides may elicit toxic or sensitivity reactions in golfers, spectators, and employees.[8] Because intake is relatively small at any one time, the symptoms and findings are seldom acute. Repeated exposure, however, predisposes to chronic complaints because of exposure through the skin and mucous membranes. Golfers, especially youngsters, occasionally ingest such chemicals by licking the ball.

Carbamate insecticides include aldicarb, carbaryl, isocarb, and propoxur. They are cholinergic and produce a clinical picture characterized by constricted pupils, sweating, increased bronchial secretions, vomiting, and diarrhea. Toxic reactions usually respond to atropine or pralidoxime. Organophosphates such as parathion, malathion, diazinon, dichlorvos, and mipafox are also cholinergic but produce much more severe symptoms. Chlorinated hydrocarbons (for example, chlordane, aldrin, DDT, lindane, mirex, and pardichlorobenzene) produce respiratory and central nervous system reactions.

Thiram is an effective fungicide and may be a constituent of turf fungicide used on golf courses. A severe, eczematous skin eruption caused by thiram has been reported in a golfer who tested strongly positive on a patch test.[16] Thiram also causes ethanol sensitivity reactions.

Industrial Medicine

The accidents and illnesses already discussed, when they affect employees of the golf club, support service personnel, volunteers, and media representatives, could be considered part of the field of industrial medicine. Except for emergencies, those persons who live in the area of the course will be managed by their personal physician, but the services of tournament physicians and physical therapists may be required for those who are not local residents.

A principal difference in the spectrum of medical problems that will be encountered in this group is that they may experience more (and possibly more severe) equipment-related injuries. Those who apply toxic chemicals to the course also may suffer greater effects if precautions are inadequate.

Crowd Medicine

Crowd medicine will make up the greatest number and variety of medical problems confronting medical and paramedical personnel at a major tournament. People of all ages may be included among the spectators, and many will bring health problems with them. A high incidence of allergic events may be expected, for example. Young mothers who travel with the players often have children who mingle with the spectators, some of whom bring children themselves. The high exposure to infectious agents in this group, together with the stress of travel and changing weather, diet, and water, may all produce acute problems.

For the most part, tournament physicians should have to deal only with emergency diagnosis and first aid. Other medical problems can be referred to local physicians, medical facilities, and hospitals. Treatment of those persons who are part of the entourage of the tour presents an exception to this rule.

SUMMARY

- A number of medical problems may arise in golfers and others present at a golf tournament. Some are incidental to the setting, but many will be brought out by the environment of the golf course and the activity of the players and spectators. Careful planning of medical services and facilities in preparation for such events, using a team approach involving a number of medical specialties and support personnel, and ensuring close cooperation with local emergency systems and hospitals should be effective in providing optimal care.

REFERENCES

1. Appelberg, DB, Masters, FW, and Robinson, DW: Pathophysiology and treatment of lightning injuries. J Trauma 17, 1977.
2. Centers for Disease Control: Lyme Disease— Connecticut. MMWR 37:1–3, 1988.
3. Cooper, MA: Lightning injuries: Prognostic signs for death. Ann Emerg Med 9(3):134–138, 1980.
4. Golf Course Management, April 1990, p 128.
5. Hamilton, DR: Lyme disease: The hidden pandemic. Postgrad Med 85(5):303–314, 1989.
6. Kappus, KD: Rabies. In Merck Manual, 14th ed. Merck and Co, Rahway, NJ, 1982, pp 214–218.
7. Kurecki, BA III and Brownlee, HJ Jr: Venomous snakebite in the United States. J Fam Pract 25(4):386–392, 1987.
8. McGuigan, M: Treatment of poisoning. CIBA-Clinical Symposia 36(5):24–26, 1984.
9. Montgomery, WH, Donegan, J, and McIntyre, KM: 1985 National Conference on standards and guidelines for cardiopulmonary resuscitation and emergency cardiac care. JAMA 255:2906–2981, 1986.
10. Pennell, T, Babu, S, and Meredith, J: The management of snake and spider bites in the southeastern United States. Am Surg 53:198–204, 1987.
11. Piesmon, J, et al: Duration of tick attachment and Borrelia burgdorferi transmission. J Clin Microbiol 25:557–558, 1987.
12. Rowland, S: The management of snake (pit viper) bites. In Green, DP (ed): Operative Hand Surgery. Churchill Livingstone, New York, 1982.
13. Rubenstein, E: Heatstroke. Scientific American Medical Textbook 8:102, 1984.
14. Rubin, DB: Office management of anaphylaxis. Am Fam Physician 3:179–183, Sept 1986.
15. Sanders, AB, et al: New concepts in cardiopulmonary resuscitation. Cardiac Impulse 7(6):1–3, 1986.
16. Shelley, WB: Golf-course dermatitis due to thiram fungicide. JAMA 188:415–417, 1964.
17. Steere, AC: Lyme disease. N Engl J Med 321:586–596, 1989.
18. Steere, AC, et al: The early clinical manifestations of Lyme disease. Ann Intern Med 99:76–82, 1983.
19. Steere, AC, et al: Lyme carditis: Cardiac abnormality of Lyme disease. Ann Intern Med 93:8–16, 1980.
20. Strosser, E, Davis, RM, and Menchey, MJ: Lightning injuries. J Trauma 17(4):315–319, 1977.
21. Tsai, TS, Bailey, RE, and Moore, PS: National surveillance of Lyme disease 1987–1988. Conn Med 53:324–326, 1989.
22. United States Golf Association and The Royal and Ancient Golf Club of St. Andrews, Scotland: The Rules of Golf 1991. The United States Golf Association, Far Hills, NJ, 1987.
23. Voss, MW: A medical support system for a professional golf tournament. Phys Sportsmed 10(8):63–69, 1982.
24. Voss, MW: When an athlete's life is in danger. In Birrer, RB (ed): Sports Medicine for the Primary Care Physician. Appleton-Century-Crofts, Norwalk, CT, 1984, p 140.
25. Wilkerson, MG: Actinin keratoses. Am Fam Physician 30(1):103–108, 1984.

Rehabilitation of the Injured Golfer

· ·

Walter L. Jenkins, MS, PT, ATC
Paul Callaway, PT
Terry R. Malone, EdD, PT, ATC

INJURY SITES
Low Back
Neck
Shoulder
Elbow, Forearm, Wrist, and Hand
FOOT ORTHOTICS
MANUAL THERAPY
ELECTRICAL STIMULATION
OTHER FORMS OF THERAPY

G olf is a unique sport that requires a delicate balance between the mental and physical states. Fourteen clubs are available to the golfer, each allowing a variety of shots. The motor control required may be among the most demanding in any sporting event. Professional golfers hit hundreds of golf balls daily to develop and maintain their shot-making ability. This constant repetition leads to consistency but also to overuse syndromes. Because of the specific demands of the golf swing, muscular patterning must be normal to allow appropriate stroke mechanics (see Chapter 3). It is imperative to facilitate normalization of muscular action via pain modulation if successful treatment is to be accomplished.

A physical therapist's role in the management of golf injuries is very similar to his or her role with many other athletic events and their related injuries. As with running injuries, for instance, a good working knowledge of normal mechanics is essential for proper treatment of overuse inflammatory conditions. Similarly, when one cares for post-traumatic injuries, a knowledge of golf swing mechanics can be helpful in preventing overuse syndromes from occurring secondary to mechanical swing faults during the rehabilitation period. Simply knowing the game and the stresses placed on various body parts is crucial to designing an accurate functional progression postinjury.

Although physical therapy services can be helpful to many injured golfers, it is not essential that all patients be sent to a physical therapist. If used appropriately, many techniques described in this chapter can be performed on a variety of patients by other health care professionals, provided the proper indications are followed.

Included in this chapter are physical therapy management of spinal and upper-extremity injuries, indications for the use of foot orthotics, and the selection of the proper physical therapy modalities to care for golf-induced injury.

INJURY SITES

Low Back

Lumbar pain is a very common complaint among golfers of all ages and abilities. Consequently, over the last several years much more attention has been focused on the biomechanics of the golf swing and how it contributes to back injuries. In most cases, the combination of forward bending with rotation done repeatedly and forcefully during each swing is a primary cause of back pain in golfers.[18] (see Chapter 11).

As with all musculoskeletal injuries found with golfers, the specific diagnosis made by the physician and the clinical assessment of the dysfunction made by the physical therapist are essential before an appropriate treatment and rehabilitation program can be carried out. Frequently, professional and avid amateur golfers develop gradual, degenerative changes to their lumbar spine because of the many hours of practice and regular play, in contrast to the sudden, traumatic injuries encountered by weekend golfers. The tissues commonly involved are the joint complex including the intervertebral disc, facet (apophyseal) joints and supportive joint capsules, rather than the soft tissues of the muscles, tendons, or ligaments. These developing arthritic joint conditions are accompanied by postural adaptations of surrounding soft-tissue structures, however, which may confuse the clinician's ability to specify the origin of the golfer's pain and may retard the golfer's progress in treatment if the postural asymmetries are not adequately addressed.[18]

Treatment therefore should focus on reestablishing the correct biomechanics of the lumbar spine necessary to perform a proper golf swing. Providing adequate functional segmental mobility to the appropriate spinal segments adjacent to regions of hypermobility can be quite difficult, and it often requires a physical therapist skilled in specific manual therapy (hands-on mobilization) techniques. Generalized trunk stabilization techniques (Fig. 18-1) can be readily employed, however, followed by isometric or isotonic strengthening exercises for the important muscles connected to the lumbodorsal fascia, hip, and pelvis.

Full-body flexibility exercises also should be initiated, stressing the maintenance of the "neutral" lumbar spine concept developed during the trunk stabilization phase of treatment. The neutral lumbar spine concept involves keeping the low back in a slight amount of extension while performing exercises or functional tasks (Fig. 18-2). Most

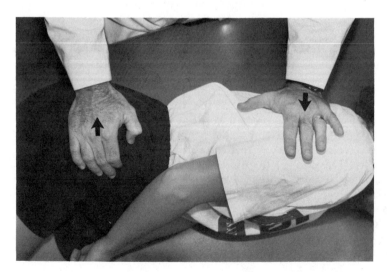

Figure 18-1. Manual technique for trunk stabilization or strengthening.

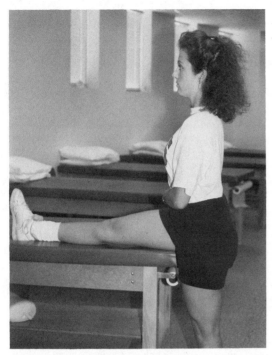

Figure 18–2. Stretching of the hamstrings while maintaining a "neutral" lumbar spine.

lumbar spine conditions in golf are benefited by a gradual improvement in the amount of lumbar extension flexibility.[18] Lumbar extension exercises such as press-ups and prone-on-elbows are very helpful in improving this functional movement (Fig. 18–3).

Lumbar extension exercises are a form of stretching exercises. Thus each repetition needs to be held in the terminal position for approximately 20 to 30 seconds, with three to five repetitions performed during each treatment session.

A balance among all necessary golf movements should be proportionately shared by all spinal segments, however. The therapeutic program can only be considered complete when the injured golfer has thoroughly demonstrated a proper understanding of swing mechanics, using postural stability (lumbar control), and has functional strength and flexibility to return to the stresses of his or her level of golf and enough endurance to prevent biomechanical breakdowns during play, risking further lumbar injury.

Neck

Injuries to the cervical spine are also frequently referred for physical therapy treatment. As is true with low back or upper extremity injuries in golf, understanding neck injuries and providing proper treatment depends on a sound awareness of the golf swing and its effect on normal cervical and upper thoracic joint mechanics. Furthermore, the contribution of the scapulohumeral and scapulothoracic joint complexes to cervical dysfunction has great significance.[3]

The repeated trauma within and around the cervical region during years of practice and play eventually contributes to gradual postural changes including a forward head,

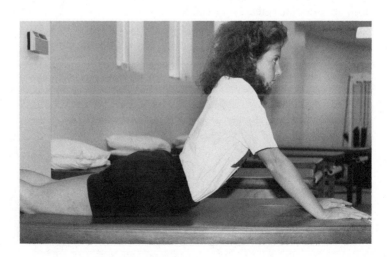

Figure 18–3. Extension of the lumbar spine in a prone position.

increased upper thoracic kyphosis and forward or elevated shoulders, with one shoulder often held higher than the other. The forward head position is most detrimental because of the narrowed posterior cervical joint spaces, which often impinge on nerve roots and compromise blood flow to important muscles controlling neck motion. Moreover, degenerative changes in the intervertebral disc, facet joints, and joint linings may be accelerated.

Cervical rotation is functionally the most important neck motion required to make a full turn during a golf swing. The full turn in a golf swing occurs as a result of the shoulders moving away from the ball while the head remains stationary. This causes a maximal rotation of the cervical spine in the opposite direction to the turn. Often the cervicothoracic junction is injured secondary to the torsional stresses from the full turn.

The muscles most affected symptomatically with respect to pain, spasm, and tightness are the trapezius, levator scapulae, scalenus, and sternocleidomastoids. The muscle groups can develop pronounced myofascial trigger points with specific referred pain patterns.[26] Consequently, treatment provided to the trigger points of the cervical rotators may allow a golfer to participate, if needed, while further treatment would address other joint and muscular dysfunctions.

Trigger point treatment can be provided with a combination of electrical muscle stimulation, ice massage, and gentle stretching during the acute stages of neck pain and stiffness. Postural balancing techniques, including gentle joint and soft-tissue mobilization, myofascial release, and active stretch-

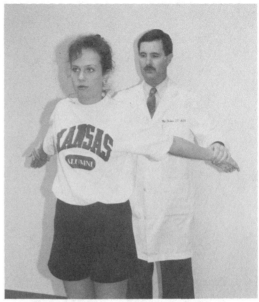

Figure 18–5. Bilateral anterior shoulder stretch. The patient is stretched into horizontal abduction of the shoulder. This position is held for 20 to 30 seconds at a point where there is a mild to moderate stretch felt by the patient. Care should be taken to avoid any anterior or posterior shoulder pain during this exercise.

ing, should begin as soon as possible. Supine positioned "neck tucks" (posterior dorsal gliding) (Fig. 18–4) and chest stretching (Fig. 18–5) help to allow posterior repositioning of the scapula and head, thus reducing the inappropriate forward head posture.

Finally, acute strengthening of the scapular stabilizing muscles of the upper and middle back may begin when full, pain-free cervical range of motion is available (Fig. 18–6A and B). This treatment plan, in com-

Figure 18–4. "Neck tucks" are performed by actively pushing the middle cervical spine into the table. The patient is asked to hold this position for 15 to 20 seconds on each repetition, with three to five repetitions performed in each treatment session.

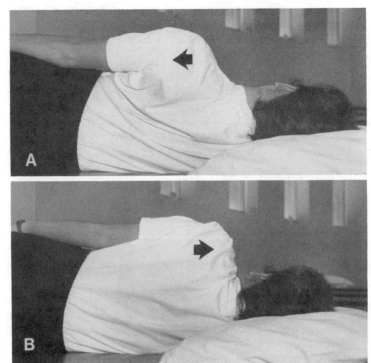

Figure 18-6. (*A*) Starting position for scapular elevation exercises. (*B*) Terminal position for scapular elevation exercises.

bination with a biomechanical swing analysis and functional progression of gradual practice and play, has proven very successful for most golfers with neck pain.

Shoulder

As with other injuries, the treatment of shoulder injuries requires a precise diagnosis by the physician and a thorough evaluation by the physical therapist. A knowledge of golf swing mechanics and muscles used is an important aspect of treatment and rehabilitation. Research in the last several years has been helpful in gaining a greater understanding of the golf swing from a kinesiologic point of view[12,22] (see Chapter 13).

Soft-tissue disorders of the shoulder make up the majority of golfers' lesions referred to a physical therapist. Traumatic and overuse lesions involving the rotator cuff, glenoid labrum, joint capsule, and the shoulder musculature are often seen in a physical therapy clinic. Rotator cuff tears treated conservatively or surgically require patience and a thorough knowledge of the patient's postural and anatomic abnormalities leading to the onset of symptoms.[3] Without this knowl-

edge, attempts to correct the musculotendinous problems of the rotator cuff may have an initial success but a poor long-term result.

Particular attention should be paid to the cervical spine and scapular posture whenever a patient is referred with a shoulder injury. An example of this is seen in a patient with a forward head with rounded shoulders predisposing him or her to an anterior impingement of the rotator cuff musculature, with eventual weakness resulting from this posture. Rehabilitation exercises should emphasize scapular stabilization (Fig. 18-7) and biceps (Fig. 18-8) and triceps strengthening (Fig. 18-9), as well as rotator cuff strengthening (Fig. 18-10). Several authors have performed electromyograms (EMGs) to determine which muscles are functioning during specific strengthening activities.[4,22,25] A working knowledge of these findings can be very helpful in setting up a thorough exercise program. Home programs can be effective if good patient compliance is achieved, but each patient needs an individualized program of strength, range-of-motion (ROM), and flexibility exercises. Standardized programs for all patients can

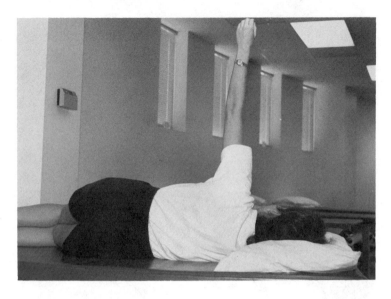

Figure 18–7. Scapular stabilization exercise for abduction of the scapula. This position may be held for several minutes.

be helpful but remain limited in their approach.

Glenoid labrum tears have become a more common diagnosis with the advent of arthroscopy.[2] Once the lesion has been re-moved, an aggressive rehabilitation program may be initiated. After arthroscopy, the patient may begin ROM exercises under a physical therapist's supervision as early as one day postoperatively. Rehabilitation should include emphasis on the rotator cuff musculature, biceps, triceps, and scapular stability, just as with rotator cuff tears. Rotator cuff, biceps, and triceps emphasis will help to decrease possible problems with shoulder instability, which are often associated with glenoid labrum lesions. Postural and mechanical considerations are also necessary in the complete treatment of these patients.

Active range of motion in the shoulder in several planes is very helpful in restoration of pain-free movement, particularly early in rehabilitation. Frontal and sagittal plane movements within the pain-free arch of motion are most effective in these circumstances.

Repairs of the glenoid labrum require a more conservative approach to rehabilitation. Range of motion may be limited for several weeks, with strength training initiated only after a full healing response has taken place. Repair of superior labrum anterior posterior (SLAP) lesions[24] in the superior aspect of the glenoid labrum may require immobilization of the shoulder, with ROM exercises beginning in a limited fashion from 3 to 6 weeks postoperatively. Strength training for patients after SLAP

Figure 18–8. Biceps curls.

Figure 18–9. Triceps extensions.

lesion repair may begin 6 to 8 weeks post-operatively.

Shoulder instability may or may not require surgical intervention. Conservative, as well as surgical, treatment and rehabilitation consist of a well-balanced strengthening, ROM exercises, and postural program (Fig. 18–11). In planning rehabilitation, while emphasizing the internal rotators in the case of an anterior/inferior instability, the therapist should also be careful not to neglect the external rotators, biceps, triceps, and the scapular musculature. External rotators atrophy very quickly postsurgically or post-immobilization and require a great deal of work to return the musculature to full strength. It must be noted that the posterior glenohumeral musculature, including the infraspinatus, teres minor, and posterior deltoid, are also helpful in pulling the humerus posteriorly in the event of an anterior instability at this joint. Likewise, the restoration of proper scapulohumeral rhythm is important in returning a golfer to his or her competition.[14] Without proper scapulohumeral strength, and thus proper scapular position, the glenoid fossa can become positioned inappropriately for a particular movement, creating undue stress on the glenohumeral joint capsule and musculature during functional movements.

Therapeutic exercise designed to strengthen the shoulder, or other selected body parts, needs to follow certain princi-

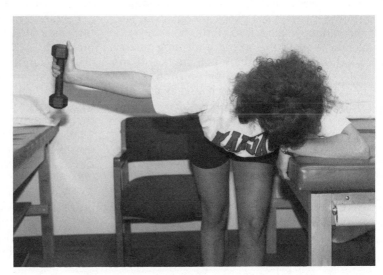

Figure 18–10. Infraspinatus strengthening is performed by horizontal abduction of the arm with the shoulder held in an externally rotated position.

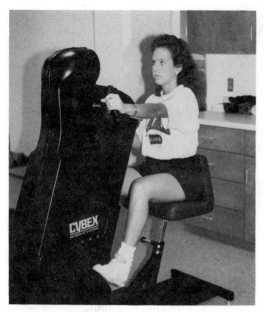

Figure 18–11. An upper body ergometer for shoulder range of motion and strengthening.

ples. Most injuries respond to the submaximal or endurance type of exercise because of a selective atrophy in the "slow twitch" muscle fibers.[8] To perform submaximal strengthening exercise one should use weight or resistance that can be moved through a ROM from 15 to 30 times or more. The exercises are performed in bouts or sets, with two to four sets used in each treatment session.

After a good base of muscular endurance has been laid, pure muscle strengthening may be performed. Training for muscular strength involves using a weight that the patient can move from 6 to 10 times in one set. Weight used in the strength-training phase of rehabilitation is therefore higher than that used in the submaximal portion. Care should be taken to use mechanically correct positions and movements on each repetition. When using higher amounts of weight it is very easy to substitute the use of incorrect mechanics, with a resultant increase in potential for injury.

Elderly patients will most commonly need the submaximal phase of rehabilitation. The strengthening portion, while worthwhile in a younger individual, is too risky for the elderly patient. Moderate strength gains can be achieved in the elderly patient by using a weight that can be moved through a ROM 10 to 15 times in a set, with two to three sets performed in each treatment session.

Elbow, Forearm, Wrist, and Hand

Upper-extremity injuries from the elbow to the hand are not quite as common in golfers as are injuries to the spine and shoulder. Nevertheless, the pain, dysfunction, and persistence of these injuries may easily rival the more common maladies. Of the most troublesome lesions occurring in the elbow, forearm, wrist or hand, tendinitis is the most commonly treated (see Chapters 14 and 15).

"Tennis elbow" (lateral epicondylitis); "golfer's elbow" (medial epicondylitis); tendinitis in the ulnar or radial aspects of the wrist; and tendinitis in the thumb are rarely caused by single traumatic occurrences.[14] Although an acute sprain may occur when the golfer hits a rock, tree root, or hard ground, tendinitis more commonly develops insidiously with excessive practice, new equipment (change in grip size, length, lie, or weight of club), a change in swing mechanics, or swing techniques that are altogether improper. With the exception of golfer's elbow, which develops most often at the medial epicondyle of the right elbow, most inflammatory conditions in right-handed golfers occur in the left arm because the left arm and hand endure most of the stresses during the swing, from the initial gripping of the club to the ultimate club impact with ball and ground. Subsequently, a detailed patient history and a thorough understanding of golf equipment and swing mechanics will greatly facilitate the physician's diagnosis and the physical therapist's rehabilitation progression.

Lateral epicondylitis can occur secondary to a poor grip, which results in overuse of the wrist extensors during the downswing. The wrist extensors act in a complex manner during this portion of the golf swing. First, the wrist extensors work as stabilizers of the wrist to counteract the tendency of the long wrist and finger flexors to bring the wrist into flexion. Second, the wrist extensors of the left hand must contract concentrically when accelerating the club head prior to impact. Third, the wrist extensors must contract eccentrically at the point of impact or ball strike, in order to absorb the force of striking the stationary ball. Complex movements of this nature have a small margin of error (considering the timing and sequencing of a golf swing). The fragile nature of the wrist extensor muscle likewise plays an important role in the development of lateral epicondylitis.

The medial epicondyle can also become injured during the impact portion of the swing. This injury occurs in the right hand, as the hand grips the club with the long flexors of the fingers while the wrist flexors are accelerating the club toward the ball. At the moment of impact, the wrist flexors must eccentrically contract to absorb the force of ball strike.

It is important to note that eccentric contraction of the forearm musculature is a component of injury in both the flexors and extensors of the wrist. Curwin and Stanish[6] have thoroughly explained the eccentric mechanism in athletic and nonathletic activity. As will be discussed in more detail later in this chapter, eccentric activity is also necessary to rehabilitate golfers following injuries in this and other portions of the body.

Early stages of therapy for acute tendinitis or sprains include ice, oral nonsteroidal anti-inflammatory medications, and electrical stimulation for pain, edema, and muscle spasm in affected tissue. Modified rest is advisable for tendon problems, in contrast to complete immobilization for more severely sprained ligaments. Transverse friction massage may also provide help during the initial stages of healing.[7] Simple, active ROM exercises may also be used to help facilitate the blood supply and laying down of new collagen without increasing the inflammatory response in an acutely inflamed structure. Active wrist flexion and extension, first without the effects of gravity, and later in the treatment progression working against gravity, are helpful with inflammatory disorders of the wrist and elbow.

When tissue conditions allow, gentle stretching of the involved structures should begin, to help model newly formed scar tissue and assure functional joint motion. Strengthening exercises should follow, with emphasis placed on pain-free movements. All muscle groups from the scapular stabi-

Figure 18–12. Shoulder internal rotation strengthening with wrist flexion stabilization using surgical tubing.

lizers to the wrist and hand muscles should be included in the strengthening program. Materials like surgical tubing (Fig. 18–12), rubber balls (Fig. 18–13), and dumbbell weights (Fig. 18–14) all work nicely. An excellent display of upper-extremity strengthening exercises for golf can be found in *Thirty Exercises for Better Golf.*[11] (See also Chapter 4, on training and conditioning.)

The eccentric or muscle-lengthening contraction should be emphasized during rehabilitation.[6] If the injury takes place secondary to eccentric overloading, some form of eccentric control must be performed prior to returning to golf. Submaximal eccentric loading is very helpful provided the patient can perform these exercises in a pain-free

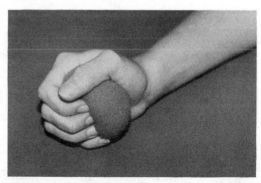

Figure 18–13. Grip strengthening using a foam ball.

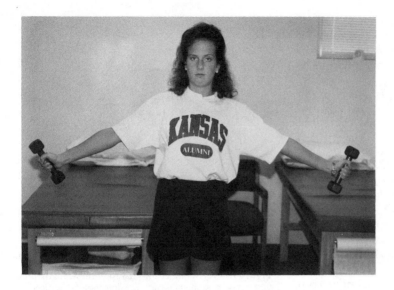

Figure 18–14. Shoulder abduction exercises using dumbbell weights.

fashion without increasing swelling.[6] To use eccentric exercise for the wrist extensors, the patient holds a weight in one hand, with the forearm supported by a table. The wrist and hand hang over the edge of the table, the palm facing the floor. The patient is asked to assist the musculature with the contralateral limb during the concentric (muscle-shortening) phase, by pulling up with the contralateral hand, to place the wrist in an extended position. From this position, the patient is asked to lower the weight by eccentrically contracting the wrist extensors.

Finally, a gradual return to practice and play may begin with adequate supervision by an experienced golf coach or instructor so that the principal mechanism of injury already mentioned can be avoided. Counterforce bracing for elbow tendinitis (Fig. 18–15), as well as taping or bracing for wrist and finger injuries, may be beneficial at any time during treatment, rehabilitation, and functional progression. Care must be taken, however, to avoid player dependencies on brace devices in lieu of proper rehabilitation.

FOOT ORTHOTICS

The use of foot orthotics may be essential for proper lower extremity proprioception and pain-free function in those individuals who have foot and lower-extremity dysfunction.[19,27] Golfers who suffer from lower-extremity overuse syndromes such as posterior tibialis tendinitis, plantar fasciitis, or patellofemoral chondrosis may benefit from some type of foot orthotic management. Individ-

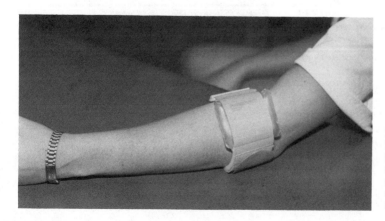

Figure 18–15. Counterforce bracing for the wrist extensors. By placing the brace distal to the origin of the impaired muscle–tendon unit, the pressure of the brace helps to dissipate the force of muscular contraction away from the injured area.

uals who have congenital malalignment of the subtalar and/or midtarsal joints in the presence of foot or lower extremity overuse syndromes are often rendered symptom-free following this type of treatment.

Prior to the use of a foot orthotic, one must treat any associated lesions in the lower extremity. Muscular weakness and tight lower extremity musculature often accompany overuse injury. It follows that a proper exercise routine involving stretching and/or strengthening of the involved musculature should be performed prior to foot orthotic management.

Foot orthotics are helpful in restoring proprioception to the lower extremity because they position a patient's foot in the proper anatomic position for that individual. Positioning the patient's foot in this "neutral position" allows for the proper length-tension relationship to be restored in the ligaments, joint capsule, and musculature, which are imbalanced in an individual with subtalar or midtarsal joint malformation. Balance and proprioception are key factors in the golf swing.

Foot malformations such as forefoot or rearfoot varus and forefoot valgus predispose an individual to many overuse syndromes of the lower extremity. Excessive walking over even and uneven terrain can lead to a breakdown of the soft-tissue structures of the foot, lower leg, knee, hip and even the low back. Plantar fasciitis, stress fractures, posterior tibialis tendinitis, and patellofemoral chondrosis may be at least in part linked to foot malformations. Treatment of the pathology begins with primary care, with evaluation for foot orthotics later in the treatment progression.

Foot orthotics can be classified as soft, semirigid, and rigid.[19,27] There is wide disagreement over which type of orthotic device to use with various foot types. Regardless of the pathology, the proper prescription of orthotic should be based on an individual evaluation.

MANUAL THERAPY

There are many philosophies and approaches to the treatment of musculoskeletal dysfunctions using manual therapy, or hands-on techniques. Essential to the safety and success of whichever manual therapy philosophy is employed is a complete understanding of the properties of normal and pathologic human anatomy, kinesiology, osteokinematics, and arthrokinematics. Furthermore, of equal importance are the evaluative steps taken to specify the origin and degree of severity of the lesion and the associated dysfunction.

The manual therapy techniques used for the treatment of golf injuries depend on the specific medical diagnosis, the degree of severity, and the clinical expertise of the therapist. Gentle superficial massage or deeper massage, sometimes known as myofascial release, may be most beneficial in conjunction with the judicious use of appropriate electrical modalities during the early inflammatory control stages of treatment for conditions of joint hypomobility.

Later, when the condition has stabilized and normalization of joint movement is desired, passive ROM exercises (Fig. 18–16) may be appropriate. Joint mobilization techniques with varying grades of motion and force, which take into account the accessory movements necessary for full return of motion, may also be used in the subacute or later stages of treatment. Typical lesions in golf requiring assistive mobilization include capsular adhesions secondary to chronically inflamed synovial joints such as the shoulder, the elbow, the wrist, and the apophyseal (facet) joints in the spine.

Joint mobilization uses gliding or accessory movements to restore full motion to a joint.[13] When analyzing the movements of joints, it is important to recognize that motion is most often broken up into rolling and gliding. Rolling or osteokinematic motion is the portion of joint movement that is readily observable by a clinician, whereas gliding or arthrokinematic motions are impossible to visualize and must be understood prior to assessing the patient. Each joint has specific rolling and gliding occurring with each physiologic motion.[13]

An example of proper indications for the use of joint mobilization occurs when a shoulder has been immobilized with resultant losses of motion. A patient who has lost ROM needs to have both the osteokinematic motion (passive ROM) and arthrokinematic motion (joint mobilization) restored. Passive ROM of the shoulder into flexion (sagittal plane motion) will help to restore the osteokinematic movement. Joint mobilization,

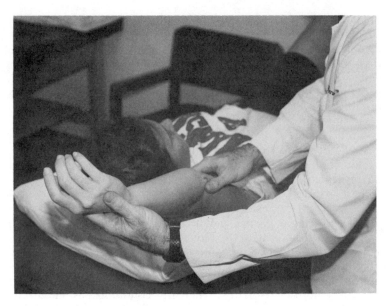

Figure 18–16. Passive shoulder flexion exercises.

gliding of the humerus posteriorly on the glenoid fossa, will further help to increase the lost physiologic movement, flexion (Fig. 18–17).

If a loss of external rotation is noted, passive external rotation may be indicated within pain-free limits of movement. A joint mobilization technique for restoration of external rotation is anterior gliding of the humerus on the glenoid fossa (Fig. 18–18). Contraindications to mobilization and manipulation of joints are listed in Table 18–1.[11]

Manual therapy techniques most appropriate for hypermobility or unstable joint conditions, as in the shoulder secondary to glenoid labrum tears or in spinal segments adjacent to regions of hypomobility, are those that are designed to promote functional stability. Early stages of treatment for muscular, capsular, or ligamentous trauma contributing to excessive joint play or laxity require immobilization of the tissues involved and appropriate use of ice and electrical modalities to decrease localized inflammation and promote healing of stabilizing structures. After the necessary stages of soft-tissue healing are complete, gentle proprioceptive neuromuscular facilitation (PNF)[16] using rhythmic stabilization (Fig.

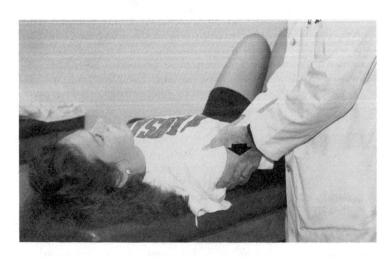

Figure 18–17. Posterior glide of the humerus on the glenoid fossa for restoration of shoulder flexion.

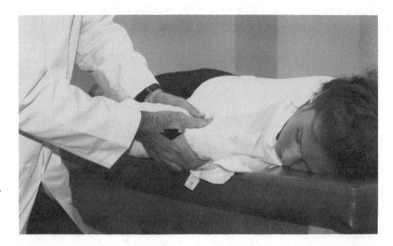

Figure 18–18. Anterior glide of the humerus on the glenoid fossa for restoration of shoulder external rotation.

18–19) or other "muscle energy" techniques may facilitate joint stabilization without reinjuring the supportive structures.

Rhythmic stabilization is a manual technique used in strengthening specific areas. It is performed by having the patient push into the hands of the therapist, first in one direction and then in another. The patient is asked to move the extremity against one hand and then the other in an oscillatory fashion. The hands work in opposite directions, alternating resistance against the injured extremity. Resistance varies depending on the stage of healing and the strength of the involved extremity.

ELECTRICAL STIMULATION

Electrical stimulation can be used in the treatment of traumatic or overuse injuries, whether acute or chronic.[23] There are sev-

TABLE 18–1. Contraindications to Joint Mobilization

Bone disease
Malignancy in bone or soft-tissue structures to be treated
Infection
Inflammatory arthritis
Central nervous system involvement
Vascular disease in the areas to be treated
Joint instability
Pregnancy
Severe joint pain
Muscle spasm

eral types of electrical stimulation, with specific physiologic effects for each of the particular types.

High-voltage stimulation, sometimes known as high-voltage galvanic stimulation, can be used in reduction of edema and modulation of pain.[1] Edema secondary to a disruption of blood vessels may be decreased via a muscle-pumping action. Muscle pumping may be attained by active muscular contraction or involuntarily by electrical stimulation. High-voltage stimulation is used with a low frequency and with intensity within the patient's tolerance. The low frequency allows for a muscular contraction in a muscle-pumping fashion. A "muscle twitch" is observed with the low frequency if the intensity is turned up to the threshold of contraction for that muscle. This muscle-pumping action is passive to the patient, with the effects being similar to those seen with continuous passive motion.[23]

High-voltage stimulation, as well as other forms of electrical stimulation, also has been proven effective in the modulation of pain. The Gate Control theory and the Endogenous Opiate theory are the two mechanisms most frequently associated with pain relief.[1,23] The Gate Control theory[21] is based on the idea that both nonnoxious sensory and pain-conducting fibers must pass through the same pathway in the spinal cord. The electrical stimulation facilitates conduction in the large sensory nerve fibers and inhibits conduction in the smaller pain fibers. When using the Gate Control theory,

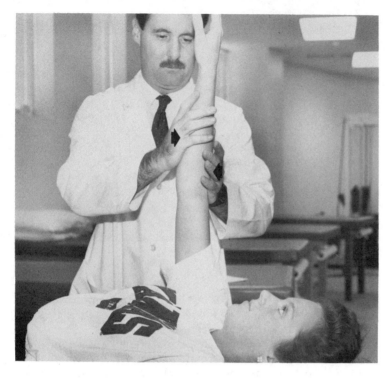

Figure 18–19. Rhythmic stabilization technique for strengthening the shoulder joint.

the clinician should apply the electrodes directly over the injured area, using a continuous setting, a high frequency, and with intensity increased until sensory stimulation is perceived.

The Endogenous Opiate theory[21] describes endogenous peptides that may be used in the control of pain. Endorphins and enkephalins are the most widely known of these endogenous substances. Enkephalins are found in the brain, spinal cord, nerve terminals, and throughout the intestine. Stimulation of enkephalins results in immediate but short-term relief of symptoms. Endorphins are neurohormones that have delayed response and provide a longer duration of relief on stimulation. Activation of enkephalins can be provided by directly stimulating the injured area at a high frequency and intensity. Endorphin release can be achieved by stimulating the injury site with low-frequency, high-intensity electrical stimulation.

The use of transcutaneous electrical nerve stimulation (TENS) has been found very effective in the reduction of pain.[23] The theories used in pain control with TENS are the same as those just discussed. Use of TENS is aided by the portable nature of the units, with stimulation being performed before, during, and after the event.

Medium-frequency electrical stimulation, Russian stimulation, has become prominent in the prevention of muscle atrophy since being brought to the United States via an exchange with Canada in the early 1980s.[21] It has been effectively used in decreasing atrophy postsurgically, during the post-immobilization period. Patients who have difficulty with voluntary muscle contractions despite having intact innervation to the atrophied muscle are excellent candidates for this type of electrical stimulation. The Russian electrical stimulation works by facilitation of the nerve innervating a particular muscle and should not be confused with direct current (DC) stimulation, which is used for denervated muscle. Use of Russian stimulation has been effective as early as several hours postoperatively to minimize atrophy.

A bipolar technique using two active electrode pads for stimulation is commonly used with Russian technique in stimulating the involved muscle, with electrodes of equal size used at each end of the muscle. The electrical current passes between the electrodes and facilitates a contraction of the muscle. Parameters for effective use of Russian stimulation include a fast onset of stimulation, a rate of at least 20 to 25 pps, a duration of 15 to 20 minutes, and frequency of one to two times daily. The fast onset of stimulation is necessary to impart a muscle contraction because muscle or nerve will accommodate to electrical stimulation. The longer the onset time, the less likely the contraction will be strong enough for therapeutic effects. A rate of 20 to 25 pps is necessary for a tetanic muscular contraction. The duration of treatment must not exceed the point of muscle fatigue. One or two daily treatments have been found to be most effective in minimizing atrophy.

Many stimulation devices are available that provide a variety of treatment techniques. Computer-assisted units facilitate tissue healing and pain modulation. Although tissue healing is imperative for a complete recovery, pain modulation allows the golfer to return to activity at the earliest possible time.

OTHER FORMS OF THERAPY

Heat therapy may be divided into superficial or deep according to tissue response and penetration. Superficial sources include hydrotherapy, hydrocollator, paraffin, fluidotherapy, and heat lamp. The unit or source selected should be suitable to the body part and ease of application. Superficial heat is used most frequently in treating golfers with subacute or chronic conditions. The primary outcome is decreased pain, allowing exercise and more appropriate muscular function. Normalization of function is the desired result of heat therapy.

The most commonly used deep heating modality is ultrasound. This is used primarily for selective tissue heating.[20,23] Ultrasound has been shown to increase temperatures at depths of 5 cm or more, with tissue changes including increased tissue extensibility, blood flow, metabolism, and pain threshold.[10,20,23] Because bone and ligament are primarily collagen, they absorb a high level of ultrasound energy. Thus, rehabilitation professionals frequently use ultrasound on patients with nonacute problems to pro-

vide desired changes in periarticular joint structures.[17]

Ultrasound frequently is used as a precursor to stretching and therapeutic exercise. This may provide pain modulation, which allows functional activity. Such activity is vital because a golfer must practice if he or she is to play well.

In patients presenting with inflammatory conditions, ultrasound is often used in conjunction with local steroid cream to allow an enhanced anti-inflammatory effect. The steroid cream is driven into the inflamed tissue by the ultrasound. The combination of ultrasound and steroid cream is known as "phonophoresis."[9,15] Although basic science research is conflicting, the use of phonophoresis has increased in many clinics following positive patient reactions.[5,15] Many clinicians prefer phonophoresis in an attempt to avoid the deleterious effects of corticosteroid injection. One recent pilot study reports that phonophoresis did not cause a decrease in tensile strength or other structural changes in tendons.[9] Acute bursal or capsular problems may respond quite favorably to this combination treatment.

Cold therapy (cryotherapy) is used during acute phases of injury management, when decreased vascularity and metabolic activity is desired. In most clinics, cryotherapy is applied through ice massage, ice pack, cold hydrotherapy, or cold pack. The patient will commonly report feeling four distinct, sequential phases during the application of cold therapy: cold, burning, aching, and numbness. Cryotherapy is frequently used in conjunction with exercise (cryokinetics) in the fourth phase of cryotherapy, to allow pain-free movements. Ice is used in most clinical circumstances; cryokinetics are quite helpful with subacute as well as acute problems.

"Spray and stretch" is another combination treatment quite useful in treating chronic myofascial injuries in golfers. These techniques have been described in detail and are valuable adjuncts.[26] According to Travell and Simons,[26] spray and stretch can be used to increase the extensibility of the myofascial trigger point and thus increase ROM and decrease pain. Spray and stretch may be used in a variety of anatomic areas, but it is particularly effective in the cervical and lumbar regions. Fluoromethane spray is first applied longitudinally to the muscle tendon unit, followed by a manual stretching of the involved muscle. The procedure may be repeated several times in one session, with multiple sessions of spray and stretch usually performed.

SUMMARY

Golfers of all ages and levels of expertise can become injured traumatically and through overuse. Relief of pain and inflammation can be provided by the application of specific manual, electrical, heat, and cold modalities. Because of their unique background involving biomechanical analysis, therapeutic exercise, and manual therapy, physical therapists can be very helpful in the treatment of golf-related disorders.

REFERENCES

1. Alon, G: High Voltage Stimulation: An Integrated Approach to Clinical Electrotherapy. Chattanooga Corporation, Chattanooga, 1987.
2. Andrews, JR and Carson, WG: Operative arthroscopy of the shoulder in the throwing athlete. In Zarins, B, Andrews, JR, and Carson, WG (eds): Injuries to the Throwing Arm. WB Saunders, Philadelphia, 1985.
3. Ayub, E: Posture and the upper quarter. In Donatelli, R (ed): Physical Therapy of the Shoulder. Churchill Livingstone, New York, 1987.
4. Blackburn, TA, et al: EMG analysis of posterior rotator cuff exercises. Ath Training 25(1):40–45, 1990.
5. Chantraine, A, Ludy, JP, and Berger, D: Is cortisone iontophoresis possible? Arch Phys Med Rehabil 67:38–40, 1986.
6. Curwin, S and Stanish, WD: Tendonitis: Its Etiology and Treatment. The Collamore Press, DC Heath and Co, Lexington, MA, 1984.
7. Cyriax, J: Textbook of Orthopedic Medicine: Treatment by Manipulation, Massage and Injection, Vol 2. Tindall Publishers, London, 1984.
8. Davies, G: A Compendium of Isokinetics in Clinical Usage, ed 3. S and S Publishers, Onalaska, WI, 1987.
9. Druffel, CM: Phonophoresis and Iontophoresis: A Pilot Study on the Tensile Strength in Histology of the Patellar Tendon in Rabbits. Master's thesis, Duke University, 1988.
10. Gersten, J: Effect of ultrasound on tendon extensibility. Am J Phys Med 34(2):362–369, 1955.
11. Jobe, FW and Moynes, D: Thirty Exercises for Better Golf. Champion Press, Inglewood, CA, 1986.
12. Jobe, FW, Moynes, DR, and Antonelli, DJ: Rotator cuff function during a golf swing. Am J Sports Med 14:388–392, 1986.
13. Kaltenborn, FM: Mobilization of the Extremity Joints and Basic Treatment Techniques. Olaf Norlis Bokhandel, Oslo, 1980.
14. Kessler, RM and Hertling, D: Management of Common Musculoskeletal Disorders. Harper and Row, Philadelphia, 1983.
15. Kleinkort, JA and Wood, F: Phonophoresis with 1% vs. 10% hydrocortisone. Phys Ther 55:1320–1324, 1975.
16. Knott, M and Voss, DE: Proprioceptive Neuromuscular Facilitation, 2nd ed. Harper and Row, New York, 1968.
17. Lehmann, JF: Ultrasound therapy. In Licht, S (ed): Therapeutic Heat and Cold, 2nd ed. Williams and Wilkins, Baltimore, 1965.
18. McKenzie, RA: The Lumbar Spine Mechanics, Diagnosis, and Therapy. New Zealand Spinal Publications, Waikanae, 1981.
19. McPoil, TG and Brocato, RS: The foot and ankle: Biomechanical evaluation and treatment. In Gould, J and Davies, G (eds): Orthopaedic and Sports Physical Therapy. CV Mosby, St Louis, 1985, pp 313–341.
20. Michlovitz, SL (ed): Thermal Agents in Rehabilitation. FA Davis, Philadelphia, 1986.
21. Nelson, RM and Currier, DP: Clinical Electrotherapy. Appleton and Lange, Norwalk, CT, 1987.
22. Pink, M, Jobe, FW, and Perry, J: Electromyographic analysis of the shoulder during the golf swing. Am J Sports Med 18(2):137–140, 1990.
23. Prentice, WE (ed): Therapeutic Modalities in Sports Medicine. Times Mirror/Mosby, St Louis, 1986.
24. Snyder, S, et al: SLAP Lesions of the Shoulder. Arthroscopy Assoc of North Am 6(4):274–279, 1990.
25. Townsend, H, et al: Electromyographic analysis of the glenohumeral muscles during a baseball rehabilitation program. Am J Sports Med 19(3):264–272, 1991.
26. Travell, J and Simons, DG: Myofascial Pain and Dysfunction: The Trigger Point Manual. Williams and Wilkins, Baltimore, 1983.
27. Wu, KK: Foot Orthoses. Williams and Wilkins, Baltimore, 1990.

Index

An "f" following a page number indicates a figure; a "t" indicates a table.